S0-ABA-288

RITES AND SYMBOLS OF INITIATION

The Mysteries of Birth and Rebirth

RITES AND SYMBOLS
OF INITIATION

The Mysteries of Birth and Rebirth

MIRCEA ELIADE

**Translated from the French
by Willard R. Trask**

And with a New Foreword
by Michael Meade

**Spring Publications
Woodstock, Connecticut**

RITES AND SYMBOLS OF INITIATION

Copyright © 1958 by Mircea Eliade. All rights reserved.

Published by arrangement with Harper Collins Publishers, Inc., who also kindly gave permission to use their typography.

"Foreword to the New Edition" © by Michael Meade. All rights reserved

Published by Spring Publications, Inc.; 299 East Quassett Road, Woodstock, CT 06281.

Second Spring Publications Printing 1995.

Printed in the United States of America, text on acid free paper. Cover designed and produced by Slobodan Trajkovic. The cover image, by Slobodan Trajkovic, is "Symbol," ink on paper, 1993

Distributed in the United States by the Continuum Publishing Group; in Canada by McClelland and Stewart; in the United Kingdom, Eire, and Europe by Airlift Book Co.; in Austrailia by Astam Books Pty Ltd; in Europe by Daimon Verlag; and in South Africa by Feffer and Simons

Library of Congress Cataloging-in-Publication Data

Eliade, Mircea, 1907-
    [Naissances mystiques. English]
    Rites and symbols of initiation : the mysteries of birth and
rebirth / Mircea Eliade : translated from the French by Willard R.
Trask ; and with a new foreward by Michael Meade.
        p. cm.
    Originally published: New York : Harper Bros., 1958, in series:
The Library of religion and culture.
    ISBN 0-88214-358-1 (alk. paper)
    1. Initiation rites—Religious aspects.   I. Title.
BL615.E4   1994
291.3'8—dc20   93-3049
                                                         CIP

CONTENTS

FOREWORD   vii

INTRODUCTION   ix

FOREWORD TO THE NEW EDITION   xvii

I INITIATION MYSTERIES IN PRIMITIVE RELIGIONS   1

Preliminary Remarks—The Sacred Ground—Separation
from the Mother—The Kurnai Initiation Mystery—Supreme
Being and Initiation Among the Yuin—Symbolism of
Initiatory Death—Meaning of the Initiatory Ordeals—
Initiation and Collective Regeneration

II THE INITIATORY ORDEALS   21

The Bull-Roarer and Circumcision—Symbolism of Subincision—Initiation in Tierra del Fuego—Scenarios of Initiatory Death—Being Swallowed by a Monster

III FROM TRIBAL RITES TO SECRET CULTS   41

Initiation of Girls—Degrees in Female Initiations—An
Extant Australian Secret Cult—Initiatory Symbolisms of
Return to the Womb—Symbolism of New Birth in Indian
Initiations—Multiple Meanings of the Symbolism of the
Embryo

IV INDIVIDUAL INITIATIONS AND SECRET SOCIETIES   61

Descent to the Underworld and Heroic Initiations—Initi-
atory Symbolism of the Symplegades—Individual Initiations:
North America—Kwakiutl Dancing Societies—Men's Secret
Societies—Initiatory Motifs Common to Puberty Rites and
Secret Societies

V HEROIC AND SHAMANIC INITIATIONS   81

Going Berserk — Cuchulainn's Initiation — Symbolism of
Magical Heat—Shamanic Initiations—Initiatory Ordeals of

Siberian Shamans—Public Rites of Shamanic Initiations—
Techniques of Ecstasy—Initiations of Australian Medicine
Men—Asiatic Influences in Australia

VI PATTERNS OF INITIATION IN HIGHER RELIGIONS   103

India—Traces of Puberty Rites in Ancient Greece—Eleusis
and the Hellenistic Mysteries—Christianity and Initiation
—Survival of Initiatory Motifs in Christian Europe—
Patterns of Initiation and Literary Themes—Concluding
Remarks—Epilogue

NOTES   137

INDEX   167

FOREWORD

This book represents the Haskell Lectures which I was privileged to deliver at the University of Chicago in the fall of 1956 under the title "Patterns of Initiation." In preparing the text for publication, I have added an Introduction and some notes and bibliographical references, but I have adhered to the presentation demanded by the original oral delivery. As I conceive it, the book is addressed to any nonspecialist reader interested in the spiritual history of humanity. It is for this reason that I have limited myself to depicting the complex phenomenon of initiation only in broadest outline. More detailed studies of certain aspects are contained in some of my earlier publications.[1] I shall return to the problem in a book now in preparation, *Death and Initiation.*

I wish once again to express my gratitude here to the Chancellor of the University of Chicago, to the Committee for the Haskell Lectures, and to the Dean of the Federated Theological Faculty of the University of Chicago for the honor that they conferred on me by inviting me to give the 1956 Haskell Lectures. The Bollingen Foundation has generously undertaken to defray the expense of the English translation; may the Trustees rest assured of my gratitude. I also wish to thank my translator, Mr. Willard R. Trask, for the pains he took to provide a faithful reproduction of my thought and my text in speakable English.

MIRCEA ELIADE

Department of History of Religions
University of Chicago
April, 1958

INTRODUCTION

It has often been said that one of the characteristics of the modern world is the disappearance of any meaningful rites of initiation. Of primary importance in traditional societies, in the modern Western world significant initiation is practically nonexistent. To be sure, the several Christian communions preserve, in varying degrees, vestiges of a mystery that is initiatory in structure. Baptism is essentially an initiatory rite; ordination to the priesthood comprises an initiation. But it must not be forgotten that Christianity triumphed in the world and became a universal religion only because it detached itself from the climate of the Greco-Oriental mysteries and proclaimed itself a religion of salvation accessible to all.

Then, too, we may well ask whether the modern world as a whole can still justifiably be called Christian. If a "modern man" does indeed exist, it is in so far as he refuses to recognize himself in terms familiar to the Christian view of man or, as European scholars express it, in terms of Christian "anthropology." Modern man's originality, his newness in comparison with traditional societies, lies precisely in his determination to regard himself as a purely historical being, in his wish to live in a basically desacralized cosmos. To what extent modern man has succeeded in realizing his ideal is another problem, into which we shall not enter here. But the fact remains that his ideal no longer has anything in common with the Christian message, and that it is equally foreign to the image of himself conceived by the man of the traditional societies.

It is through the initiation rite that the man of the traditional societies comes to know and to assume this image. Obviously there are numerous types and countless variants of initiation, corresponding to different social structures and cultural horizons. But the important fact is that all premodern societies (that is, those that lasted in Western Europe to the end of the Middle Ages, and in the rest of the world to the first World War) accord primary importance to the ideology and techniques of initiation.

The term initiation in the most general sense denotes a body of rites and oral teachings whose purpose is to produce a decisive alteration in the religious and social status of the person to be initiated. In philosophical terms, initiation is equivalent to a basic change in existential condition; the novice emerges from his ordeal endowed with a totally different being from that which he possessed before his initiation; he has become *another*. Among the various categories of initiation, the puberty initiation is particularly important for an understanding of premodern man. These "transition rites"[1] are obligatory for all the youth of the tribe. To gain the right to be admitted among adults, the adolescent has to pass through a series of initiatory ordeals: it is by virtue of these rites, and of the revelations that they entail, that he will be recognized as a responsible member of the society. Initiation introduces the candidate into the human community and into the world of spiritual and cultural values. He learns not only the behavior patterns, the techniques, and the institutions of adults but also the sacred myths and traditions of the tribe, the names of the gods and the history of their works; above all, he learns the mystical relations between the tribe and the Supernatural Beings as those relations were established at the beginning of Time.

Every primitive society possesses a consistent body of mythical traditions, a "conception of the world"; and it is this conception that is gradually revealed to the novice in the course of his initiation. What is involved is not simply instruction in the modern sense of the word. In order to become worthy of the sacred teaching, the novice must first be prepared spiritually. For what he learns concerning the world and human life does not constitute knowledge in the modern sense of the term, objective and compartmentalized information, subject to indefinite correction and addition. The world is the work of Supernatural Beings—a divine work and hence sacred in its very structure. Man lives in a universe that is not only supernatural in origin, but is no less sacred in its form, sometimes even in its substance. The world has a "history": first, its creation by Supernatural Beings; then, everything that took place after that —the coming of the civilizing Hero or the mythical Ancestor, their cultural activities, their demiurgic adventures, and at last their disappearance.

This "sacred history"—mythology—is exemplary, paradigmatic:

not only does it relate how things came to be; it also lays the foundations for all human behavior and all social and cultural institutions. From the fact that man was created and civilized by Supernatural Beings, it follows that the sum of his behavior and activities belongs to sacred history; and this history must be carefully preserved and transmitted intact to succeeding generations. Basically, man is what he is because, at the dawn of Time, certain things happened to him, the things narrated by the myths. Just as modern man proclaims himself a historical being, constituted by the whole history of humanity, so the man of archaic societies considers himself the end product of a mythical history, that is, of a series of events that took place *in illo tempore,* at the beginning of Time. But whereas modern man sees in the history that precedes him a purely human work and, more especially, believes that he has the power to continue and perfect it indefinitely, for the man of traditional societies everything significant—that is, everything creative and powerful—that has ever happened took place *in the beginning,* in the Time of the myths.

In one sense it could almost be said that for the man of archaic societies history is "closed"; that it exhausted itself in the few stupendous events of the beginning. By revealing the different modes of deep-sea fishing to the Polynesians at the beginning of Time, the mythical Hero exhausted all the possible forms of that activity at a single stroke; since then, whenever they go fishing, the Polynesians repeat the exemplary gesture of the mythical Hero, that is, they imitate a transhuman model.

But, properly considered, this history preserved in the myths is closed only in appearance. If the man of primitive societies had contented himself with forever imitating the few exemplary gestures revealed by the myths, there would be no explaining the countless innovations that he has accepted during the course of Time. No such thing as an absolutely closed primitive society exists. We know of none that has not borrowed some cultural elements from outside; none that, as the result of these borrowings, has not changed at least some aspects of its institutions; none that, in short, has had no history. But, in contrast to modern society, primitive societies have accepted all innovations as so many "revelations," hence as having a superhuman origin. The objects or weapons that were borrowed, the behavior patterns and institutions that were imitated, the myths or beliefs that were assimilated, were believed to be charged with magico-religious power; indeed, it was for this reason that they had been noticed and the effort made to acquire them. Nor is this all.

These elements were adopted because it was believed that the Ancestors had received the first cultural revelations from Supernatural Beings. And since traditional societies have no historical memory in the strict sense, it took only a few generations, sometimes even less, for a recent innovation to be invested with all the prestige of the primordial revelations.

In the last analysis we could say that, though they are "open" to history, traditional societies tend to project every new acquisition into the primordial Time, to telescope all events in the same atemporal horizon of the mythical beginnings. Primitive societies too are changed by their history, although sometimes only to a very small degree; but what radically differentiates them from modern society is the absence of historical consciousness in them. Indeed, its absence is inevitable, in view of the conception of Time and the anthropology that are characteristic of all pre-Judaic humanity.

It is to this traditional knowledge that the novices gain access. They receive protracted instruction from their teachers, witness secret ceremonies, undergo a series of ordeals. And it is primarily these ordeals that constitute the religious experience of initiation— the encounter with the sacred. The majority of initiatory ordeals more or less clearly imply a ritual death followed by resurrection or a new birth. The central moment of every initiation is represented by the ceremony symbolizing the death of the novice and his return to the fellowship of the living. But he returns to life a new man, assuming another mode of being. Initiatory death signifies the end at once of childhood, of ignorance, and of the profane condition.

For archaic thought, nothing better expresses the idea of an end, of the final completion of anything, than death, just as nothing better expresses the idea of creation, of making, building, constructing, than the cosmogony. The cosmogonic myth serves as the paradigm, the exemplary model, for every kind of making. Nothing better ensures the success of any creation (a village, a house, a child) than the fact of copying it after the greatest of all creations, the cosmogony. Nor is this all. Since in the eyes of the primitives the cosmogony primarily represents the manifestation of the creative power of the gods, and therefore a prodigious irruption of the sacred, it is periodically reiterated in order to regenerate the world and human society. For symbolic repetition of the creation implies a reactualization of the primordial event, hence the presence of the Gods and their creative energies. The return to beginnings finds expression in a reactivation of the sacred forces that had then been manifested for the first time. If the world was restored to the state in which it had been at the moment when it came to birth, if the gestures that the Gods had made *for the first time* in the beginning were reproduced, society and the entire cosmos became what they had been then—pure, powerful, effectual, with all their possibilities intact.

Every ritual repetition of the cosmogony is preceded by a symbolic retrogression to Chaos. In order to be created anew, the old world must first be annihilated. The various rites performed in connection with the New Year can be put in two chief categories: (1) those that signify the return to Chaos (e.g., extinguishing fires, expelling "evil" and sins, reversal of habitual behavior, orgies, return of the dead); (2) those that symbolize the cosmogony (e.g., lighting new fires, departure of the dead, repetition of the acts by which the Gods created the world, solemn prediction of the weather for the ensuing year). In the scenario of initiatory rites, "death" corresponds to the temporary return to Chaos; hence it is the paradigmatic expression of the *end of a mode of being*—the mode of ignorance and of the child's irresponsibility. Initiatory death provides the clean slate on which will be written the successive revelations whose end is the formation of a new man. We shall later describe the different modalities of birth to a new, spiritual life. But now we must note that this new life is conceived as the true human existence, for it is open to the values of spirit. What is understood by the generic term "culture," comprising all the values of spirit, is accessible only to those who have been initiated. Hence participation in spiritual life is made possible by virtue of the religious experiences released during initiation.

All the rites of rebirth or resurrection, and the symbols that they imply, indicate that the novice has attained to another mode of existence, inaccessible to those who have not undergone the initiatory ordeals, who have not tasted death. We must note this characteristic of the archaic mentality: the belief that a state cannot be changed without first being *annihilated*—in the present instance, without the child's dying to childhood. It is impossible to exaggerate the importance of this obsession with beginnings, which, in sum, is the obsession with the absolute beginning, the cosmogony. For a thing to be well done, it must be done as it was done *the first time*. But the first time, the thing—this class of objects, this animal, this particular behavior—did not exist: when, in the beginning, this object, this animal, this institution, came into existence, it was as if, through the power of the Gods, being arose from nonbeing.

Initiatory death is indispensable for the beginning of spiritual life. Its function must be understood in relation to what it prepares: birth to a higher mode of being. As we shall see farther on, initiatory death is often symbolized, for example, by darkness, by cosmic night, by the telluric womb, the hut, the belly of a monster. All these images express regression to a preformal state, to a latent mode of being (complementary to the precosmogonic Chaos), rather than total annihilation (in the sense in which, for example, a member of the modern societies conceives death). These images and symbols of ritual death are inextricably connected with germination, with embryology; they already indicate a new life in course of preparation. Obviously, as we shall show later, there are other valuations of initiatory death—for example, joining the company of the dead and the Ancestors. But here again we can discern the same symbolism of the beginning: the beginning of spiritual life, made possible in this case by a meeting with spirits.

For archaic thought, then, man is *made*—he does not make himself all by himself. It is the old initiates, the spiritual masters, who make him. But these masters apply what was revealed to them at the beginning of Time by the Supernatural Beings. They are only the representatives of those Beings; indeed, in many cases they incarnate them. This is as much as to say that in order to become a man, it is necessary to resemble a mythical model. Man recognizes himself as such (that is, as man) to the extent to which he is no longer a "natural man," to which he is made a second time, in obedience to a paradigmatic and transhuman canon. The initiatory new birth is not natural, though it is sometimes expressed in obstetric symbols. This birth requires rites instituted by the Supernatural Beings; hence it is a divine work, created by the power and will of those Beings; it belongs, not to nature (in the modern, secularized sense of the term), but to sacred history. The second, initiatory birth does not repeat the first, biological birth. To attain the initiate's mode of being demands knowing realities that are not a part of nature but of the biography of the Supernatural Beings, hence of the sacred history preserved in the myths.

Even when they appear to be dealing only with natural phenomena—with the course of the sun, for example—the myths refer to a reality that is no longer the reality of Nature as modern man knows it today. For the primitive, nature is not simply natural; it is at the same time supernature, that is, manifestation of sacred forces and figure of transcendental realities. To know the myths is not (as was thought in the past century) to become aware of the regularity of certain cosmic phenomena (the course of the sun, the lunar cycle, the rhythm of vegetation, and the like); it is, first of all, to know what has happened in the world, has *really* happened, what the Gods and the civilizing Heroes *did*—their works, adventures, dramas. Thus it is to know a divine history—which nonetheless remains a "history," that is, a series of events that are unforeseeable, though consistent and significant.

In modern terms we could say that initiation puts an end to the natural man and introduces the novice to culture. But for archaic societies, culture is not a human product, its origin is supernatural. Nor is this all. It is through culture that man re-establishes contact with the world of the Gods and other Supernatural Beings and participates in their creative energies. The world of Supernatural Beings is the world in which things took place for the first time— the world in which the first tree and the first animal came into existence; in which an act, thenceforth religiously repeated, was performed for the first time (to walk in a particular posture, to dig a particular edible root, to go hunting during a particular phase of the moon); in which the Gods or the Heroes, for example, had such and such an encounter, suffered such and such a misadventure, uttered particular words, proclaimed particular norms. The myths lead us into a world that cannot be described but only "narrated," for it consists in the history of acts freely undertaken, of unforeseeable decisions, of fabulous transformations, and the like. It is, in short, the history of everything significant that has happened since the Creation of the world, of all the events that contributed to making man as he is today. The novice whom intiation introduces to the mythological traditions of the tribe is introduced to the sacred history of the world and humanity.

It is for this reason that initiation is of such importance for a knowledge of premodern man. It reveals the almost awesome seriousness with which the man of archaic societies assumed the responsibility of receiving and transmitting spiritual values.

FOREWORD TO THE NEW EDITION

The close of the twentieth century can be looked at simply, even fundamentally, as "The End," or else can be seen into as a thorough change, a period of radical alteration, a rush of endings and beginnings. The distinctions between the ways we view change and death become more important at the end of eras, at funeral rites and at births. The attitudes of mourners have a crucial effect on a funeral, and the manner of the attendants at a birth can help or harm the new life. Mid-wives once assisted the newborn into this world and helped the newly dead on to the "other world." Willingly, or not, we are all attendants at the funeral of the last era and the birth of the next. We are all mid-wives placing the shroud on a body soon to disappear and anointing the next birth with our prayers, fears, denials and hopes.

The radical dismantling of institutions, boundaries, beliefs and ecosystems that characterizes the end of the era is an extended funeral that we can consciously attend or try to deny. At some level we each know that huge shifts in nature and culture are affecting us daily. But, without some spiritual vision and ritual structure we lose the capacity to handle death and embrace life fully. Instead, we build walls of denial to hold off terror and confusion and try to cover our helplessness with displays of force and greed. Denial arises as a primary symptom of the age because of the scope of changes already under way and as a defense against the flood of losses and endings. The cost of mass denial can be found in the increase of random violence, increased abuse of drugs, the collapse of medicine, and the confusion in personal, gender and national identities. And the momentum of loss increases because a death unmourned becomes a lingering ghost that haunts the living until it receives its allotment of attention and tears. Meanwhile, each birth unprepared and uncared for invites the reckless spirits of chaos to feed on the next generation.

Through his writings, Mircea Eliade fervently worked at keeping the doors of perception open to the world of sacred symbols and creative ritual. Through his insistence that we are each the necessary inheritors

of a vast sacred heritage, he has acted as a spiritual elder and distant
mentor to me and many students of myth and ritual. Like an archeologist
of symbols, he has unearthed, preserved and found new meanings in
the rites of our ancestors. As we sort out which cultural artifacts to carry
across the threshold of the millennium, his practice of keeping the local
and specific details while seeking the cross-cultural meanings will be
increasingly valuable.

Rites and Symbols of Initiation was first published in 1958 on the
eve of an onslaught of social, sexual and spiritual changes in American
culture. At first titled *Birth and Rebirth*, it served as an academic text
for many years. Now, it finds regeneration as Mircea Eliade intended
it: ". . . addressed to any non-specialist reader interested in the spiritual
history of humanity." This renewal in print comes at a time of even greater
upheaval: the end of the millennium when underlying patterns of initiatory death and rebirth erupt through the surface of cultures and
disrupt cycles of nature. There may be no time more suited to the study
of rites of passage than the threshold between the end of modernity
and the uncertain future of humanity. As old proverbs remind: "We can
only see as far forward as we remember back." The future is contained
in the past; and the past is carried within us like seeds of memory waiting
for the waters of attention.

When looking behind before moving ahead, our usual mistake lies
in not looking back far enough. In his labors on behalf of the "sacred
world," Eliade doesn't make that mistake. He reaches all the way back
and down to the roots of the mysteries of birth and death, seeking the
parts they play in times of change and renewal. The rebirth of this book
in print is also a regeneration of the spirit of Eliade's work on ritual,
transformation and shamanism. This volume seems to function as an
offshoot, a renewable branch that sprouts from the great body of his
work. It also serves as a divining rod to find taproots of the "tree of
the knowledge of life and death."

This book is a meditation on initiation and rites that open pathways
between the withering "daily world" and the sacred "other world," where
root images can restore the flow of life again. From it arises a pageant,
a bold procession of images and ideas in which the faces of birth, death
and resurrection appear in sundry masks and guises. Symbols and rites
from many places and various stages of cultural ascendancy and decline
appear. Some are finely shaped and glisten with intelligent meaning,
while others are partly broken, poorly fashioned, twisted with loss. The
study of initiation rites becomes a tracing of the lines of "spiritual history."
When rites of passage disappear in the storm of modern, material

cultures, Eliade tracks the survival of the rites and symbols in the realms of dream, alchemy, literature and psychotherapy.

Eliade establishes initiation as a universal rite, an archetypal form that surfaces and influences life wherever events have the spirit of beginning or the weight of an end. "As if initiation and its patterns were indissolubly linked with the very structure of spiritual life . . . an indispensable process in every attempt at . . . regeneration." As an elemental pattern or archetypal style, initiation is a "whole way" of seeing into the world, one that sees death as part of the fabric of life. On the ground of initiation, death is the opposite of birth, not the opposite of life. Life includes both, and the spirit of life regenerates in the land of death. Archaic rites of initiation show the basic pattern for genuine change. For any transformation to be meaningful it must be thorough, and to be thorough requires both the ache of loss and a spirit of restoration.

Eliade writes that ". . . it is only in initiation that death is given a positive value." More than an empty tomb, death becomes also the womb of change. In dreams and dramas of initiation, death represents change for the entire psyche and life of a person. It means change inside and out, not a simple adaptation or switch in "lifestyle." Initiation includes death and rebirth, a radical altering of a person's "mode of being"; a shattering and shaking all the way to the ground of the soul. The initiate becomes as another person: more fully in life emotionally and more spiritually aware. Loss of identity and even feeling betrayal of one's self are essential to rites of passage. In that sense, every initiation causes a funeral and a birth; a mourning appropriate to death and a joyous celebration for the restoration of full life. Without conscious rituals of loss and renewal, individuals and societies lose the capacity to experience the sorrows and joy that are essential for feeling fully human. Without them life flattens out, and meaning drains from both living and dying. Soon there is a death of meaning and an increase in meaningless deaths.

Traditional rites of passage were based in the hard knowledge that the sanctity of life and the making of a meaningful death must be struggled for by each person and that the entire drama must be recast for each generation. Participating in "ordeals of finding meaning" was both an inheritance and a requirement that made each child a central figure in his or her own dream and in the life of the tribe. In contrast to our practice of criticizing young people for unnecessarily drawing attention to themselves, an awareness of initiation draws everyone to the young people to see the future breaking out of them. Youth naturally feel drawn to thresholds of the "unconscious" and the unfinished; they are both knowing and unknowing. If our first birth is a fall into life, this "second birth" falls toward death and the underworld. It requires a return to the roots of knowledge, the roots of consciousness and the seeds of meaning hidden in each person. Only by a descent and a series of adventures along the dark roads of the unconscious can the inner life fully awaken. Rites of initiation intended to make the inevitable descent a direct opening of the spirit and soul in the life of each youth. Through that opening the woman comes out of the girl, and the man separates from the boy. The story of childhood ends and the next drama begins.

Initiation means beginning the revelation of one's true self. It includes the opening up of the inner life of the spirit and releasing the potentials and possibilities within the individual. Beyond that, the initiations of youth always imply an opportunity for the cleansing and restoration of the life force of the community and the society. The initiation of youths into full life also represents a critical opportunity for a society to sustain meaning and teach life-affirming values. As Eliade says, "this meaning is always religious." Or as we now might say, the meaning is always spiritual, elementally spiritual before becoming religious. During initiation the individual becomes bound through spiritual experience to the future of the society on one hand and open to the origins and ancestral beginnings of the group in the past. For a time, the initiate steps out of being simply himself or herself and becomes an ancestral, dream-time hero or heroine re-entering the origin stories of the culture. By shedding the skin of their limited sense of self, marked by the time they were born into and the family they were born amongst, the initiates encounter the sacred. Temporarily, they walk in the footsteps of heroes and heroines engaged in elemental struggles, touched by mystery, learning to sustain life and face death.

When rites of passage disappear from conscious presentation, they nonetheless appear in unconscious and semi-conscious guises. They surface as misguided and mis-informed attempts to change one's own life. They become mis-carriages of meaning, tragic acts or empty forms and ghostly shapes. For, underlying the surface structures of schools, fraternities, sororities, maternity groups, military organizations, street gangs, rap bands, crack houses, meditation centers and prisons lie the bones and sinews of initiatory rites and symbols. Whenever life gets stuck or reaches a dead end, where people are caught in rites of addiction, possessed by destructive images, compelled to violent acts or pulled apart by grief and loss, the process of initiation presses to break through. The most important reason to study rites of passage may be to see in the events erupting in the streets and at the borders and crossroads of our post-historic era the archaic energies of life renewing itself. As old walls fall and institutions rattle, even older forces of change and renewal gather to pour through the cracks.

Learning the language of initiation means finding in the inevitable struggles of our own lives ". . . certain types of real ordeals . . . the spiritual crises, the solitude and despair through which every human being must pass in order to attain to a responsible, genuine, and creative life. Even if the initiatory character of these ordeals is not apprehended as such, it remains true nonetheless that man becomes *himself* [and woman herself] only after having solved a series of desperately difficult and even dangerous situations; that is, after having undergone 'tortures' and 'death,' followed by an awakening to another life. . . . If we look closely, we see that every human life is made up of a series of ordeals, of 'deaths,' and of 'resurrections.'"

Seen with an eye for initiation and mystery, addictions are rites of substitution, where "tortures and death" occur on a "junk" level that can't quite create a breakthrough. The ritual revolves around a "cracked quest" for spiritual relief, but keeps repeating the same alchemical mistake and moves toward actual death when real change was the desire. In Eliade's descriptions of shamanic dismemberment and dazed–crazed out of body wanderings can be seen the "spirit afflictions" of the hordes of homeless psyches and homeless people that increasingly haunt the cracking streets of modern cities. Like scenes from initiatory rituals, the unconscious breaks through, the psyche turns inside-out and inner sufferings become outer dramas. But, unlike the conscious efforts of rites of passage, the sacrifice doesn't work; a spiritual home in the heart of the tribe is not found.

Without a ritual to contain and inform the wounds of life, pain and suffering increase, yet meaningful change doesn't occur. Where drops of blood once symbolized life trying to change, pools of blood stain street after street without renewing the spirit of life. Instead of ritual descent and emotional resurrection, complete death occurs; actual corpses pile up. Instead of the startling hum of bullroarers twirled by unpredictable elders, the wail of sirens, the crack of bullets and whirl of flashing lights bring the "underworld" to life each night. Instead of participating in a prepared rite for leaving childhood games through ordeals of emotional struggle and spiritual alertness, gangs of blindly wounded youth hurl their woundedness at the darkness and spit angry bullets at groups that are their mirror image, attacking masks of themselves. The sacrificial blood once offered by those trying to glimpse mysteries at the thresholds of the stages of life has become bloody "street sacrifices" of entire generations. An unconscious, chaotic amassing of death gathers where the passage required some honest suffering, a scar to mark the event and a community to accept and acknowledge the change. Denying that each individual must struggle at the thresholds of spiritual and emotional self-discovery eventually destroys any shared awareness of the sanctity of life.

In the symbolic mind and in the ritual imagination of most peoples, a small amount of blood exposed to the outside world represents the immediate, mutual presence of life and death. The metaphor of showing blood to make a change brings present the death of what was contained and the birth of something that was hidden. In the history of initiation, woundings, beatings, scarifications and hair-cutting represent dying by losing some part of the living world to the "other world" of death. In order to gain an increase of life for the individual evolving and for the community involved with that individual, something must be sacrificed or "made sacred." When a culture, for whatever reason, loses its ability to make real changes out of symbolic sacrifices and make new meaning out of individual suffering, then the quantity of violence, blood spilling and actual death increases for everyone.

Behind all involvements of young people with actual death hides the desire to find full life through a symbolic death that reveals a core of meaning and purpose in their lives. The beatings administered to prospective members of modern street gangs are semi-conscious reflections of ancient rites of separation. The foolish dramas of fraternity and military hazings increasingly miss and obscure the actual need to experience "spiritual hazards." Unguided by ritual elders and genuine spiritual aims, all groups become simple "gangs." In contrast, Eliade offers many examples of complete rituals of separation, ordeals, death and return of the "twice-born." In one pattern, the ritual beating of the initiate is followed by a fall into narcotic sleep and a funeral service. Family and friends mourn the death of their loved one, who undergoes partial burial in a grave. During the burial time he receives specific spiritual and psychological instruction, has time to reflect on the past and an opportunity to view the future from the grave. Eventually, there follows the resurrection of the new person, more fully in life by feeling a "little death."

Now, it seems that we increasingly live only the first half of these rites, unconsciously enacting the wounding, narcotic sleep and spiritual death. Living becomes profane, a "half-life," a modern tragedy of pointless suffering, abuse or addiction, loss of identity and death-like isolation. Descents and ordeals occur randomly, without a ritual surrounding, without the benefit of the love and instruction necessary to guide a person toward the chance of a second birth. When the inner purpose and spirit of a person do not get revealed, re-valued and acknowledged by an appropriate community, people increasingly feel like victims and act like outcasts. When the rites of change are incomplete, there is an increasing sense of chaos and loss of the possibility of restoring the community through the shared joy over the return of "the dead."

When the death-side of life is denied, the birth-side becomes obscured and some of the importance of each life is lost right at birth, at the beginning. In this process of loss, women's rites and mysteries get diminished and the womb seems to lose its place at the center of life. Although *Rites and Symbols* frequently focuses on rituals for men and primarily uses male pronouns, there are descriptions of rites that reflect women's symbols and experiences. Eliade acknowledges that there has been more hearsay than direct observation of women's rituals. Early studies were often done by men who may have lacked interest and surely lacked access to women's rites. He also points at the rapid destruction and decline of women's mystery groups and puberty rituals when exposed to Western influences.

Puberty rites often begin the psychological and spiritual division of rights and powers between the genders, and rites of separation often distinguish different paths for each. Boys often get called to initiatory events as part of a group that forms when there happen to be enough eligible age-mates. By contrast, a girl often begins her rite of passage individually when the mystery of her menses breaks the seal of her inner world and indicates that the spirit of a woman wants to come out. When rites of coming out are lost, the girl loses touch with her place in the community. What has been lost over time is the sense that each daughter represents the psychic as well as genetic womb of the tribe. Each represents the well of ancestral memories and the creative crucible from which the future will come. During initiation the womb manifests as symbol of renewal and generativity showing the body to be a spiritual vessel, necessary for understanding the body of nature and for carrying knowledge of the tribe.

When the daughter of the tribe temporarily separates from the village, she becomes as a fetus in the womb of Mother Nature. She enters a time of segregation and isolation in darkness that represents a return to the womb. Dwelling in the dark may occur in a cave, a hut with no windows or within the hollow enclosure of a sacred tree. Each daughter must find a mysterious and unique connection to the darkness from which all life originates. The hollow tree stands symbolically as a tomb in which the daughter disappears and as a womb of the tree of life from which the woman will step. During isolation, the female initiate may not be allowed to feed or care for herself. Rather, she retreats into a still meditation on the origins of life while she is being nourished and sustained by older women. These spiritual and psychological mothers hold her in a fetal crucible prior to the second birth.

What begins as an individual and very personal break in the world of childhood typically ends as a unifying public celebration upon the return of the initiated woman. The one who disappeared into Mother Nature returns adorned with new clothes, wrapped in the knowledge of the old women of the tribe and acknowledged as a carrier of life and deep creative will. At the return, all of the village would be present to recognize, admire and acknowledge the birth of a woman from the blood and trials of a girl.

When rites of this kind are not enacted, or if they lose genuine spiritual elements, reverence for the feminine is lost and brutality toward women and girls increases. Another loss can be seen in the lack of understanding and respect for body, for nature and for the mysteries of birth. Hidden behind many current afflictions of the feminine—anorexia, bulimia and obsession with surface beauty—is a ritual emptiness, a lack of being seen, a spiritual omission. The woundings that occur during initiations can be rejected as brutal, but I would argue that greater brutality results where there are no "ordeals of meaning" and no rites of acceptance into the adult community.

Toward the end of the book, Eliade writes, "It does not fall to us to determine to what extent traditional initiations fulfilled their promises. The important fact is that they proclaimed their intention, and professed to possess the means, of transmuting human life." The intention of this book includes keeping alive the symbols and rites necessary for renewing a life and for surviving the onslaught of changes at the end of an age. Being alive at the end of this millennium means getting caught in fundamental crises that call into question every aspect of life and death. It becomes essential to have an eye for the symbolic and a feel for ritual as radical changes affect both time and place, both culture and nature. Eliade again: "In such moments of total crisis, only one hope seems to offer any issue—the hope of beginning life over again." Anyone caught in a total crisis feels that he or she is brushing against death, and anyone "undergoing such a crisis dreams of new, regenerated life, fully realized and significant." Amongst the sadness, loss and litter at the end of the age, Eliade reminds us that "the hope and dream of these moments of total crisis are to obtain a definitive and total *renovatio*, a renewal capable of transmuting life."

MICHAEL MEADE

CHAPTER I

Initiation Mysteries in Primitive Religions

Preliminary Remarks

In this book I shall present the most important types of initiation, seeking above all to decipher their deeper meaning. The meaning is always religious, for the change of existential status in the novice is produced by a religious experience. The initiate becomes another man because he has had a crucial revelation of the world and life. I shall therefore treat this important and difficult problem in the perspective of the history of religion and not, as is usually done, in the perspectives of cultural anthropology or of sociology. Several excellent studies have been written from these points of view; I need only mention two at this time, those of Heinrich Schurtz and Hutton Webster.[1] The historian of religion will always make use—and most profitable use—of the results attained by the ethnologist and the sociologist; but he has to complement these results and give them their due place in a different and broader perspective. The ethnologist is concerned only with the societies that we call primitive, whereas the historian of religion will include the entire religious history of humanity in his field of investigation, from the earliest cults in palaeolithic times of which we have records down to modern religious movements. To understand the meaning and the role of initiation, the historian of religion will cite not only the rituals of primitive peoples but also the ceremonies of the Greco-Oriental mysteries or of Indo-Tibetan Tantrism, the initiation rites of the Scandinavian berserkers or the initiatory ordeals that are still traceable even in the experiences of the great mystics.

1

The historian of religion parts company with the sociologist too, since his primary concern is to understand the religious experience of initiation and to interpret the deeper meaning of the symbolisms present in initiatory myths and rites. In short, the ambition of the historian of religion is to arrive at the existential situation assumed by religious man in the experience of initiation, and to make that primordial experience intelligible to his contemporaries.

Generally speaking, the history of religion distinguishes three categories, or types, of initiations. The first category comprises the collective rituals whose function is to effect the transition from childhood or adolescence to adulthood, and which are obligatory for all members of a particular society. Ethnological literature terms these rituals "puberty rites," "tribal initiation," or "initiation into an age group."

The other two categories of initiations differ from puberty initiations in that they are not obligatory for all members of the community and that most of them are performed individually or for comparatively small groups. The second category includes all types of rites for entering a secret society, a *Bund*, or a confraternity. These secret societies are limited to one sex and are extremely jealous of their respective secrets. Most of them are male and constitute secret fraternities (*Männerbünde*); but there are also some female secret societies. On the level of primitive cultures, societies open to both sexes are extremely rare; where they exist, they usually represent a phenomenon of degeneration. But in the ancient Mediterranean and Near Eastern world, the mysteries were open to both sexes; and although they are a little different in type, we can put the Greco-Oriental mysteries in the category of secret confraternities.

Finally, there is a third category of initiation—the type that occurs in connection with a mystical vocation; that is, on the level of primitive religions, the vocation of the medicine man or the shaman. A specific characteristic of this third category is the importance that personal experience assumes in it. Broadly speaking, we can say that those who submit themselves to the ordeals typical of this third kind of initiation are—whether voluntarily of involuntarily—destined to participate in a more intense religious experience than is accessible to the rest of the community. I said "voluntarily or involuntarily" because a member of a community can become a medicine man or a shaman not only in consequence of a personal decision to acquire religious powers (the process called "the quest") but also through vocation ("the call"), that is, because he is *forced* by Superhuman Beings to become a medicine man or shaman.

I may add that these last two categories—initiation imposed upon entrance to a secret society, and initiation requisite for obtaining a higher religious status—have a good deal in common. They might even be regarded as two varieties of a single class. What principally tends to distinguish them is the element of ecstasy, which is of great importance in shamanic initiations. I may add too that there is a sort of structural common denominator among all these categories of initiation, with the result that, from a certain point of view, all initiations are much alike. But it seemed best to begin by drawing a few guiding lines in this extremely wide field, for without them we might easily get lost. In the course of the following pages, I shall have occasion to supplement and amend these few preliminary remarks.

Initiation represents one of the most significant spiritual phenomena in the history of humanity. It is an act that involves not only the religious life of the individual, in the modern meaning of the word "religion"; it involves his *entire* life. It is through initiation that, in primitive and archaic societies, man becomes what he is and what he should be—a being open to the life of the spirit, hence one who participates in the culture into which he was born. For as we shall soon see, *the puberty initiation represents above all the revelation of the sacred—and, for the primitive world, the sacred means not only everything that we now understand by religion, but also the whole body of the tribe's mythological and cultural traditions.* In a great many cases puberty rites, in one way or another, imply the revelation of sexuality—but, for the entire premodern world, sexuality too participates in the sacred. In short, through initiation, the candidate passes beyond the natural mode—the mode of the child—and gains access to the cultural mode; that is, he is introduced to spiritual values. From a certain point of view it could almost be said that, for the primitive world, it is through initiation that men attain the status of human beings; before initiation, they do not yet fully share in the human condition precisely because they do not yet have access to the religious life. This is why initiation represents a decisive experience for any individual who is a member of a premodern society; it is a fundamental existential experience because through it a man becomes able to assume his mode of being in its entirety.

As we shall presently see, the puberty initiation begins with an act of rupture—the child or the adolescent is separated from his mother, and sometimes the separation is performed in a decidedly brutal way. But the initiation is not the concern only of the young novices. The ceremony involves the tribe as a whole. A new generation is instructed, is made fit to be integrated into the community of adults. And on this occasion, through the repetition, the *reactualization,* of the traditional rites, the entire community is regenerated. This is why, in primitive societies, initiations are among the most important of religious festivals.

The Sacred Ground

Since the Australian puberty ceremonies represent a comparatively archaic form of initiation, I shall turn to them for our first examples. Usually a considerable number of tribes take part in the ceremony, hence the preparations for an initiation festival require a long time. Several months pass between the time when the older men decide to assemble the tribes and the beginning of the ceremony proper. The headman of the inviting tribe sends messengers, carrying bull-roarers (long, thin, narrow pieces of wood attached to a string; when whirled through the air, they make a roaring sound), to the other headmen, to whom they announce the decision. Since the Australian tribes are divided into two intermarrying "classes," class A undertakes the initiation of the youths of class B, and vice versa.[2] In short, the novices are initiated by their potential fathers-in-law.[3] It is unnecessary to rehearse all the details of the preparation for the "bora," as the ceremony is called among the tribes of eastern Australia. Only one fact requires mention; in everything that is done, the greatest precautions are taken to keep the women from knowing what is afoot.

Broadly speaking, the initiation ceremony comprises the following phases: first, the preparation of the "sacred ground," where the men will remain in isolation during the festival; second, the separation of the novices from their mothers and, in general, from all women; third, their segregation in the bush, or in a special isolated camp, where they will be instructed in the religious traditions of the tribe; fourth, certain operations performed on the novices, usually circumcision, the extraction of a tooth, or subincision, but sometimes scarring or pulling out the hair. Throughout the period of the initiation, the novices must behave in a special way; they undergo a number of ordeals, and are subjected to various dietary taboos and prohibitions. Each element of this complex initiatory scenario has a religious meaning. It is primarily these meanings, and their articulation into a religious vision of the world, that I hope to bring out in these pages.

As we just saw, the bora always involves the preliminary preparation of a sacred ground. The Yuin, the Wiradjuri, the Kamilaroi, and some of the Queensland tribes prepare a circular ring of earth, in which the preliminary ceremonies will later take place, and, at some distance from it, a small sacred enclosure. These two constructions are connected by a path, along which the men of the inviting tribe set up various images and sacred emblems. As the tribal contingents arrive, the men are led along the path and shown the images. There is dancing every night, sometimes continuing for several weeks, until the last contingent arrives.[4]

Mathews gives a quite detailed description of the sacred ground as prepared by the Kamilaroi. It consists of two circles. The larger, which is seventy feet in diameter, has a pole three yards high in the center "with a bunch of emu's feathers tied on the top."[5] In the smaller circle two young trees are fixed in the ground with their roots in the air. After the ritual separation from the women, two older men—sometimes described as wizards—climb these trees and there chant the traditions of the bora.[6] (These trees, which are anointed with human blood,[7] have a symbolism that we shall investigate later.) The two circles are connected by a path. On either side of the path a number of figures are drawn on the ground or modeled in clay. The largest, which is fifteen feet in height, is that of the Supreme Being, Baiamai. A couple represents the mythical Ancestors, and a group of twelve human figures stands for the young men who were with Baiamai in his first camp. Other figures represent animals and nests. The neophytes are not allowed to look at these images, which will be destroyed by fire before the end of their initiation. But they can examine them on the occasion of the next bora.[8] This detail is interesting; it shows that religious instruction does not end with initiation, but continues and has several degrees.

According to Mathews, the "bora ground represents Baiamai's first camp, the people who were with him while there and the gifts he presented them with."[9] This is to say that the participants in the initiation ceremony reactualize the mythical period in which the bora was held for the first time. Not only does the sacred ground imitate the exemplary model, Baiamai's first camp, but the ritual performed reiterates Baiamai's gestures and acts. In short, what is involved is a reactualization of Baiamai's creative work, and hence a regeneration of the world. For the sacred ground is at once an image of the world (*imago mundi*) and a world sanctified by the presence of the Divine Being. During the bora the participants return to the mythical, sacred time when Baiamai was present on earth and founded the mysteries that are now being performed. The participants become in some sort contemporaries of the first bora, the bora that took place in the beginning, in the Dream Time (*bugari* or "Alchera times"), to use the Australian expression. This is why the initiation ceremonies are so important in the lives of the aborigines; by performing them, they reintegrate the sacred Time of the beginning of things, they commune with the presence of Baiamai and the other mythical Beings, and, finally, they regenerate the world, for the world is renewed by the reproduction of its exemplary model, Baiamai's first camp.

Since the initiation ceremonies were founded by the Divine Beings or the mythical Ancestors, the primordial Time is reintegrated whenever they are performed. This is true not only for the Australians, but for the entire primitive world. For what is involved here is a fundamental conception in archaic religions—the repetition of a ritual founded by Divine Beings implies the reactualization of the original Time when the rite was first performed. This is why a rite has efficacy—it participates in the completeness of the sacred primordial Time. The rite makes the myth present. Everything that the myth tells of the Time of beginning, the *"bugari* times," the rite reactualizes, shows it as happening, *here and now*. When the Bâd, a West Kimberley tribe, prepare to initiate the boys, the old men withdraw to the forest and look for the *ganbor* tree "under which Djamar"—their Supreme Being—"rested in ancestral times." A witch doctor, who goes ahead, "has the task to discover the tree." When it is found, the men surround it, singing, and then cut it down with their flint knives.[10] The mythical tree is made present.

All the gestures and operations that succeed one another during the initiation are only the repetition of exemplary models—that is, gestures and operations that were performed, in mythical times, by the founders of the ceremonies. This very fact makes them sacred, and their periodical reiteration regenerates the entire religious life of the community. Sometimes there are gestures whose meaning seems to have been forgotten, but which are still repeated because they were made by the mythical beings when the ceremony was

inaugurated. Among the Arunta, at a particular point in the ceremony a woman lifts the novice onto her shoulders; and the explanation given is that, by performing this gesture, she is imitating what
the Unthippa women did in the mythical Time (*alcheringa*).[11]

To return to our subject: the sacred ground plays an essential
role in Australian initiation ceremonies because it represents the
image of the primordial world as it was when the Divine Being was
on earth. The women, children, and uninitiated are kept at a distance, and even the novices will acquire merely a superficial knowledge of it. Only as initiates, at the time of the next bora, will they
examine the images set along the path between the two circles.
Having been taught the mythology of the tribe, they will be able to
understand the symbols.

Separation from the Mother

The separation of the novices from their mothers takes place
more or less dramatically, in accordance with the customs of different tribes. The least dramatic method is found among the Kurnai,
where the initiation ceremony is in any case quite simple. The
mothers sit behind the novices; the men come forward in single file
between the two groups and so separate them. The instructors raise
the novices into the air several times, the novices stretching their
arms as far as possible toward the sky. The meaning of this gesture
is clear; the neophytes are being consecrated to the Sky God. They
are then led into the sacred enclosure, where, lying on their backs
with their arms crossed on their chests, they are covered with rugs.
From then on they see and hear nothing. After a montonous song,
they fall asleep; later, the women withdraw. "If a woman," a
Kurnai headman said to Howitt, "were to see these things, or hear
what we tell the boys, I would kill her."[12]

Among the Yuin—as among some other Australian tribes—the
novice is put under the charge of two guardians. Throughout the
initiation, these guardians prepare his food, bring him water, and
instruct him in the traditional myths and legends, the powers of
the medicine man, and his duties to the tribe. One night a great fire
is lighted and the guardians carry the novices to it on their shoulders.
The novices are told to look at the fire and not to move, no matter
what may happen. Behind them their mothers gather, completely
covered with branches. For ten or twelve minutes the boys are
"roasted" at the fire.[13] When the chief medicine man considers that
this first ordeal has lasted long enough and that the novices have

been sufficiently roasted, the bull-roarers are sounded behind the row of women. At this signal the guardians make the boys run to the sacred enclosure, where they are ordered to lie down with their faces to the ground and are covered with opossum skins and rugs. Soon afterward the women are given permission to rise, and they retire a few miles away, where they set up a new camp. The first initiation ceremony, comprising the separation from the women and the ordeal by fire, is thus completed. From that night on the novices share only in the life of the men.[14]

Among the Murring, the separation is more abrupt and dramatic. Covered with blankets, the women sit down on the ground with their boys in front of them. At a particular moment the novices are seized by the men, who come up running, and they run away together.[15]

The Wiradjuri call the initiation ceremonies *Guringal,* "belonging to the bush." The scenario is the same: according to Howitt, the women are covered with branches and blankets; the novices are seized by their guardians and carried off to the forest, where they are daubed with red ocher.[16] Mathews gives a fuller and livelier description: a group of men arrives from the direction of the sacred ground, sounding bull-roarers, beating the ground with rods, and throwing burning sticks. Meanwhile, other men quietly seize the boys and lead them some distance away. When the women and children are allowed to look, they see nothing but ashes and burning sticks all about them, and they are told that Daramulun tried to burn them when he came to take the novices.[17]

The meaning of this first part of the ceremony, the separation of the neophytes from their mothers, seems quite clear. What we have is a break, sometimes quite a violent break, with the world of childhood—which is at once the maternal and female world and the child's state of irresponsibility and happiness, of ignorance and asexuality. The break is made in such a way as to produce a strong impression both on the mothers and the novices. In fact, in the case of nearly all Australian tribes the mothers are convinced that their sons will be killed and eaten by a hostile and mysterious divinity, whose name they do not know, but whose voice they have heard in the terrifying sound of the bull-roarers. They are assured, of course, that the divinity will soon resuscitate the novices in the form of grown men, that is, of initiates. But in any case the novices die to childhood, and the mothers have a foreboding that the boys will never again be what they were before initiation: *their* children.

When the lads finally come back to the camp, the mothers touch them to make sure that they are really their sons. Among some Australian tribes—as among other peoples too—the mothers mourn over the initiands as the dead are mourned.

As for the novices, their experience is still more decisive. For the first time they feel religious fear and terror, for they are told beforehand that they will be captured and killed by Divine Beings. As long as they were considered to be children, they took no part in the religious life of the tribe. If by chance they had heard references to the mysterious Beings, and scraps of myths and legends, they did not realize what was in question. They had perhaps seen dead people, but it did not occur to them that death was something that concerned themselves. For them, it was an exterior "thing," a mysterious event that happened to other people, especially to the old. Now, suddenly, they are torn from their blissful childhood unconsciousness, and are told that they are to die, that they will be killed by the divinity. The very act of separation from their mothers fills them with forebodings of death—for they are seized by unknown, often masked men, carried far from their familiar surroundings, laid on the ground, and covered with branches.

For the first time they face an unfamiliar experience of darkness. This is not the darkness that they have known hitherto, the natural phenomenon of night—a night that was never wholly dark, for there were the stars, the moon, fires—but an absolute and menacing darkness, peopled with mysterious beings and above all made terrifying by the approach of the divinity announced by the bull-roarers. This experience of darkness, of death, and of the nearness of Divine Beings will be continually repeated and deepened throughout the initiation. As we shall see, a considerable number of initiation rites and ordeals reactualize the motif of death in darkness and at the hands of Divine Beings. But it is important to emphasize that the very first act of the ceremony already implies the experience of death, for the novices are violently flung into an unknown world, where the presence of Divine Beings is sensed through the terror that they inspire.

The maternal universe was that of the profane world. The universe that the novices now enter is that of the sacred world. Between the two, there is a break, a rupture of continuity. Passing from the profane to the sacred world in some sort implies the experience of death; he who makes the passage dies to one life in order to gain access to another. In the example we are considering, the novice dies to childhood and to the irresponsibility of the child's existence —that is, profane existence—in order to gain access to a higher life, the life where participation in the sacred becomes possible.

The Kurnai Initiation Mystery

All this will be more clearly apparent when we see what happens to the novices after they have been taken in charge by their instructors. To give a better idea of the interconnections between the various ritual and ideological moments that go to make up an initiation ceremony, I shall describe some of these ceremonies in their entirety, that is, without dividing them up in order to discuss their motifs separately. This inevitably involves a certain amount of repetition, but I know no other way to display the succession of ritual moments and, in so doing, to bring out the structures of different initiation ceremonies. I shall begin with the simplest and least dramatic, the ceremony performed by the Kurnai. You will remember that we left the novices, sitting on the ground in the sacred enclosure and covered with rugs, falling asleep after a monotonous chant. When they wake they are invested with a "belt of manhood," and their instruction begins.

The central mystery of the initiation is called "Showing the Grandfather." One day the novices are again made to lie on the ground and rugs are put over their heads. The men approach, whirling bull-roarers. The headman tells the novices to throw off the rugs and to look at the sky and then at the men who are carrying the bull-roarers. Then two old men say to them: "You must never tell this. You must not tell your mother, nor your sister, nor any who is not *jeraeil*," that is, who is not initiated. They are shown the two bull-roarers—one of which is larger, the other smaller, and which are called "man" and "woman"—and the headman tells them the myth of the origin of the initiation. Long, long ago, a Divine Being, Mungan-Ngaua, lived on earth. It was he who civilized the Kurnai. His son Tundum is the direct ancestor of the Kurnai. Mungan-Ngaua instituted the initiation mysteries and his son conducted them for the first time, using the two bull-roarers that bear his name and that of his wife. But a traitor revealed the *jeraeil* mysteries to women. In his anger, Mungan-Ngaua brought on a cosmic cataclysm in which almost the entire human race perished, and soon after he ascended into the sky.[18] His son Tundum and Tundum's wife were turned into porpoises. While telling them this myth, the old men hand the bull-roarers to the neophytes and tell them to whirl them.

After this mystery is revealed, all return to the camp. But the teaching continues. The neophytes are especially instructed in the duties of the adult. They also attend a number of dramatic representations, illustrating the events of mythical times. The final rite involves a fresh act of separation from the mother; she asks her son for water to drink, but he "splashes water over her." The women then withdraw to their camp. Howitt saw a mother crying for her son as if he were dead. As for the neophytes, they will remain in the bush with their tutors for several more months.[19]

The essence of this ceremony lies in the communication of the name and myth of the Supreme Being, and the revelation of his relation to the bull-roarers and to the initiation mystery The Kurnai *jeraeil* involves no kind of operation or mutilation. Instead, the initiation is confined to religious, moral, and social instruction. This form of initiation has been seen as not only the simplest but also the oldest in Australia.[20] And the absence of violent ordeals and the peaceful nature of the ceremony in general is indeed striking.

Supreme Being and Initiation Among the Yuin

With other Australian tribes, dramatic elements play a more important role. For example, among the Yuin and the Murring, after the novices have been separated from their mothers, the ceremony continues as follows. The men whirl bull-roarers and point with raised arms to the sky; this gesture signifies "the Great Master" (*biamban*), the Supreme Being, whose real name—unknown to the uninitiated and to women—is Daramulun. The instructors tell the novices the myths of Daramulun, and forbid them ever to speak of these things before women or children. Soon after, all set out in procession for the mountains.[21] At each halt magic dances are performed. The medicine men cause their magical influence to enter the novices, thus making them pleasing to Daramulun. When they are close to the mountains the guardians and novices make a camp by themselves, while the other men prepare a cleared ground in the forest. When this is ready, the novices are brought to it by their tutors. As usual, they look at nothing but the ground between their feet. When they are suddenly ordered to raise their eyes, they see before them masked and disguised men, and to one side, carved on a tree, the figure of Daramulun, three feet high. Presently their guardians cover their eyes, the chief medicine man approaches dancing, seizes the head of each novice in turn, and knocks out one of his incisors with a chisel and a small hammer. The boy is not allowed to spit blood, or else the wound will not heal.

Usually the novices endure this ordeal with admirable indifference. They are then led to the tree bearing the image of Daramulun, and the great secret is revealed to them. Daramulun lives beyond the sky, and from there watches what men are doing. It is he who takes care of men after they die. It was he who instituted the initiation ceremony and taught it to their ancestors. The medicine men receive their powers from Daramulun. "He is the great *Biamban* who can do anything and go anywhere, and he gave the tribal laws to their fathers, who have handed them down from father to son until now."[22] The medicine man warns the novices that he will kill them if they reproduce the image of Daramulun in the main camp. Each novice receives a "man's belt" ("a long cord of opossum-fur string"). After this, all return to the small camp at the edge of the forest, where many dances and pantomimes, imitating the behavior of various animals, are performed.

As Spencer and Gillen have pointed out in connection with the Arunta, these dances and pantomimes have a deep religious meaning, "for each performer represents an ancestral individual who lived in the Alcheringa."[23] Hence there is a reactualization of mythical events, which enables the new initiates to assimilate the religious heritage of the tribe. The dances are continued until three o'clock in the morning, and are resumed the next day. A final pantomime symbolizes death and resurrection. A medicine man is buried in a grave, and invocations are chanted to Daramulun. Suddenly the medicine man rises from his grave, with "magical substances" (*joïas*) in his mouth, substances that he claims to have just received from Daramulun. At noon, the entire group bathe in a stream. "Everything belonging to the bush work is washed away, so that the women may not know anything about it."[24] The initiates are now shown the bull-roarers, and then all return to the main camp. Smeared with red ocher, the initiates now resemble the other men. The women wait for them, each mother having "a band of white clay across her face as a sign of mourning."[25] Afterward the young initiates will live in the bush, eating only certain kinds of small animals, for they are under a number of dietary prohibitions. They will remain in the bush for six or seven months, under the supervision of their tutors, who visit them from time to time.[26]

In this long and varied initiation ceremony, certain features first strike us. Particularly noticeable are the insistence upon secrecy and above all the dramatic quality of the ritual. This is in the form of a scenario with several principal moments: dances by the medicine men and exhibition of their magical powers, dramatic revelation of the name and myth of the Supreme Being, violent extraction of the novice's incisor. Daramulun has a role of the first importance; the Divine Being is present both in the bull-roarers and in the image carved in the tree. As for the pantomime of the medicine man's death and resurrection, it shows not only that Daramulun himself resuscitates him, but also that he personally receives the medicine man and gives him magical substances. No other Australian puberty ceremony gives such a important role to the Supreme Being. Everything to which the novice is subjected is done in the name of Daramulun, and all the revelations concern his acts and his powers.

Symbolism of Initiatory Death

The role of the Supreme Being is also of considerable importance in the Wiradjuri initiation ceremonies.[27] When the novices have been taken to the forest, they are instructed by their tutors and witness the dances of the medicine men, who, daubed with ashes, display their magical powers, exhibiting objects that they claim to extract from their entrails. In one of the most spectacular performances, the chief medicine man disappears for a short time, then returns clothed in branches and leaves, which he says that he has gathered in Baiame's camp. For the Wiradjuri, Daramulun is no longer what he is for the Yuin, a Supreme Being, but the son or servant of Baiame, the highest of the Gods. However, Daramulun plays the principal role in the rite of extracting the incisor. According to Mathews' description,[28] the novices are covered with blankets and are told that Daramulun is coming to burn them. While the tooth is being knocked out, the bull-roarer sounds. The blankets are suddenly removed, and the tutors point to the bull-roarer, crying, "That is Daramulun!" The novices are allowed to touch the bull-roarers, which are then destroyed or carefully burned. According to a myth summarized by Mathews,[29] Daramulun told his father, or master, Baiame, that during initiation he killed the boys, cut them to pieces, burned them, and then restored them to life, "new beings, but each with a tooth missing." Other variants of the myth make him swallow them, then disgorge them alive.

This extremely important initiatory motif—being swallowed by a Divine Being or a monster—will occupy our attention later. For the moment, I will add that other tribes too believe that Daramulun kills and resuscitates the boys during their initiation. The Wonghibon, a Wiradjuri subtribe, say that Thurmulun seizes the novice, kills him, sometimes tears him to pieces, and then resuscitates him with one tooth missing.[30] Among the Turrbal, when the bull-roarer is heard at night the women and children believe that the medicine men are eating the novices.[31] In this example the magicians are merged with the mythical Being incarnated in the bull-roarer and institutor of the rite. According to Spencer and Gillen, among the Unmatjera, the Kaitish, and the Binbinga of the Gulf of Carpentaria region, the women and children are convinced that the noise of the bull-roarers is the voice of a spirit who eats the novices, or who kills and resuscitates them.[32] For the moment, let us note this connection between initiatory death at the hands of a Divine Being and the sound of the bull-roarer. We shall later see that this sound is the symbol of a divinity who bestows not only death but also life, sexuality, and fertility.

To return to the Wiradjuri, Howitt, describing the period passed in the forest, records a detail that is highly significant; the men cut a spiral piece from the bark of a tree to symbolize the path between sky and earth. In my opinion this represents a mystical *reactivation* of the connections between the human world and the divine world of the sky. According to the myths the first man, created by Baiame, ascended to the sky by a path and conversed with his Creator.[33] The role of the bark spiral in the initiation festival is thus clear—as symbol of ascension it reinforces the connection with the sky world of Baiame. We shall see that the symbol of ascent into the sky occurs in other types of Australian initiations. To conclude our description of the Wiradjuri ceremony, when the novices come back to the main camp, their mothers treat them as strangers. They beat them with branches; the novices flee to the bush, where this time they will remain for almost a year. This is their definitive separation from their mothers. Under the supervision of their guardians, they are subjected to numerous dietary taboos. They are forbidden to go near the camp, to look at women, or to go to bed before "the Milky Way is straight across the sky."[34]

Meaning of the Initiatory Ordeals

This last detail is important—the Wiradjuri novices must not go to bed until late in the night. This is an initiatory ordeal that is documented more or less all over the world, even in comparatively highly developed religions. Not to sleep is not only to conquer physical fatigue, but is above all to show proof of will and spiritual strength; to remain awake is to be conscious, present in the world, responsible. Among the Yuri-ulu, the novices are constantly shaken so that they cannot fall asleep.[35] Among the Narriniyeri, the novices are taken to the bush in the middle of the night, after which they neither eat nor sleep for three days. And during the remainder of their period of segregation, they are allowed to drink water only by "sucking it through a reed."[36] This is certainly an extremely archaic custom, for it is found among the initiation ceremonies of the Fuegians.[37] Its purpose is to accustom the boy to drinking very little, just as the countless dietary prohibitions are intended to prepare him for a hard life. All these ordeals involving physical resistance[38]—prohibitions against sleeping, drinking, and eating during the first three or four days—are also found among the Yamana of Tierra del Fuego[39] and the Indian tribes of western California.[40] In all probability this shows that they belong to an extremely archaic cultural stratum.

But dietary prohibitions also have a quite complex religious function, into which I shall not enter here. I will only observe that in some tribes dietary prohibitions are successively removed as myths, dances, and pantomimes teach the novice the religious origin of each kind of food. There is also the ritual prohibition against touching food with the fingers. Among the Ngarigo, for example, during the six months that the novice spends in the bush his guardian feeds him, putting the food into his mouth.[41] The inference would seem to be that the novice is regarded as a newborn infant and hence cannot feed himself without help. For, as we shall see later, in some puberty ceremonies the novice is assimilated to a baby unable to use its hands or to talk. But in other parts of the world the prohibition against using the hands forces the novices to take their food directly with their mouths, as most animals do and as the souls of the dead are supposed to do. This is perfectly understandable, for in their isolation in the bush the novices are actually regarded as dead and are assimilated to ghosts. Let us even now note the ambivalence in the symbolism of segregation in the jungle; there is always the idea of a death to the profane condition, but this signifies transformation into a ghost, as well as the beginning of a new life comparable to that of the infant.

The prohibition against speech is open to the same twofold interpretation—as death, and as return to earliest infancy. The neophyte is either dead, or scarcely born—more precisely, he is *being born*. There is no need to cite examples—almost everywhere in Australia the novices are enjoined to maintain silence. They are allowed only to answer their tutors' questions. Among some tribes the initiands, lying on the ground—hence symbolically dead —are not even permitted to use words, but only sounds imitating the cries of birds and animals. The Karadjeri novices make a special sound and then use gestures to indicate what they need.[42] The various prohibitions against the use of sight are to be interpreted in a similar way. The initiands are allowed to look only at the ground between their feet, they always walk with their heads bent, or they are covered with leaves and blankets, or are blindfolded. Darkness is a symbol of the other world, whether the world of death or of the fetal state. Whatever meaning we give to segregation in the bush— whether we see it as a death or as a return to the prenatal condition —it is clear that the novice is no longer in the profane world.

But all these prohibitions—fasting, silence, darkness, complete suppression of sight or its restriction to the ground between the novice's feet—also constitute so many ascetic exercises. The novice is forced to concentrate, to meditate. Hence the various physical ordeals also have a spiritual meaning. The neophyte is at once prepared for the responsibilities of adult life and progressively awakened to the life of the spirit. For the ordeals and restrictions are accompanied by instruction through myths, dances, panto-mimes. The physical ordeals have a spiritual goal—to introduce the youth into the tribal culture, to make him "open" to spiritual values. Ethnologists have been struck by the intense interest with which novices listen to mythical traditions and take part in ceremonial life. "The avidity," Norman B. Tindale writes, "with which the newly initiated youth enters into ceremonial life and the acquiring of the hidden significance of the mythological traditions and prac-tices of the tribe is remarkable."[43] Before or after circumcision the novice, with his guardians, takes long journeys, following the route of the mythical Beings; and during all this time, he must avoid meeting human beings, especially women.[44] In some cases the novice is not allowed to speak, and he swings his bull-roarer to warn away anyone who might be on the road.[45] As the Musgrave Ranges aborigines express it, the novice is a *Wangarapa,* "a boy in hiding."[46]

Among Australian initiatory ordeals, "throwing fire over the heads" of the novices and the "tossing" of novices are especially noteworthy. The latter ceremony is found only among the Arunta, for whom it is the first act in a very long initiation, which will continue for several years.[47] Throwing fire is probably a purificatory rite connected with lightning, but it also has a sexual meaning. As for the tossing of the novices, the ritual can be interpreted in two ways—as offering the novice to the Sky God or as a symbol of ascension. But the two meanings are complementary; both involve the presentation of the novice to the Sky Being. This ceremony is, I think, of the same nature as other ascension rites found in initiation ceremonies. During the *Umba* ceremony, for example, the novice has to climb a young tree that has been stripped of its branches. When he gets to the top of it, all those on the ground burst into cheers.[48] Among the Kurnai, just before the return to the camp, what is called the "opossum game" is played. A tree about twenty feet high is stripped of its branches and fashioned into a pole; one after the other, the instructors climb it, imitating the climbing technique of the opossum;[49] but this explanation is probably secondary. A similar custom is found among the Wiradjuri.[50] Among the Karadjeri, the tree climbing constitutes a special initiatory ceremony, called *laribuga;* in the forest, the neophyte climbs a tree while the men chant a sacred song.

Piddington says that the subject of the song is connected with a myth of the tree, but that the Karadjeri have forgotten its meaning.[51] Yet the meaning of the ritual can be divined: the tree symbolizes the axis of the cosmos, the World Tree; by climbing it, the neophyte reaches the sky. Probably, then, we here have an ascension, such as those that the medicine men accomplish, often in connection with initiation ceremonies. An example occurs in the bora performed by the Chepara. A young tree is fixed in the ground, roots up; around it are set several trees that have been stripped of their bark, painted with ocher, and tied together with bark bands. A medicine man sits on top of the inverted tree, with a cord hanging from his mouth. He claims to represent the Supreme Being, Maamba. The tribesmen believe that during the night he goes up to the sky to see Maamba and talk with him about the tribe's affairs. The medicine men show the novices a quartz crystal and tell them that they received it from Maamba and that anyone who swallows a piece of it will be able to fly to the sky.[52]

To climb into the sky by the aid of a tree, to fly by the virtue of a quartz crystal, are specifically shamanic motifs, quite frequent in Australia, but also found elsewhere.[53] They will be examined in greater detail when we come to shamanic initiations (Chapter V). For the moment, I would observe that the symbolism of ascension, as we see it in the rites of tossing and tree climbing, dominates some Australian puberty ceremonies. Two conclusions seem to me to follow from this. First, Supreme Beings of the sky must in the past have played a role of considerable importance in these ceremonies; for rites of ascension are archaic and, in our day, as we just saw, their original meaning has become obscured if not entirely lost. Secondly, the medicine men obtain their magical powers from Beings of the sky, they often represent them in the ceremonies, and it is the medicine men who reveal to the novices the traditions of these divine Beings who have now withdrawn to the sky. In other words, the symbols of ascent found in puberty rites would seem to indicate that in earlier periods there was a closer relation between the Gods of the sky and initiation ceremonies.

Initiation and Collective Regeneration

The tribes that have so far provided our examples of puberty rites perform no initiatory operation except the extraction of an incisor. But in a considerable part of Australia, the specific tribal rite is circumcision, usually followed by another operation, subincision. Other initiatory mutilations are also documented in Australia —tattooing, tearing out the hair, scarring the skin of the back. Since circumcision and subincision are fraught with quite complex meanings and imply the revelation of the religious values of blood and sexuality, I shall take them up in the next chapter, in which, in general, I shall continue the description of puberty rites, presenting examples taken from other primitive religions, and emphasizing the symbolism of mystical rebirth.

For, in order not to overcomplicate this first chapter, I have here chiefly stressed the symbolism of death. It was important to make it clear that puberty rites, precisely because they bring about the neophyte's introduction into the realm of the sacred, imply death to the profane condition, that is, death to childhood. But we have seen that this initiatory death of the boys is at the same time the occasion for an intertribal festival that regenerates the collective religious life.

Hence Australian initiations are episodes in a cosmic mystery. Initiates and novices leave behind the familiar landscape of the common camp and, on the sacred ground or in the bush, relive the primordial events, the mythical history of the tribe. Reactualizing the myths of origin implies, as we saw, participation in the

Dream Times, in the Time sanctified by the mystical presence of the Divine Beings and the Ancestors. For our purpose, it is not important that the Supreme Beings of the sky do not everywhere play the leading role in initiation ceremonies; nor, as we shall see in greater detail in the next chapter, that among some peoples this role falls to the Ancestors or to other mythical figures, some of them with a demonic aspect. To me, it seems extremely important that, whatever the identity of these Superhuman Beings may be, for the respective tribes they represent the world of transcendent and sacred realities. Equally important is the fact that the collective initiation ceremonies reactualize the mythical times in which these Divine Beings were creating or organizing the earth; in other words, initiation is considered to be performed by these Divine Beings or in their presence. Hence the mystical death of the novices is not something negative. On the contrary, their death to childhood, to asexuality, to ignorance—in short, to the profane condition —is the occasion for a total regeneration of the cosmos and the collectivity. Because their gestures are repeated, the Gods, the civilizing Heroes, the mythical Ancestors, are again present and active on earth. The mystical death of the boys and their awakening in the community of initiated men thus form part of a grandiose reiteration of the cosmogony, of the anthropogony, and of all the creations that were characteristic of the primordial epoch, the Dream Times. Initiation recapitulates the sacred history of the world. And through this recapitulation, the whole world is sanctified anew. The boys die to their profane condition and are resuscitated in a new world; for, through the revelation they have received during their initiation, they can perceive the world as a sacred work, a creation of the Gods.

Let us mark and remember this fact, which is as it were a fundamental motif, documented in every kind of initiation: the experience of initiatory death and resurrection not only basically changes the neophyte's fundamental mode of being, but at the same time reveals to him the sacredness of human life and of the world, by revealing to him the great mystery, common to all religions, that men, with the cosmos, with all forms of life, are the creation of the Gods or of Superhuman Beings. This revelation is conveyed by the origin myths. Learning how things came into existence, the novice at the same time learns that he is the creation of Another, the result of such-and-such a primordial event, the consequence of a series of

mythological occurrences, in short, of a sacred history. This discovery that man is part and parcel of a sacred history which can be
communicated only to initiates constitutes the point of departure
for a long-continued flowering of religious forms.

CHAPTER II

The Initiatory Ordeals

The Bull-Roarer and Circumcision

In the parts of Australia where the extraction of an incisor is not practiced, puberty initiations usually include circumcision, followed, after some time, by another operation, subincision.[1] Some ethnologists regard Australian circumcision as a recent cultural phenomenon.[2] According to Wilhelm Schmidt, the custom was brought to Australia by a cultural wave from New Guinea.[3] Whatever the case may be as to its origin, circumcision is the outstanding puberty rite not only throughout Oceania but in Africa too, and it is also documented among some peoples of both North and South America.[4] As an initiatory rite of puberty, circumcision is extremely widespread, we might also say universal. The problem does not demand our attention in all its complexity. I shall of necessity confine myself to one or two aspects of it, especially to the relations between the rite of circumcision and the revelation of religious realities.

The first aspect that strikes us, in Australia as elsewhere, is the fact that circumcision is believed to be performed not by men but by divine or "demonic" Beings. Here we have not merely the repetition of an act instituted by the Gods or by civilizing Heroes in mythical times; we have the active presence of these Superhuman Beings themselves during the initiation. Among the Arunta, when the women and children hear the bull-roarers, they believe that they are hearing the voice of the Great Spirit Twanyirrika, come to take the boys. And when the boys are circumcised, they are given bull-roarers (*churingas*).[5] Hence it is the Great Spirit himself who is

21

supposed to perform the operation. According to Strehlow, the Arunta imagine that the ceremony takes place in the following way. The novice is led before Tuanjiraka, who says to him, "Look at the stars!" When the boy looks up, the Great Spirit cuts off his head. He gives it back to him the next day, when the head begins to decompose, and resuscitates him.[6] Among the Pitjandara, a man comes rushing out of the forest with a "broken flint," circumcises the novices, and immediately disappears.[7] Among the Karadjeri, the novice is circumcised in a sitting position, his eyes blindfolded and his ears stopped up; immediately after the operation, he is shown the bull-roarers, and—after the blood of his wound has dried—the flint instruments with which the operation was performed.[8] The Kukata perform the circumcision while the bull-roarers are whirled and after the women and children have fled in terror.[9] The Anula women think that the noise of the bull-roarers is the voice of the Great Spirit Gnabaia, who swallows the novices and later disgorges them as initiates.[10]

There is no need to multiply examples.[11] To sum up, circumcision appears as a sacred act, performed in the name of Gods or of Superhuman Beings incarnated in, or represented by, the operators and their ritual tools. The whirling of the bull-roarers before or during circumcision expresses the presence of the Divine Beings. It was stated that among the Yuin, the Kurnai, and the other tribes of southeastern Australia, where circumcision is not practiced, the central mystery of the initiation includes, among other things, the revelation of the bull-roarer as the instrument or the voice of the Sky God or of his son or servant. This identification of the noise of the bull-roarer with the voice of the God is an extremely old religious idea; we find it among the Indian tribes of California and among the Ituri pygmies, that is, in regions that the historico-cultural school regards as belonging to the earliest culture (*Urkultur*).[12] As for the complementary idea that the sound of the bull-roarer represents thunder, it is even more widespread, since it is documented among many peoples in Oceania, Africa, and the two Americas, and also in ancient Greece, where the *rhombos* was held to be the "thunder of Zagreus."[13] Hence it is highly probable that in the theology and mythology of the bull-roarer we have one of mankind's oldest religious conceptions. The fact that in southeastern Australia bull-roarers are present at initiations performed under the sign of the Supreme Being of the sky is yet another proof of the archaism of this form of initiation.[14]

But we have just seen that in the Australian circumcision ceremonies the bull-roarer signifies the presence of the superhuman
Being who performs the operation. And since circumcision is
equivalent to a mystical death, the novice is believed to be killed
by this Superhuman Being. The structure of these masters of
initiation quite clearly shows that they no longer belong to the
class of the Supreme Sky Beings of southeastern Australia; they are,
moreover, regarded as either sons or servants of the Supreme
Beings, or as the mythical Ancestors of the tribes, sometimes
appearing in animal form. We see, then, that in Australia the
initiatory rite of circumcision has its place in a mythology that is
more complex, more dramatic, and presumably more recent than
the mythologies of the forms of initiation in which there is no
circumcision. Particularly striking is the terrifying nature of these
masters of initiation, who manifest their presence by the sound
of the bull-roarers. A similar situation is found outside of Australia: the Divine Beings who play a part in initation ceremonies are
usually imagined in the form of beasts of prey—lions and leopards
(initiatory animals par excellence) in Africa, jaguars in South
America, crocodiles and marine monsters in Oceania. From the
historico-cultural point of view, the connection between the animal
masters of initiation and the bull-roarer would prove that this type
of initiation is the creation of the archaic hunter culture.[15] This
comes out quite clearly in African initiation ceremonies; here too
circumcision is equivalent to death, and the operators are dressed
in lion skins and leopard skins; they incarnate the divinities in
animal form who in mythical times first performed initiatory murder. The operators wear the claws of beasts of prey and their
knives are barbed. They attack the novices' genital organs, which
shows that the intention is to kill them. The act of circumcision
symbolizes the destruction of the genital organs by the animal
master of the initiation. The operators are sometimes called lions
and circumcision is expressed by the verb "to kill." But soon
afterward the novices are themselves dressed in leopard or lion
skins; that is, they assimilate the divine essence of the initiatory
animal and hence are restored to life in it.[16]

From this pattern of African initiation by circumcision, certain
elements emerge which we shall do well to note and remember.
First, the masters of initiation are divinities in animal form, which
supports the hypothesis that, structurally, the ritual belongs to an
archaic hunter culture. Second, the divine beasts of prey are incar-

nated by the operators, who "kill" the novices by circumcising them. Third, this initiatory murder is justified by an origin myth, which tells of a primordial Animal who killed human beings in order to resuscitate them; in the end, the Animal was itself killed, and this event, which took place in the beginning, is ritually reiterated by the circumcision of the novices. Fourth, "killed" by the beast of prey, the novice is nevertheless resuscitated by putting on its skin, which means that in the end he becomes both the victim and the murderer; in short, the initiation is equivalent to the revelation of this mythical event—a revelation that enables the novice to share in the twofold nature of the human victim of the primordial Animal, and of the same Animal as, in its turn, the victim of other divine figures.[17] Hence, in Africa too, circumcision is believed to be performed by a primordial Being, incarnated by the operator, and represents the ritual reiteration of a mythical event.

All these data concerning the ritual function of the bull-roarers, circumcision, and the Supernatural Beings who are believed to perform the initiation indicate the existence of a mythico-ritual theme whose essential features can be summarized as follows: (1) mythical Beings, identified with or manifesting themselves through the bull-roarers, kill, eat, swallow, or burn the novice; (2) they resuscitate him, but changed—in short, a new man; (3) these Beings also manifest themselves in animal form or are closely connected with an animal mythology; (4) their fate is, in essence, identical with that of the initiates,[18] for when they lived on earth, they too were killed and resuscitated, but by their resurrection they established a new mode of existence. This entire mythico-ritual theme is of primary importance for an understanding of the phenomena of initiation, and we shall constantly encounter it in the course of our investigation.

The suffering consequent upon circumcision—sometimes an extremely painful operation—is an expression of initiatory death. However, it must be emphasized that the real terror is religious in nature; it arises from the fear of being killed by Divine Beings. But it is always the Divine Being who resuscitates the novices; and then they do not go back to their childhood life, but share in a higher existence—higher because it is open to knowledge, to the sacred, and to sexuality. The relations between initiation and sexual maturity are obvious. The uninitiated are assimilated to infants and young girls, and hence are supposed to be unable to conceive, or, among some peoples, their children are not accepted into the clan.[19]

Among the Magwanda and Bapedi peoples of Africa the master of the initiation addresses the novices in these words: "Until now, you have been in the darkness of childhood; you were like women and you knew nothing!"[20] Very often, especially in Africa and Oceania, the young initiates are allowed great sexual freedom after they have been circumcised.[21] But we must beware of misinterpreting these licentious excesses, for what is in question here is not sexual freedom, in the modern, desacralized sense of the term. In premodern societies, sexuality, like all the other functions of life, is fraught with sacredness. It is a way of participating in the fundamental mystery of life and fertility. Through his initiation, the novice has gained access to the sacred; he now knows that the world, life, and fertility are sacred realities, for they are the work of Divine Beings. Hence, for the novice, his introduction to sexual life is equivalent to sharing in the sacredness of the world and of human life.

Symbolism of Subincision

In Australia, as we saw, circumcision is followed by subincision. The interval between the two operations varies, from five or six weeks among the Arunta to two or three years among the Karadjeri. For the ethnologist and the psychologist, this mysterious operation raises a number of problems. There is no need to go into them here; I will confine myself to two of the religious meanings of subincision. The first is the idea of bisexuality. The second is the religious value of blood. According to Winthuis, the purpose of subincision is symbolically to give the neophyte a female sex organ, so that he will resemble the divinities, who, Winthuis asserts, are always bisexual.[22] The first thing to be said in this connection is that divine bisexuality is not documented in the oldest Australian cultural strata, for it is precisely in these archaic cultures that the gods are called Fathers. Nor is divine bisexuality found in other really primitive religions. The concept of divine bisexuality appears to be comparatively recent; in Australia, it was probably introduced by cultural waves from Melanesia and Indonesia.[23]

However, there is an element of truth in Winthuis' hypothesis, and that is the idea of *divine totality*. This idea, which is found in a number of primitive religions, naturally implies the coexistence of all the divine attributes, and hence also the coalescence of sexes.[24]

As to the symbolic transformation of the initiand into a woman by means of subincision, only a few clear cases of this have been found in Australia. W. E. Roth, for example, observed that the

Pitta-Pitta and the Boubia of northwest central Queensland assimilate the wound from subincision to the vulva, and also refer to the
novice on whom the operation has recently been performed as "one
with a vulva."[25] R. M. Berndt, studying the Kunapipi cult in northern Australia, gives the same interpretation: "Symbolically, then,"
he writes, "the subincised member represents both the female and
the male organs, essential in the process of fructification."[26] It
should be added that in this last example we probably have a more
recent idea, brought to Australia with the waves of Melanesian culture, for the great majority of Australian tribes are ignorant that
there is a causal relation between the sexual act and conception.[27]

It will help us to understand these Australian data if we remember that the novice's ritual transformation into a woman during
his initiation is a rather common phenomenon in other cultural
areas. In Africa, for example, among the Masai, the Nandi, the
Nuba, and other tribes, the novices are dressed as girls; while
among the South African Sotho, girls who are being initiated
wear men's clothing.[28] Similarly the novices to be initiated into the
Arioi Society in Tahiti are dressed as women.[29] According to
Wilhelm Schmidt[30] and Paul Wirz,[31] ritual transformation into
women is practiced in New Guinea. And Haddon has found it in
Torres Strait.[32] Even the quite widespread custom of ritual nudity
during the period of segregation in the bush can be interpreted as
symbolizing the novice's asexuality. I suggest that the religious
meaning of all these customs is this: the novice has a better chance
of attaining to a particular mode of being—for example, becoming
a man, a woman—if he first symbolically becomes a totality. For
mythical thought, a particular mode of being is necessarily preceded by a *total* mode of being. The androgyne is considered
superior to the two sexes just because it incarnates totality and
hence perfection. For this reason we are justified in interpreting
the ritual transformation of novices into women—whether by
assuming women's dress or by subincision—as the desire to recover
a primordial situation of totality and perfection.

But in Australia and the nearby regions, the primary purpose of
initiatory subincision appears to be obtaining fresh blood. Throughout the world, blood is a symbol of strength and fertility. In Australia as elsewhere, the novices are daubed with red ocher—a substitute for blood—or sprinkled with fresh blood. Among the
Dieiri, for example, the men open veins and let the blood flow
over the novices' bodies to make them brave.[33] Among the Karad-

jeri, the Itchumundi, and other Australian tribes, the novice also drinks blood;[34] and the same custom is found in New Guinea, where the explanation given for it is that the novice has to be strengthened with male blood because the blood he has had so far was entirely his mother's.[35]

In this last example we have to do with two different but connected ideas. First, since the fetus is fed on its mother's blood, all its blood is female. Hence, secondly, the initiation, which definitively separates the boy from his mother, must supply him with male blood. In northeastern New Guinea, where the initiatory operation of subincision has been replaced by incision of the sexual organ, the novices are told that this is a way of getting rid of their mother's blood, so that they will grow strong and handsome.[36] Among the Vangla-Papua of the Bismarck Archipelago, the maternal blood is removed by perforating the nose,[37] an operation that symbolically corresponds to mutilating the genitals. The same custom is found among the Kuman of New Guinea, where the chief initiatory operation consists in perforating "the inner septum of the [candidate's] nose." As a native explained to John Nilles: "This is done to release the bad blood accumulated since he was in his mother's womb, his inheritance from the woman."[38]

M. F. Ashley-Montagu thinks that such beliefs are the explanation for subincision.[39] In his view, men had observed that women get rid of "bad blood" by menstruation, and tried to imitate them by inflicting a genital wound that made the male genital organ resemble the female. If this is so, we have here not merely the idea of expelling the mother's blood, but especially the wish to regenerate the blood by periodically eliminating it after the manner of women. Subincision makes it possible for men to obtain a certain quantity of blood by periodically opening their wounds. This is done especially at critical times, and also in connection with initiations.[40]

The phenomenon of subincision is too complex to be adequately discussed in a few pages. For our purpose, one fact is of primary interest. The novice is initiated into the mystery of blood—that is, his instructors reveal to him the connections (both mystical and physiological) which still bind him to his mother, and the ritual which will enable him to transform himself into a man. Since female blood is the product of female feeding, the novice, as we saw, is subjected to numerous dietary prohibitions. The mystical interconnection between food, blood, and sexuality constitutes an initiatory pattern that is specifically Melanesian and Indonesian,[41] but which is also found elsewhere. What we should note is the fact that the novice is radically regenerated as the result of these sanguinary mutilations. In short, all these operations find their explanation and justification on the religious plane, for the idea of regeneration is a religious idea. Hence we must guard against being misled by the aberrant aspect of some initiatory mutilations or tortures. We must not forget that, on the level both of primitive and of more developed cultures, the strange and the monstrous are expressions frequently used to emphasize the transcendence of the spiritual.

Initiation in Tierra del Fuego

Access to spiritual life, seen as the first result of initiation, is proclaimed by many symbols of regeneration and new birth. A frequent custom is that of giving the novice a new name immediately after his initiation. In addition to being widespread, it is archaic, for we find it among the tribes of southeastern Australia.[42] Now for all premodern societies the individual's name is equivalent to his true existence, to his existence as a spiritual being. It is interesting to note that the initiatory symbolism of new birth is documented even among very primitive peoples, for example, the Yamana and the Halakwulup of Tierra del Fuego, whose puberty rites are simple in the extreme. For, according to the investigations of Gusinde and W. Koppers, the Yamana and the Halakwulup initiation is rather a course of moral, social, and religious instruction than a secret ceremony involving more or less dramatic ordeals. The girls are initiated with the boys, although each sex also receives separate teaching from old men and women. Among the Halakwulup there is no initiatory secrecy. Schmidt considers this collective initiation of the two sexes to be the most ancient of existing forms, and stresses the fact that it involves no corporal mutilation, being principally confined to instruction regarding the nature and activities of the Supreme Being.[43] He further holds that the Yamana and the Halakwulup initiation represents an even older form than the initiation ceremony of the Australian Kurnai, giving as his reason the fact that the Fuegians do not practice separation of the sexes.[44]

Whether this chronology is correct, and whether the extreme simplicity of the Yamana and the Halakwulup initiation reflects a primitive state or, on the other hand, an impoverishment of rites, are questions that need not be decided here. But it is significant that among these Fuegian tribes we find a perfectly clear and consistent initiatory pattern, which already includes the motifs of segregation, mystical death and resurrection, and revelation of the Supreme Beings. The initiation is performed at a great distance from the village; the one that Gusinde and Koppers attended in 1922 took place "in a lonely spot on the Island of Navarino."[45] The novices are taken from their parents—above all, from their mothers—whose guardianship is replaced by that of their "sponsors." They are subjected to a physical and moral discipline in which it is easy to recognize the structure of initiatory ordeals—for example, they must fast, maintain a particular body posture, speak little and in a low voice, fix their eyes on the ground, and, above all, keep long vigils. That the Yamana regard their initiation as a rebirth is shown by the fact that Koppers, when he attended the ceremony, was given a new name to indicate that he was reborn into the tribe.[46] According to the information collected by Gusinde, the Yamana initiation includes a certain number of esoteric moments. The boys are segregated in a cabin, and an evil spirit, the Earth Spirit Yetaita, plays an important role. He is believed to eat men. During the ceremony Yetaita is represented by one of the instructors, painted red and white. Springing from behind the curtain, he attacks the novices, e.g., maltreats them, throws them up into the air.[47] The instructors enjoin the strictest secrecy concerning the appearance and actions of Yetaita and in general concerning everything that takes place in the cabin. It is true that during the initiation period the instructors continually refer to the Supreme Being, Watauineiwa, who is also believed to have established the ceremony; but, ritually speaking, Yetaita's role is the more dramatic. Quite often these two supernatural figures are regarded as equal in power. We may suppose that before becoming the Earth Spirit (*Erdgeist*) he is today, Yetaita was the tribe's mythical Ancestor[48]—hence the initiatory master par excellence—and that he acquired his aggressive character from the men's secret festivals of the Selknam.

For among the Selknam the puberty initiation was long ago transformed into a secret ceremony reserved exclusively for men.[49] An origin myth tells that in the beginning—under the leadership of Kra, Moon Woman and powerful sorceress—women terrorized men because they knew how to change themselves into "spirits"; that is, knew the arts of making and using masks. But one day Kran, the Sun Man, discovered the women's secret and told it to the men. Infuriated, they killed all the women except little girls, and since then they have organized secret ceremonies, with masks and dramatic rituals, to terrorize the women in their turn. This festival continues for from four to six months, and during the ceremonies the evil female spirit, Xalpen, tortures the initiates and "kills" them; but another spirit, Olim, a great medicine man, resuscitates them.[50] Hence in Tierra del Fuego, as in Australia, puberty rites tend to become increasingly dramatic and especially to intensify the terrifying nature of the scenarios of initiatory death. But the dramatic elaboration of rituals and the introduction of striking and even sensational mythologies do not occur in the name of the Supreme Beings. On the contrary, these innovations result in lessening the importance of the Supreme Beings, and even in almost completely eliminating their active presence in the cult. Their place is taken by demonic Beings and, in general, by mythical figures that are in some way connected with a terrible but decisive moment in the history of humanity. These Beings revealed certain sacred mysteries or certain patterns of social behavior which radically altered men's mode of existence and, consequently, their religious and social institutions. Although supernatural, in the time of beginnings these mythical Beings lived a life in some sort comparable to the life of men; more precisely, they experienced tension, conflicts, drama, aggression, suffering, and, generally, death—and by living all this for the first time on earth, they instituted mankind's present way of being. Initiation reveals these primordial adventures to the novices, and they ritually reactualize the most dramatic moments in the mythology of the Supernatural Beings.

This phenomenon becomes more marked when we leave the extreme regions of the inhabited world—Australia, Tierra del Fuego—and study the religions of Melanesia, Africa, and North America. The rites become more complex and various; the ordeals more sensational; physical suffering rises to the horrors of torture; the mystical death is suggested by a ritual aggressiveness when the novice is separated from his mother. Among the Hottentots, for example, the initiate is allowed to insult and even to manhandle his mother,[51] in token of his emancipation from her tutelage. In some parts of Papua the novice walks over his mother's body, deliberately stepping on her belly,[52] and this gesture confirms his definitive separation from her.

Scenarios of Initiatory Death

The rites of initiatory death grow longer and more complex, sometimes becoming real dramatic scenarios. In the Congo and on the Loango coast, the boys between ten and twelve years old drink a potion that makes them unconscious. They are then carried into the jungle and circumcised. Bastian reports that they are buried in the fetish house, and that when they wake they seem to have forgotten their past life. During their seclusion in the jungle they are painted white (certainly a sign that they have become ghosts), they are allowed to steal, are taught the tribal traditions, and learn a new language.[53]

Characteristic here are death symbolized by loss of consciousness, by circumcision, and by burial; forgetting the past; assimilation of the novices to ghosts; learning a new language. Each of these motifs recurs in numerous puberty rites of Africa, Oceania, and North America. As it is impossible to cite them all, I shall confine myself for the moment to a few examples of forgetting the past after initiation. In Liberia, when the novices—who are supposed to have been killed by the Forest Spirit—are resuscitated to a new life, tattooed, and given a new name, they seem to have entirely forgotten their past existence. They recognize neither their families nor their friends, they do not even remember their own names, and they behave as if they had forgotten how to perform even the most elementary acts—washing themselves, for example.[54] Similarly, initiates into some Sudanese secret societies forget their language.[55] Among the Makua the novices spend several months in a hut far from the village and are given new names; when they return to the village they have forgotten their family relationships. As Karl Weule puts it: by his stay in the bush, the son is dead in his mother's eyes.[56] Forgetting is a symbol of death, but it can also be interpreted as betokening earliest infancy. Among the Patasiva of western Ceram, for example, the women are shown the bloody lances with which the spirit is supposed to have killed the novices. When the novices come back to the village, they behave like infants —they do not speak, and pick things up by the wrong end.[57] Whatever may be said of their sincerity, these attitudes and types of behavior have a definite purpose—they proclaim to the whole community that the novices are new beings. ·

The dramatic structure of certain puberty rites comes out more clearly in cases where we have detailed and accurate descriptions. A good example is the Pangwe, whose initiatory rites are the subject of an excellent study by Günther Tessmann. Four days before the ceremony the novices are marked, and the mark is called "consecration to death." On the day of the festival they are given a nauseating potion to drink, and any novice who vomits it up is chased through the village with cries of "You must die!" The novices are then taken to a house full of ants' nests, and are made to remain inside it for some time, during which they are badly bitten; meanwhile their guardians cry, "You will be killed, now you must die!" The tutors then lead the novices to "death" in a cabin in the jungle, where, for a whole month, they will live completely naked and in absolute solitude. They use a xylophone to announce their presence, so that no one will have the bad luck to meet them. At the end of the month they are painted white and are allowed to return to the village to take part in the dances, but they must sleep in the cabin in the bush. They are forbidden to let women see them eat because, Tessmann writes, "of course the dead do not eat." They remain in the bush for three months. Among the southern Pangwe, the ceremony is even more dramatic. An excavation representing the grave is covered by a clay figure, usually in the form of a mask. The excavation symbolizes the belly of the cult divinity, and the novices pass over it, thus indicating their new birth.[58]

Here we have a well developed scenario, comprising several moments: consecration to death; initiatory torture; death itself, symbolized by segregation in the bush and ritual nudity; imitation of the behavior of ghosts, for the novices are considered to be in the other world and are assimilated to the dead; finally, the ritual of rebirth and the return to the village. Probably a considerable number of African and other peoples still have scenarios as elaborate as that of the Pangwe, even in our day. But explorers, especially those of the nineteenth century, have not always recorded the details of these ceremonies. Generally they say no more than that they encountered a death and resurrection ritual.

But we find a number of other African ceremonies in which the dramatic element is of primary importance. Here, for example, is what Torday and Joyce tell us about the Bushongo puberty rites. A long ditch is dug, in which there are four niches. Four men hide in these, disguised respectively as a leopard, a warrior, a smith, and a monkey. The novices are made to walk through the ditch; at a certain moment they fall into a pool of water. Another ceremony, *Ganda,* is still more terrifying. A man disappears into a tunnel and shakes several poles whose tops can be seen from a great distance. The novices believe that he has been attacked by spirits in the tunnel and is fighting for his life. After secretly

rubbing his body with goat's blood, the man comes out of the
tunnel as if he were severely wounded and exhausted. He collapses
on the ground, and the other men immediately carry him far away
from the spot. The novices are then ordered to enter the tunnel,
one after the other. But in the greatest terror, they usually beg to
be let off. Niyami—the king, who is at the same time the master of
the initiation—consents, in return for the payment of a certain
sum.[59]

We here have a terrifying scenario, which tests the novices'
courage. This Bushongo puberty rite has very probably been
influenced by the initiation ceremonies of the secret societies
that are so important in Africa. We can suspect such an influence
whenever we find puberty initiations that are dramatic in character
and make use of masks. This is the case, for example, with the
Elema of New Guinea. Here, when the boys have reached the age
of ten or thereabouts, they are isolated in the Men's House (eravo)
and the village is invaded by masked men, the heralds of Kovave,
God of the Mountain.[60] Swinging bull-roarers by night, the masked
men literally terrorize the village; they have the right to kill any
woman or noninitiate who tries to discover their identity. Meanwhile, the other men store up great quantities of food, especially
swine's flesh, and when Kovave makes his appearance all withdraw
to the bush. One night the novices are brought into Kovave's
presence. They hear a voice in the darkness, revealing the secret
lore and threatening death to any who should betray it. They are
then taken to cabins and put under dietary taboos. They are forbidden any relations with women. On the rare occasions when they
leave their cabins, they are not allowed to speak.[61] Their initiation
comprises several degrees—which in New Guinea is already an
indication of the influence of the secret societies. The atmosphere in
which these puberty rituals are performed, with the sudden appearance of the masks and the terror of the women and the uninitiated,
suggests the tension that is characteristic of Melanesian secret
societies.

A fine example of the puberty rite developed into a dramatic
scenario is the Nanda ceremony, which used to be performed in
some parts of Fiji. The ritual began with the construction of a
stone enclosure, sometimes a hundred feet long and fifty wide, at
a great distance from the village. The stone wall might reach a
height of three feet. The structure was called Nanda, literally
"bed."[62] For our purpose, some aspects of the ceremony can be

neglected—for example, its relations to Megalithic culture, and its origin myth, according to which the Nanda was taught to the Ancestors by two strangers, black in aspect and small in stature, whose faces were respectively painted red and white. The Nanda obviously represents the sacred ground. Two years pass between its building and the first initiation, and two more years between the latter and the second ceremony, after which the neophytes are finally considered to be men. Some time before the second ceremony· large quantities of food are stored up and cabins are built near the Nanda.

On a particular day the novices, led by a priest, proceed to the Nanda in single file, with a club in one hand and a lance in the other. The old men await them in front of the walls, singing. The novices drop their weapons at the old man's feet, as symbols of gifts, and then withdraw to the cabins. On the fifth day, again led by the priests, they once more proceed to the sacred enclosure, but this time the old men are not awaiting them by the walls. They are then taken into the Nanda. There "lie a row of dead men, covered with blood, their bodies apparently cut open and their entrails protruding." The priest-guide walks over the corpses and the terrified novices follow him to the other end of the enclosure, where the chief priest awaits them. "Suddenly he blurts out a great yell, whereupon the dead men start to their feet, and run down to the river to cleanse themselves from the blood and filth with which they are besmeared."[63]

The men represent the Ancestors, resuscitated by the mysterious power of the secret cult, a power directed by the high priest but shared by all other initiates. The purpose of this scenario is not merely to terrify the novices but also to show them that the mystery of death and resurrection is enacted in the sacred enclosure. For what the chief priest reveals to them is the secrets by whose power death will always be followed by resurrection.

This example well illustrates the important role that the Ancestors finally come to play in puberty ceremonies. What we have here is, in short, a periodic return of the dead among the living for the purpose of initiating the youth. This mythico-religious theme is abundantly documented elsewhere, for example, in protohistorical Japan and among the ancient Germans.[64] The important thing for our purpose is that the idea of death and resurrection, which is fundamental in all forms of initiation, here receives a new addition—the idea that death is never final, for the dead return. As we shall see later, this idea is destined to play an essential role in secret societies.

Being Swallowed by a Monster

The strong emotions, the fear, the terror, so skillfully aroused by the scenarios just described, are to be regarded as so many initiatory tortures. We have already noticed some examples of cruel ordeals; naturally, they are far greater in number and variety. In southeastern Africa, the tutors beat the novices mercilessly, and the novices must show no signs of pain.[65] Excesses of this kind sometimes result in the death of the boy. In such cases the mother is not informed until after the period of segregation in the bush;[66] she is then told that her son was killed by the spirit,[67] or that, swallowed by a monster with the other novices, he did not succeed in escaping from its belly. In any event, the tortures are equivalent to ritual death. The blows that the novice receives, the insect bites, the itching caused by poisonous plants, the mutilations —all these various forms of torture signify precisely that he is killed by the mythical Animal which is the master of the initiation; that he is torn to pieces and crushed in its maw, "digested" in its belly.

The assimilation of initiatory tortures to the sufferings of the novice in being swallowed and digested by the monster is confirmed by the symbolism of the cabin in which the boys are isolated. Often the cabin represents the body or the open maw of a water monster,[68] a crocodile, for example, or of a snake.[69] In some parts of Ceram the opening through which the novices pass is called the snake's mouth. Being shut up in the cabin is equivalent to being imprisoned in the monster's belly. On Rooke Island, when the novices are isolated in a cabin in the jungle a number of masked men tell the women that their sons are being devoured by a terrifying Being, named Marsaba.[70]

Sometimes entering the monster's body includes quite elaborate stage effects. Among some tribes of southeastern Australia, the novice is made to lie down in a natural depression or an excavation, and before him is set a piece of wood cut in two, representing the jaws of the snake who is the master of the initiation.[71] But New Guinea furnishes the most eloquent examples of the symbolism of the initiatory cabin. A special house is built for the circumcision of the boys; it is in the form of the Monster Barlun, who is believed to swallow the novices;[72] that is, the building has a "belly" and a "tail."[73] The novice's entrance into the cabin is equivalent to entering the monster's belly. Among the Nor-Papua (north coast of central New Guinea) the novices are swallowed and later disgorged by a spirit whose voice sounds like a flute. Plastically, the spirit is also represented both by masks and by small leaf huts into which the initiands enter.[74] The initiatory cabins of the Kai and the Jabim have two entrances—one, representing the monster's mouth, is quite large; the other, which is much smaller, symbolizes its tail.[75]

An equivalent rite is entrance into a dummy resembling an aquatic monster (crocodile, whale, large fish). Among the Papuans of New Guinea, for example, a monstrous dummy called Kaiemunu is built of raffia; during initiation the novice has to enter the monster's belly. But in our day the initiatory meaning of the act has been lost; the boy enters Kaiemunu while his father is still finishing its construction.[76]

We shall have occasion to return to the symbolism of entrance into a monster's belly. For this initiatory pattern attained the widest dissemination and has been constantly reinterpreted in various cultural contexts. For the moment, let us say that the symbolism of the cabin is considerably more complex than these first examples have shown. The initiatory cabin represents not only the belly of the devouring monster but also the womb.[77] The novice's death signifies a return to the embryonic state. This is not to be understood merely in terms of human physiology but also in cosmological terms. It is not only a repetition of the first gestation and of carnal birth from the mother; it is also a temporary return to the virtual, precosmic mode (symbolized by night and darkness), followed by a rebirth that can be homologized with a "creation of the world."[78] This need to repeat the cosmogony periodically, and to homologize human experiences with the great cosmic moments, is, furthermore, a characteristic of primitive and archaic thought.

The memory of the secluded initiatory hut, far away in the forest, was preserved in popular tales, even in those of Europe, long after puberty rites had ceased to be performed. Psychologists have shown the importance of certain archetypal images; and the cabin, the forest, and darkness are such images—they express the eternal psychodrama of a violent death followed by rebirth. The bush symbolizes both hell and cosmic night, hence death and virtualities; the cabin is the maw of the devouring monster, in which the neophyte is eaten and digested, but it is also a nourishing womb, in which he is engendered anew. The symbols of initiatory death and of rebirth are complementary.

As we saw earlier, some peoples assimilate the segregated novices in the forest to the souls of the dead. They are often rubbed with a white powder to make them resemble ghosts.[79] They do not eat with their fingers, because the dead do not use their fingers.[80] To give only a few examples, in some parts of Africa (the Babali Negroes of Ituri)[81] and of New Guinea,[82] the novices eat with a little stick. In Samoa they are obliged to use such sticks until the wound from their circumcision has healed.[83] But this sojourn among the dead is not without its rewards. The novices will receive revelations of secret lore. For the dead know more than the living. Here we have our first example of the religious importance of the dead. The cult of the Ancestors is increasingly stressed, and the figures of the Celestial Beings almost disappear from living religious practice. Ritual death tends to be valuated not only as an initiatory ordeal necessary for a new birth but also as a privileged situation in itself, for it allows the novices to live in the company of the Ancestors. This new conception is destined to play a major role in the religious history of mankind. Even in developed societies the dead will be regarded as the possessors of arcane knowledge, and prophecy or poetic inspiration will be sought where the dead lie buried.

The Degrees of Revelation

But as we have seen, *all* forms of puberty initiation, even the most elementary, involve the revelation of a secret and sacred knowledge. Some peoples call their initiates "the knowing ones."[84] In addition to the tribal traditions, the novices learn a new language, which they will later use to communicate with one another.

A special language—or at least a vocabulary inaccessible to women and the uninitiated—is the token of a cultural phenomenon that will find its full development in the secret societies. There is a progressive transformation of the community of initiates into an even more closed confraternity, with new rites of admission and many degrees of initiation. Now this phenomenon is already present in rudimentary form in the most archaic cultures. To confine our examples to Australia, in some tribes the puberty initiation consists of a series of rituals sometimes separated by an interval of several years,[85] and—still more significant—not all the novices are allowed to take part in them. Where subincision is customary it is sometimes performed several years after circumcision, and represents a new degree of initiation. Among the Dieiri, for example, subincision is the last of the five chief initiatory rites, and is not open to all initiates.[86] Among the Karadjeri the rites succeed one another over a period of time that may be as long as ten years. The reason for these long intervals is religious. As Tindale expresses it, "many of the most important parts of the ritual are only revealed to [the aspirant] after years have elapsed: it depends upon his prestige and his power of learning."[87] In other words, access to the religious traditions of the tribe also depends upon the candidate's spiritual powers, on his capacity to experience the sacred and to understand the mysteries.

Here we find the explanation not only for the appearance of secret societies but also for the organization of the confraternities of medicine men, shamans, and mystics of all kinds. The underlying idea is both simple and fundamental: if the sacred is accessible to every human being, including women, it is not exhausted in its first revelations. Religious experience and knowledge have degrees, higher and yet higher planes, which, by their very nature, cannot be attained by all. Deeper religious experience and knowledge demand a special vocation, or exceptional will power and intelligence. Just as a man cannot become a shaman or a mystic simply by wanting to, so he cannot rise to certain initiatory degrees unless he demonstrates that he possesses spiritual qualities. In some secret societies higher degrees can also be obtained through lavish gifts; but we must not forget that for the primitive world, wealth is a prestige that is magico-religious in nature.

The successive groups of facts that we have reviewed in this chapter have enabled us to realize the complexity of puberty rites. We saw that as a Supreme Being or his son is supplanted as director of initiation by the Ancestors or Animal Gods, initiation becomes more dramatic, and its fundamental pattern—death and resurrection—develops into detailed and often terrifying scenarios. We saw too that the elementary initiatory ordeals (extraction of an incisor, circumcision) are improved upon by an increasing number of tortures, whose purpose, however, remains the same—to provide the experience of ritual death. One element gains in importance—the revelation of the sacredness of blood and sexuality. The mystery of blood is often bound up with the mystery of food. The countless dietary taboos perform a twofold function—economic, but also spiritual. For, in the puberty rites, the novices are made aware of the sacred value of food and assume the adult condition; that is, they no longer depend on their mothers and on the labor of others for nourishment. Initiation, then, is equivalent to a revelation of the sacred, of death, of sexuality, and of the struggle for food. Only after having acquired these dimensions of human existence does one become truly a man.

What also emerges for us from the facts analyzed in this chapter is the increasingly important role of the Ancestors, usually represented by masks. Just as in Australia puberty initiations are performed under the direction of the medicine men, so in New Guinea, in Africa, in North America the rites are conducted by priests or masked men; quite often, it is the representatives of the secret societies—hence representatives of the Ancestors—who direct the ceremonies throughout. Puberty initiations are performed under the sponsorship of specialists in the sacred—which comes down to saying that they are finally controlled by men with a certain religious vocation. The novices are taught not only by the old men but also, and increasingly, by priests and members of the secret societies. The most important aspects of the tribe's religion—e.g., techniques of ecstasy, the secrets and miracles of the medicine men, relations with the Ancestors—are revealed to the novices by men who themselves possess a deeper religious experience, obtained as the result of a special vocation or after a long apprenticeship. It follows that puberty initiations will conform to a pattern that depends more and more on the mystical tradition of the medicine men and of the masked societies. And this will manifest itself in one direction by an increase in secrecy, and in the other by a multiplication of initiatory degrees and by the spiritual, social, and even political predominance of a minority made up of high-degree initiates, the sole repositories of the doctrine transmitted by the Ancestors.

In this religious perspective, initiation is equivalent to introducing the novice to the mythical history of the tribe; in other words, the initiand learns the deeds of the Supernatural Beings, who, in the dream times, established the present human condition and all the religious, social, and cultural institutions of the tribe. All in all, to know this traditional lore means to know the adventures of the Ancestors and the other Supernatural Beings when they lived on earth. In Australia these adventures amount to little more than long wanderings during which the Beings of the dream times are believed to have performed a certain number of acts. As we saw, the novices are obliged to retrace these mythical journeys during their initiation. They thus relive the events of the dream times. For the Australians these primordial events represent a sort of cosmogony—although, in general, the work of the dream times is one of completing and perfecting: the mythical Ancestors do not create the world, but transform it, thereby giving it its present form; they do not create man, they civilize him. Often the terrestrial existence of these primordial Beings ended by a tragic death or by their disappearance under the earth or into the sky. This means that their existence contains a dramatic element, which was not present in the myths of the supreme celestial Beings of southeastern Australia. What is communicated to the novices is, then, a quite eventful mythical history—and less and less the revelation of the creative acts of the Supreme Beings. The doctrine transmitted through initiation is increasingly confined to the history of the Ancestor's doings, that is, to a series of dramatic events that took place in the dream times. To be initiated is equivalent to learning what *happened* in the primordial Time—and not what the Gods are and how the world and man were created. The sacred and secret lore now depends on the mythical Ancestors, no longer on the Gods. It was the mythical Ancestors who lived the primordial drama that established the world in its present form—and consequently it is they who know and can transmit this lore. In modern terms, we could say that this sacred knowledge no longer belongs to an ontology but to a mythical history.

CHAPTER III

From Tribal Rites to Secret Cults

卍

Initiation of Girls

Before examining some initiatory patterns that will show us the continuity between puberty rites and the rites for entrance into secret societies, we must give some consideration to initiations of girls. They have been less studied than the boys' initiations and hence are not very well known. It is true that female puberty rites, and especially their secret aspects, have been less accessible to ethnologists. The majority of observers have given us descriptions of them that are largely external. We have very little documentation on the religious instruction of girls during their initiation, and especially on the secret rites that they are said to undergo. Despite these gaps, it is possible to get an approximate idea of the structure and morphology of girls' initiations.

To begin, we may note three things: first, female puberty initiations are less widespread than boys' initiations, although they are already documented in the ancient stages of culture (Australia, Tierra del Fuego, and elsewhere);[1] second, the rites are decidedly less developed than those for boys' initiations; and, third, girls' initiations are individual. This last characteristic has had important consequences. It is obviously explained by the fact that female initiation begins with the first menstruation. This physiological symptom, the sign of sexual maturity, compels a break—the young girl's removal from her familiar world. She is immediately isolated, separated from the community—which reminds us of the boy's separation from his mother and segregation. In either sex, then,

41

initiation begins with a break, a rupture. But there is a difference: for girls, the segregation takes place in each case immediately after the first menstruation, hence it is individual; whereas for boys, initiation is collective, occurring for all at about the time of puberty. The individual character of the young girl's segregation, which takes place on the appearance of the signs of menstruation, explains the comparatively small number of initiatory rites. But one thing must not be overlooked: the length of the segregation varies from culture to culture—from three days (as in Australia and India) to twenty months (New Zealand) or even several years (Cambodia). In other words, the girls do in the end form a group, and then their initiation is performed collectively,[2] under the direction of their older female relatives (as in India) or of old women (Africa). These tutoresses instruct them in the secrets of sexuality and fertility, and teach them the customs of the tribe and at least some of its religious traditions—those accessible to women. The education thus given is general, but its essence is religious; it consists in a revelation of the sacrality of women. The girl is ritually prepared to assume her specific mode of being, that is, to become a creatress, and at the same time is taught her responsibilities in society and in the cosmos, responsiblities which, among primitives, are always religious in nature.

As we have noted, female initiatory rites—at least so far as they are now known to us—are less dramatic than the rites for boys. The important element in them is segregation. This takes place either in the forest (as among the Swahili) or in a special cabin, as among many North American tribes (Shushwap, Wintun, and others), in Brazil (Coroado), in the New Hebrides, in the Marshall Islands, but also among the Veddahs and among some African peoples.[3] In speaking of boys' puberty rites, we referred to the complex symbolism of the forest and the hut—a symbolism which is at once that of the beyond, hence of death, and that of the darkness of gestation in the mother's womb. The symbolism of darkness is also emphasized in the ceremonial segregation of girls, for they are isolated in a dark corner of the house, and among many peoples are forbidden to see the sun—a taboo whose explanation lies in the mystical connection between the moon and women. Elsewhere they are forbidden to let themselves be touched by anyone, or to move. A prohibition peculiar to South American societies forbids them to touch the ground; the girl novices spend their days and nights in hammocks.[4] Naturally there are some dietary restrictions almost everywhere, and among some peoples the girl novices wear a special costume.[5]

No less essential than the segregation that constitutes the first rite of initiation is the ceremony that concludes the process. Among some coast tribes of northern Australia, the girl undergoing her first menstruation is isolated in a cabin for three days, during which time she is subjected to various dietary taboos. She is then painted with ocher and richly decorated by the women. "At the climax," Berndt writes, "all the women escort her at dawn to a fresh water stream or lagoon."[6] After this ritual bath she is led in procession to the "main camp, amid a certain amount of acclamation, and is socially accepted as a woman."[7] Berndt observes that before the Mission was established in Arnhem Land, the ritual was more complex and included songs. Modern ethnologists sometimes meet only with institutions that are on the verge of disappearing. In the case that we are studying, however, the essentials have been preserved, for the procession and the acclamation by the women at the end of the ceremony are a characteristic feature of female initiations. In some places the segregation terminates with a collective dance, and this custom is characteristic especially of the early cultivators (*Pflanzervölker*).[8] Among these same paleoagriculturalists, the girls who have been initiated are exhibited and made much of,[9] or they visit the houses of the settlement in procession to receive gifts.[10] Other external signs likewise mark the end of initiation, for example, tattooing, or blackening the teeth;[11] some ethnologists, however, consider these customs innovations due to the influence of totemic cultures.[12]

The essential rite, then, is the solemn exhibition of the girl to the entire community. It is a ceremonial announcement that the mystery has been accomplished. The girl is *shown* to be adult, that is, to be ready to assume the mode of being proper to woman. To show something ceremonially—a sign, an object, an animal, a man—is to declare a sacred presence, to acclaim the miracle of a hierophany.[13] This rite, which is so simple in itself, denotes a religious behavior that is archaic. Perhaps even before articulate language, solemnly showing an object signified that it was regarded as exceptional, singular, mysterious, sacred. Very probably this ceremonial presentation of the initiated girl represents the earliest stage of the ceremony. The collective dances mentioned earlier express the same primordial experience in a way that is at once more plastic and more dramatic.

It is clear that, even more than male rites of puberty, female initiations are related to the mystery of blood. Some scholars have even sought to explain the initiatory segregation of girls by the primitive fear of menstrual blood. Frazer emphasized this aspect of the problem and showed that women are isolated in cabins during their menses, just as girls are at the first appearance of this physiological symptom.[14] But Wilhelm Schmidt has demonstrated that the two customs do not coincide: the monthly segregation of women is a custom documented principally among nomadic hunters and pastoral peoples, that is, in societies that deal with animals and their products (meat, milk) and in which menstrual blood is regarded as unlucky; whereas the initiatory segregation of girls is a custom peculiar to matriarchal societies. And, Schmidt adds, at least among some of these matriarchal societies the initiation of girls includes festivities manifesting the public joy over the fact that the girls have reached the age of puberty and so can found families.[15] But, as we have seen, these festivities are too archaic in structure to be regarded as a creation of the matriarchal cycle, which, in Schmidt's view, is a more recent sociocultural phenomenon.

In any case, men's fear of women's blood does not explain the puberty rites for girls. The fundamental experience, which alone can enlighten us as to the genesis of the rites, is a female experience and is crystallized around the mystery of blood. Sometimes this mystery is manifested under strange aspects. Such is the case, for example, with the Dyaks, among whom the pubescent girl is isolated for an entire year in a white cabin, is dressed in white, and eats white foods. At the end of her segregation, she sucks the blood from a young man's opened vein, through a bamboo tube.[16] The meaning of this custom seems to be that during the period of segregation the girl is neither man nor woman; hence she is considered "white," "without blood."[17] Here we recognize the theme of the temporary androgynization and asexuality of novices, a theme to which reference was made in the last chapter. For cases are known in which girls are dressed as men during their initiation period, just as boys wear female clothing during their novitiate.

Degrees in Female Initiations

Among some peoples female initiation includes several degrees. Thus, among the Yao, initiation begins with the first menstruation, is repeated and elaborated during the first pregnancy, and is only concluded with the birth of the first child.[18] The mystery of blood finds its completion in childbirth. For the woman, the revelation that she is *a creator of life* constitutes a religious experience that cannot be translated into masculine terms. The example of the Yao female initiation with its three degrees enables us to understand two closely related phenomena: first, the tendency of women to organize in secret religious associations, modeled on the male confraternities; second, the importance that some cultures give to the ritual of childbirth. We shall discuss these women's associations when we come to study the organization of secret societies; we shall then see that, at least in part, female secret societies have borrowed certain morphological elements from the male confraternities. As for the ritual of childbirth, it has sometimes given rise to customs in which we can decipher the seeds (or perhaps the vestiges) of a mystery. Traces of such mystical scenarios have been preserved even in Europe. In Schleswig during the last century, on the news that a child had been born, all the women of the village went dancing and shouting to the house of the new mother. If they met men on the way, they knocked their hats off and filled them with dung; if they met a cart, they tore it to pieces and turned the horse loose. After they had all met at the new mother's house, they set out running frantically through the village, shouting, cheering, entering houses and taking whatever they wanted in the way of food and drink; if they met men, they forced them to dance.[19] Probably in early times certain secret rituals were performed in the new mother's house. We know that in the thirteenth century such rituals were current in Denmark; having gathered at the new mother's house, the women made a straw dummy, which they called the Ox, and danced with it, making lascivious gestures and singing and shouting.[20] These examples are valuable; they show us that the ritual gatherings of women on the occasion of childbirth tend to become secret associations.

To return to the girls' puberty rites, I must add that during the period of seclusion the novices learn ritual songs and dances and also certain specifically feminine skills, especially spinning and weaving. The symbolism of these crafts is highly significant; in the final phases of culture we find them raised to the rank of a principle explaining the world. The moon "spins" Time, and "weaves" human lives.[21] The Goddesses of Destiny are spinners. We detect an occult connection between the conception of the periodical creations of the world (a conception derived from a lunar mythology) and the ideas of Time and of Destiny, on the one hand, and, on the other, nocturnal work, women's work, which has to be performed far from the light of the sun and almost in secret. In some cultures, after the seclusion of the girls is ended they continue to meet in some old woman's house to spin together. Spinning is a perilous craft, and hence can be carried on only in special houses and then only during particular periods and until certain hours. In some parts of the world spinning has been given up, and even completely forgotten, because of its magical peril.[22] Similar beliefs still persist today in Europe (e.g., the Germanic fairies Perchta, Holda, Frau Holle). In some places—Japan, for example[23]—we still find the mythological memory of a permanent tension, and even conflict, between the groups of young spinning girls and the men's secret societies. At night the men and their Gods attack the spinning girls and destroy not only their work but also their shuttles and weaving apparatus.

There is a mystical connection between female initiations, spinning, and sexuality. Even in developed societies, girls enjoy a certain prenuptial freedom, and their meetings with boys take place in the house where they gather to spin. The custom was still alive in Russia at the beginning of the twentieth century.[24] It is surprising that in cultures where virginity is highly prized, meetings between young men and girls are not only tolerated but encouraged by their parents. We have here not a case of dissolute manners but a great secret—the revelation of female sacrality; the experience touches the springs of life and fertility. Prenuptial freedoms for girls are not erotic in nature, but ritual; they constitute fragments of a forgotten mystery, not profane festivities. In the Ukraine, during certain holy periods, and especially on the occasion of marriages, girls and women behave in a manner that is almost orgiastic.[25] This complete reversal of behavior—from modesty to exhibitionism—indicates a ritual goal, which concerns the entire community. It is a case of the religious need for periodical abolition of the norms that govern profane life—in other words, of the need to suspend the law that lies like a dead weight on customs, and to re-create the state of absolute spontaneity. The fact that cases of such ritual behavior have been preserved down to the twentieth century among peoples long since Christianized proves, I believe, that we are here dealing with an extremely archaic religious experience, a basic experience of woman's soul. We shall encounter other expressions of the same fundamental experience later on, when we come to examine some of the women's secret organizations.

To sum up, girls' initiations are determined by a mystery "natural" to the female sex, the appearance of menstruation, with all that this phenomenon implies for primitives: e.g., periodical purification, fecundity, curative and magical powers. The girl is to become conscious of a transformation that comes about in a natural way and to assume the mode of being that results from it, the mode of being of the adult woman. Girls' initiations do not include such typical elements in the initiations for boys as the revelation of a Divine Being, of a sacred object (the bull-roarer), and of an origin myth—in short, the revelation of an event that took place in the beginning, an integral part of the tribe's sacred history and hence belonging, not to the natural world, but to culture. It should be noted that feminine ceremonies in connection with menstruation are not based on an origin myth, as is always the case with masculine puberty rites. There are certain myths according to which the initiation ceremonies now in the possession of men originally belonged to women; but these myths have nothing to do with the pre-eminent feminine mystery, menstruation. The few myths connected with the origin of menstruation do not fall in the category of initiatory myths.

It follows from all this that, unlike women, men during their period of initiatory training are made conscious of "invisible" realities and learn a sacred history that is not evident; i.e., is not given in immediate experience. A novice understands the meaning of circumcision after having learned the origin myth. Everything that happens to him during initiation happens because certain events took place in mythical times and basically changed the human condition. For boys, initiation represents an introduction to a world that is not immediate—the world of spirit and culture. For girls, on the contrary, initiation involves a series of revelations concerning the secret meaning of a phenomenon that is apparently natural—the visible sign of their sexual maturity.

An Extant Australian Secret Cult

Let us now examine an Australian secret cult, Kunapipi, which still flourishes in Arnhem Land and in the west-central Northern Territory. From the point of view of our investigation, its interest is twofold: first, although its most important ceremonies are confined to men, the ideology of Kunapipi is dominated by female religious symbolism, especially by the figure of the Great Mother, source of universal fertility; second, although its initiatory scenario is of a structural type already known to us—for the chief moment is a ritual swallowing—it also offers some new elements. In other words, Kunapipi is an excellent point of departure for our comparative investigation into the continuity of initiatory patterns. Only young men who have already undergone the initiatory rites of puberty are eligible for initiation into the Kunapipi cult. Hence we have here not an age-grading ceremony but a higher initiation —which once again confirms primitive man's desire to deepen his religious experience and knowledge.

The ritual goal of Kunapipi is twofold: the initiation of the young men, and the renewal of the energies that ensure cosmic life and universal fertility. This renewal is obtained through the re-enactment of the original myth. The sacred power possessed by the Supernatural Beings is released by the reactualization of the acts that they performed during the "Dreaming Period."[26] We here have, then, a religious conception with which we are already more or less familiar: an origin myth forms the basis for an initi-atory ritual; to perform the ritual is to reactualize the primordial Time, to become contemporary with the Dreaming Period;[27] the novices participate in the mystery, and on this occasion the entire community and its cosmic milieu are bathed in the atmosphere of the Dreaming Period; the cosmos and society emerge regener-ated. It is clear, then, that the initiation of a group of young men affects not only their own religious situation but also that of the community. Here we find the seed of a conception that will be developed in higher religions—that the spiritual perfection of an elite exerts a beneficial influence on the rest of society.

Let us now turn to the cult proper. It is based on a rather com-plex myth, of which I need mention only the chief elements. In the Dreaming Period, the two Wauwalak Sisters, the older of whom had just borne a child, set out into the north. These two sisters are really the "dual Mothers." The name of the cult, Kunapipi, is translated "Mother" or "Old Woman." After a long journey, the Sisters stopped near a well, built a hut, and tried to cook some animals. But the animals fled from the fire and threw themselves into the well. For, the aborigines now explain, the animals knew that one of the Sisters, being impure because of her "afterbirth blood," ought not to go near the well, in which the Great Snake Julunggul lived. And indeed Julunggul, attracted by the smell of blood, emerged from his subterranean home, raised his fore part threateningly—which brought on clouds and lightning—and crawled toward the hut. The younger Sister tried to keep him away by dancing, and her dances are reactualized in the Kunapipi ceremony. Finally, the Snake poured spittle all over the hut in which the two Sisters and the child had taken refuge, swallowed it, then straightened up to his full length, his head toward the sky. Soon afterwards he disgorged the two Sisters and the child. Bitten by white ants, they returned to life—but Julunggul swallowed them again, this time for good.

This myth provides the foundation for two other rituals besides Kunapipi, one of which, the *djunggawon,* constitutes the rite of puberty initiation. The aborigines explain the origin of all these rituals thus: a python, Lu'ningu, having seen Julunggul swallow and then disgorge the two Sisters, wanted to imitate him. He went wandering about the country, swallowing young men, but when he disgorged them they were dead and sometimes reduced to skeletons. In revenge, men killed him, and later they raised a monument representing him—the two posts called *jelmalandji.* To imitate the Snake's hissing, they made bull-roarers.[28] Finally, the ceremonial headman cut his arm, saying: "We make ourselves like those two women."[29]

In the Kunapipi ritual, Berndt writes, the young novices, "leaving the main camp for the sacred ground are said to be swallowed by Lu'ningu, just as he swallowed the young men in the Dreaming Era; and in the old days they had to stop away from womenfolk from a period of two weeks to two months, symbolizing their stay inside the belly of the Snake."[30] But the two Snakes—Julunggul and Lu'ningu—are confused, for on their return to the main camp, the men tell the women, "All the young boys have gone today; Julunggul has swallowed them up."[31] But in any case, the symbolism of the ritual swallowing is more complex. On the one hand, the novices, assimilated to the two Sisters, are supposed to have been swallowed by the Snake; on the other hand, by entering the sacred ground, they symbolically return into the primordial Mother's womb. We find that they are painted with ocher and with "arm-blood," representing the blood of the two Wauwalak Sisters; "that is," Berndt writes, "for the purpose of the ritual they become the Two Sisters, and are swallowed by Julunggul; and on their emergence from the ritual, they are revivified just as were the women."[32] But then too, according to the aborigines, the "triangular dancing place" represents the Mother's womb. To quote Berndt's account again: "As the neophytes leave the camp for the sacred ground, they themselves are said to become increasingly sacred, and to enter the Mother; they go into her uterus, the ring place, as happened in the beginning. When the ritual is completed the Mother 'lets them out'; they emerge from the ring place, and pass once more into ordinary life."[33]

The symbolism of return to the womb recurs during the course of the ritual. At a certain moment, the neophytes are covered over with bark and "told to go to sleep." They remain there, the aborigines say, "covered up in the hut like the Wauwalak Sisters."[34] Finally, after an orgiastic ritual, which includes an exchange of wives, the final ceremony is performed. Two forked posts, with a thick connecting pole between them, are set up between the sacred ground and the main camp. The pole is covered with branches, and the initiates are stationed behind the branches; wholly invisible from outside, they remain there clinging to the pole with their feet on the ground, supposedly "hanging from the pole." They are, that is, in the womb, and they will emerge reborn—"their spirit comes out new."[35] Two men climb up onto the forked posts, and there cry like newborn infants, for they are "the children of Wauwalak." Finally all return to the main camp, painted with ocher and arm-blood.

I have dwelt on this Kunapipi ritual because, thanks to the work of Ronald Berndt, we are in a position to know not only a number of valuable details but also the meaning that the aborigines attribute to them. It must be added that the Kunapipi ritual does not represent an archaic state of Australian culture; very probably it has been influenced by more recent Melanesian contributions.[36] The tradition that in the beginning women possessed all cult secrets and all sacred objects, and that men later stole them,[37] indicates a matriarchal ideology. Obviously, a number of the ritual elements are pan-Australian—for example, the fire-throwing, the bull-roarer and the myth of its origin, the custom of covering women and neophytes with branches. The essential characteristic of Kunapipi, is, as we saw, the initiatory pattern of return to the womb. We found it more than once: when the neophytes enter the sacred ground; when they wait under the branches, "hanging from the pole"; finally, when they are considered to be in the two Sisters' hut. Their ritual swallowing by the Snake is also to be interpreted as a return to the womb—on the one hand, because the Snake is often described as female;[38] on the other, because entering the belly of a monster also carries a symbolism of return to the embryonic state.

The frequent reiteration of the return to the primordial Mother's womb is striking. The sexual pantomimes and especially the ritual exchange of wives—an orgiastic ceremony that plays a leading role in the Kunapipi cult—further emphasize the sacred atmosphere of the mystery of procreation and childbirth. In fact, the general impression that we receive from the whole ceremonial is that it represents not so much a ritual death followed by resurrection as a complete regeneration of the initiate through his gestation and birth by the Great Mother. This of course does not mean that the symbolism of death is completely absent, for being swallowed by the Snake and even returning to the womb necessarily imply death to the profane condition. The symbolism of return to the womb is always ambivalent. Yet it is the particular notes of generation and gestation which dominate the Kunapipi cult. We here have, then, a perfect example of an initiatory pattern organized and constructed around the idea of a new birth, and no longer around the idea of symbolic death and resurrection.

Initiatory Symbolisms of Return to the Womb

We find this same pattern in a large number of initiatory myths and rites. The idea of gestation and childbirth is expressed by a series of homologizable images—entrance into the womb of the Great Mother (Mother Earth), or into the body of a sea monster, or of a wild beast, or even of a domestic animal. Obviously, the initiatory hut also belongs to the same family of images; and I must here add an image that we have not so far encountered—the pot image. It would take far more time than is available to make an adequate study of all the groups of rites and myths which have this pattern. I must confine myself to only a few aspects. To simplify the exposition, let me begin by grouping the documents into two important categories. In the first, return to the womb, though implying a certain element of peril (such as is in any case connected with every religious act), appears as an operation that is mysterious but comparatively without danger. In the second category of documents, on the contrary, the return implies the risk of being torn to pieces in the monster's jaws (or in the *vagina dentata* of Mother Earth) and of being digested in its belly. Although the facts are actually more complex, we can cite examples illustrating these two types of initiation by return to the womb—let us call them the easy and the dramatic types. In the former, the stress is on the mystery of initiatory childbirth. In the dramatic type, the theme of new birth is accompanied, and sometimes dominated, by the idea that, as an initiatory ordeal, it must involve the risk of death. As we shall see in a moment, Brahmanic initiations fall in the category of rites that actualize a new gestation and new birth of the novice, but without implying that he must first die or even that he is in any great danger of death. (Let me repeat: the symbolism of death to the profane condition is always present; but, as we have seen, this is characteristic of every genuine religious experience.)

As to the second type of initiatory return, it includes a considerable number of forms and variants, and has produced offshoots and developments, charged with more and more subtle meanings, even in the religions, the metaphysics, and the mysticisms of highly developed societies. For we find the initiatory pattern of the perilous return to the womb, first, in the myths in which the Hero is swallowed by a sea monster and then emerges victorious by forcing his way out of its belly; second, in the myths and miraculous narratives of shamans, who during their trances are supposed to enter the belly of a giant fish or whale; third, in a number of myths of an initiatory traversal of a *vagina dentata,* or a perilous descent into a cave or crevasse assimilated to the mouth or the uterus of Mother Earth—a descent that brings the hero to the other world; fourth, and lastly, the same pattern is recognizable in the whole group of myths and symbols that have to do, for example, with a "paradoxical passage" between two millstones in constant motion, between two rocks that come together from instant to instant (see pages 64 ff.), or over a bridge narrow as a thread and sharp as a knife blade. (Paradoxical because impossible on the plane of daily experience, the passage whose images I have just cited will serve, in later mysticisms and metaphysics, to express access to a transcendental state.) What characterizes all forms of this dangerous return to the womb is that the Hero undertakes it as a living man and an adult—that is, he does not die and he does not return to the embryonic state. The stake involved in the enterprise is sometimes extraordinary—nothing less than winning immortality. And as we shall see in the myth of the Polynesian Hero Maui, it is because Maui did not succeed in coming alive out of the body of the Great Mother that humanity did not win immortality. I shall devote part of the next chapter to this whole group of initiatory myths and rites and there try to complete and refine this too rapid outline.

Symbolism of New Birth in Indian Initiations

For the moment, let me cite some examples illustrating the non-perilous type of initiatory return to the embryonic state. Let us begin with the Brahmanic initiations. I shall make no attempt to present them in their entirety; we shall confine ourselves to the theme of gestation and new birth. In ancient India the *upanayana* ceremony—that is, the boy's introduction to his teacher—is the homologue to primitive puberty initiations. Indeed, something of the behavior of novices among the primitives is still preserved in ancient India; the *brahmacarin* lives in his teacher's house, dresses in the skin of a black antelope, eats nothing but food for which he has begged, and is bound by a vow of absolute chastity. (Indeed, the name for this period of study with a teacher—*brahmacarya*—finally came to express the idea of sexual continence.) Unknown to the *Rig-Veda,* the *upanayana* is first documented in the *Atharva-Veda* (XI, 5, 3), and here the motif of gestation and rebirth is clearly expressed; the teacher is said to change the boy into an embryo and keep him in his belly for three nights. The *Shatapatha Brahmana* (XI, 5, 4, 12-13) gives the following details: the teacher conceives when he puts his hand on the boy's shoulder, and on the third day the boy is reborn as a brahman. The *Atharva-Veda* (XIX, 17) calls one who has gone through the *upanayana* "twice-born" (*dvi-ja*); and it is here that this term, which had an extraordinary career in India, appears for the first time.

Obviously, the second birth is spiritual in nature, and later texts frequently insist on this point. According to the *Laws of Manu* (II, 144), he who imparts the word of the Veda to the novice (that is, the *brahman*) shall be regarded as father and mother; between the begetter and the *brahman,* it is the latter who is the true father (II, 146); true birth, that is, birth to immortality, is given by the Savitri formula (II, 148).[39] This conception is pan-Indian and is taken up again by Buddhism; the novice forsakes his family name and becomes a "son of Buddha" (*sakya-putto*), for he has been "born among the saints" (*ariya*). As Kassapa said of himself: "Natural son of the Blessed One, born of his mouth, born of *dhamma,* fashioned by *dhamma* . . ." (*Samyutta Nikaya,* II, 221).

Buddhist imagery also preserves the memory that the second,

spiritual birth is accomplished like that of the chick, that is, "by breaking the eggshell."[40]

The initiatory symbolism of the egg and the chick is ancient; very probably it is the "twofold birth" of birds which is at the origin of the image of the *dvi-ja*. In any case, we are here in the presence of archetypal images, already documented on the level of archaic cultures. Among the Kavirondo Bantu, these words are spoken of initiates: "The white chick is now creeping out of the egg, we are like newly fired pots."[41] It is remarkable that the same image brings together two motifs that are at once embryological and intiatory, the egg and the pot—which, by the way, we shall meet again in India.

In addition to this new birth obtained through the *upanayana*, Brahmanism has an initiatory ritual, the *diksha,* which must be performed by anyone who is preparing to offer the *soma* sacrifice and which, properly speaking, consists in a return to the fetal state.[42] The *Rig-Veda* seems to know nothing of the *diksha,* but it is documented in the *Atharva-Veda.* Here the *brahmacarin*—that is, the novice undergoing the initiatory puberty rite—is called the *dikshita,* "he who practices the *diksha."* Herman Lommel[43] has rightly emphasized the importance of this passage (*Atharva-Veda,* XI, 5, 6): the novice is homologized with one in the course of being reborn to make himself worthy to perform the *soma* sacrifice. For this sacrifice implies a preliminary sanctification of the sacrificer—and to obtain it he undergoes a return to the womb. The texts are perfectly clear. According to the *Aitareya Brahmana* (I, 3): "Him to whom they give the *diksha,* the priests make into an embryo again. They sprinkle him with water; the water is man's sperm. . . . They conduct him to the special shed; the special shed is the womb of the *dikshita;* thus they make him enter the womb that befits him. . . . They cover him with a garment; the garment is the caul. . . . Above that they put the black antelope skin; verily the placenta is above the caul. . . . He closes his hands; verily the embryo has its hands closed so long as it is within, the child is born with closed hands. . . . He casts off the black antelope skin to enter the final bath; therefore embryos come into the world with the placenta cast off. He keeps on his garment to enter it and therefore a child is born with a caul upon it."

The parallel texts emphasize the embryological and obstetrical character of the rite with plentiful imagery. "The *dikshita* is an embryo, his garment is the caul," and so on, says the *Taittiriya*

Samhita (I, 3, 2). The same work (VI 2, 5, 5) also repeats the image of the *dikshita*-embryo, completed by that of the hut assimilated to the womb—an extremely ancient and widespread image; when the *dikshita* comes out of the hut, he is like the embryo emerging from the womb. The *Maitrayani-Samhita* (III, 6, 1) says that the initiate leaves this world and "is born into the world of the Gods"; the cabin is the womb for the *dikshita,* the antelope skin the placenta. The reason for this return to the womb is emphasized more than once. "In truth man is unborn. It is through sacrifice that he is born" (III, 6, 7). And it is stressed that man's true birth is spiritual: "The *dikshita* is semen," the *Maitrayani-Samhita* adds (III, 6, 1)—that is, in order to reach the spiritual state that will enable him to be reborn among the Gods, the *dikshita* must symbolically become what he has been from the beginning. He abolishes his biological existence, the years of his human life that have already passed, in order to return to a situation that is at once embryonic and primordial; he "goes back" to the state of semen, that is, of pure virtuality. This theme of going back in order to abolish the historical duration that has already elapsed and to begin a new life, with all its possibilities intact, has so obsessed humanity that we find it in a great many contexts and even in highly developed soteriologies and mysticisms.[44] Obviously, all these initiatory rites of return to the womb have a mythical model—it is Indra who, to prevent the birth of a terrifying monster after the union between the word (*Vac*) and sacrifice (*yajña*), turned himself into an embryo and entered Vac's womb.[45]

I should like to draw special attention to this point: the return to the womb represented by the *diksha* is renewable; it is accomplished each time that the *soma* sacrifice is performed. And since the sacrificer is already "twice-born" by virtue of his initiation (*upanayana*), it follows that the purpose of the *diksha* is to regenerate the sacrificer so that he can share in the sacred. This return to the womb obviously implies the abolition of past time. The texts do not say this expressly, but there is no explanation for the return to the beginning except the desire once more to begin a "pure" existence, that is, one which has not yet undergone the evil effects of Time. The same ritual is used on other occasions too; for example, the novice who has broken his vows must watch all night by the fire, wrapped in a black antelope skin out of which he crawls on his hands and knees at dawn (*Baudhayana Dharmashastra,* III, 4, 4). To be wrapped in a skin signifies gestation, and crawling out of it symbolizes a new birth. The rite and the signification are also found on other cultural levels. Among some Bantu peoples, the boy, before being circumcised, is the object of a ceremony called "being born anew." The father sacrifices a ram, and three days later wraps the boy in the animal's stomach membrane and skin. But before being wrapped up, the boy has to get into bed beside his mother and cry like an infant. He remains in the ram skin for three days. I may add that the dead are buried wrapped in ram skins and in the embryonic position.[46]

To return to India, we have still to examine another rite involving return to the womb. This, too, is performed for the purpose of obtaining a new birth, whether to attain a higher mode of being (for example, becoming a Brahman) or to obtain purification from some great defilement (for example, that represented by a journey into another country). This rite is the *Hiranyagarbha,* literally "golden embryo." First described in the *Atharva-Veda Parishishta* (XIII), it showed exceptional vitality, for it was still in use in the nineteenth century.[47] The ceremony is as follows. The person undergoing the rite is placed in a golden receptacle in the shape of a cow, upon emerging from which he is regarded as an infant and is put through the rites of birth. But as such a receptacle is too costly, a gold reproduction of the womb (*yoni*) is commonly used. The person undergoing the rite is assimilated to the golden embryo (*hiranyagarbha*). This name is also one of the cognomens of Prajapati and of Brahman—which is understandable, for, in India as elsewhere, gold is a symbol of immortality and perfection. Being transformed into a golden embryo, the person undergoing the rite in some sort appropriates to himself the indestructibility of the metal and participates in immortality. Gold is solar; then too, there is a whole mythico-iconographic complex which presents the sun as descending into darkness even as the novice, as embryo, enters the uterine darkness of the initiatory hut.[48]

But the symbolism of gold has here only overlaid an older and more universal theme, that of mythical rebirth in a cow, or in a pot in the shape of a womb. The cow is one of the epiphanies of the Great Mother. Herodotus (II, 129) relates that Mycerinus buried his daughter in a golden cow, and at Bali there are still coffins in the shape of a cow.[49] The *Rig-Veda* says nothing of the *hiranyagarbha* ritual, whether because it was not known in Vedic times or because it was not then practiced in the priestly and military circles in which the *Rig-Vedic* hymns were elaborated and circulated. The fact that the *hiranyagarbha* ritual appears in the *Atharva-Veda Parishishta,* and that, in modern times, it is practiced chiefly in southern India (Travancore, Comorin) and in Assam, indicates a probable pre-Aryan origin. It is perhaps one of the traces left by the great Afro-Asiatic culture which, between the fourth and third millennia, extended from the eastern Mediterranean and Mesopotamia to India. However this may be, the *hiranyagarbha* initiatory rite is especially important for the equivalence that it establishes between the three symbols of the Mother Goddess— cow, womb, and pot. In southern India and in Borneo, the Great Mother is frequently represented in the form of a pot.[50] That this is always a symbol of the uterus is proven, for India, by the miraculous birth of the sages Agastya and Vasishta from a pot,[51] and elsewhere in the world by burials in urns in the embryonic position.[52] All these rites and extremely complex symbolisms obviously reach beyond the sphere of initiation, but it was neces- sary to mention them briefly in order to show that we are in the presence of general conceptions of life, death, and rebirth, and that the initiatory concept with which we are concerned is only one aspect of this extensive world view.

Multiple Meanings of the Symbolism of the Embryo

It is noteworthy that the initiatory theme of return to the em- bryonic state recurs even on higher levels of culture, as, for ex- ample, in the Taoist techniques of mystical physiology. Indeed, "embryonic breathing" (*t'ai-si*), which plays a considerable role in neo-Taoism, is imagined as respiration in a closed circuit, in the manner of a fetus; the adept tries to imitate the circulation of blood and breath from mother to child and from child to mother. The Preface to the *T'ai-si k'eou kiue* ("Oral Formulas for Embry- onic Breathing") clearly expresses the goal of the technique in one sentence: "By returning to the base, by returning to the origin, one drives away old age, one returns to the fetal state."[53] A Taoist text of the modern syncretistic school puts it as follows: "That is why the (Buddha) Ju-Lai (Tathagata), in his great mercy, revealed the method of the (alchemical) work of Fire and taught men *to enter the womb again* in order to recreate their (true) nature and (the fullness of) their portion in life."[54]

The same motif is documented among Western alchemists: the adept must return to his mother's breast, or even cohabit with her. According to Paracelsus, "he who would enter the Kingdom of

God must first enter with his body into his mother and there die."[55]
Return to the womb is sometimes presented in the form of incest
with the mother. Michael Maier tells us that "Dephinas, an anony-
mous philosopher, in his treatise, the *Secretus Maximus,* speaks
very clearly of the mother, who, of natural necessity, must unite
with her son" (*cum filio ex necessitate naturae conjungenda*).[56]
Obviously, the mother symbolizes nature in the primordial state,
the *prima materia* of the alchemists. This is proof of the symbolic
plurivalence of return to the womb, a plurivalence that enables it
to be constantly revaluated in different spiritual situations and
cultural contexts.

Another whole series of initiatory rites and myths, concerning
caves and mountain crevasses as symbols of the womb of Mother
Earth, could also be cited. I will merely say that caves played a role
in prehistoric initiations, and that the primordial sacredness of the
cave is still decipherable in its semantic modifications. The Chinese
term *tong,* "cave," finally came to have the meaning "mysterious,
profound, transcendent"; that is, it became equivalent to the arcana
revealed in initiations.[57]

Although it is risky to compare religious documents belonging
to such different ages and cultures, I have taken the risk because
all these religious facts fit into a pattern. Initiations by return to
the womb have as their first aim the novice's recovery of the
embryonic situation. From this primordial situation the various
forms of initiations which we have reviewed develop in different
directions, for they pursue different ends. That is, having symbolically returned to the state of "semen" or "embryo," the novice
can do one of four things. He can resume existence, with all its
possibilities intact. (This is the goal of the *hiranyagarbha* ceremonies and of "embryonic breathing," and the same motif is amply
documented in archaic therapies.)[58] Or he can reimmerse himself
in the cosmic sacrality ruled by the Great Mother (as, for example,
in the Kunapipi ceremonies). Or he can attain to a higher state of
existence, that of the spirit (which is the goal of the *upanayana*),
or prepare himself for participation in the sacred (the goal of the
diksha). Or, finally, he can begin an entirely different, a transcendent mode of existence, homologizable to that of the Gods (the
goal of Buddhism). From all this, one common characteristic
emerges—access to the sacred and to the spirit is always figured as
an embryonic gestation and a new birth. Every initiate in this category is twice-born, and even—in the case of the Kunapipi ceremony

and the *diksha*—is born a number of times. Sacrality, spirituality, and immortality are expressed in images that, in one way or another, signify the beginning of life.

Primitives, of course, always think of the beginning of life in a cosmological context. The Creation of the world constitutes the exemplary model for all living creation. A life that begins in the absolute sense is equivalent to the birth of a world. The sun, plunging every evening into the darkness of death and into the primordial waters, symbol of the uncreated and the virtual, resembles both the embryo in the womb and the neophyte hidden in the initiatory hut. When the sun rises in the morning, the world is reborn, just as the initiate emerges from his hut. In all probability, burial in the embryonic position is explained by the mystical interconnection between death, initiation, and return to the womb. In some cultures this close connection will finally bring about the assimilation of death to initiation—the dying man is regarded as undergoing an initiation. But burial in the fetal position especially emphasizes the hope of a new beginning of life—which does not mean an existence reduced to its mere biological dimensions. For the primitive, *to live* is to share in the sacrality of the cosmos. And this will suffice to keep us from falling into the error of explaining all initiatory rites and symbols of return to the womb by the desire to prolong a merely biological existence. Such an existence is a quite recent discovery in the history of humanity—a discovery that was made possible precisely by a radical desacralization of nature. On the level on which our study is being conducted, life is still a sacred reality. And this, I think, explains the continuity between archaic rites and symbols of initiatory "new birth," on the one hand, and, on the other, techniques of longevity, of spiritual rebirth, of divinization, and even such ideas of immortality and absolute freedom as we find, in the historical period, in India and China.

The examples just given show how an initiatory scenario that originally determined puberty rites was capable of being used in ceremonies pursuing other ends. This multivalence is easy to understand; briefly, what takes place is an increasingly broad application of a paradigmatic method, especially that employed to "make" a man. Since the boy is made an adult by an initiation involving return to the womb, it is hoped that similar results will be obtained when other things are to be made—for example, when the object is to make (that is, to obtain) long life or immortality.

In the end, all kinds of making are homologized by being identified with the supreme example of the "made," the cosmogony. Attaining to another mode of being—that of spirit—is equivalent to being born a second time, to becoming a new man. The most striking expression of newness is birth. The discovery of spirit is homologized to the appearance of life, and the appearance of life to the appearance of the world, to the cosmogony.

In the dialectic that made all these homologies possible, we discern the emotion of primitive man discovering the life of spirit. The newness of the spiritual life, its autonomy, could find no better expression than the images of an "absolute beginning," images whose structure is anthropocosmic, deriving at once from embryology and from cosmogony.

CHAPTER IV

Individual Initiations and Secret Societies

卐

Descent to the Underworld and Heroic Initiations

Part of the last chapter was devoted to initiatory rites of return to the womb implying the initiand's symbolic transformation into an embryo. In all these contexts, the return to the mother signifies return to the chthonian Great Mother. The initiand is born again from the womb of Mother Earth (*Terra Mater*). But as I had occasion to mention before, other myths and beliefs exist in which this initiatory pattern displays two new elements: first, the Hero enters the Great Mother's womb without returning to the embryonic state; second, the enterprise is particularly dangerous. There is a Polynesian myth which admirably illustrates this type of initiatory return to the womb. After a life full of adventures, Maui, the great Maori Hero, returned to his native country and the house of his ancestress Hine-mi-te-po, the Great Lady (of Night). He found her asleep and, throwing off his clothes, entered the giantess' body. He made his way through it without being stopped, but when he was about to emerge—that is, when half his body was still inside her mouth—the birds that were accompanying him burst out laughing. Waking suddenly, the Great Lady (of Night) clenched her teeth and cut the Hero in two, killing him. It is because of this, the Maoris say, that man is mortal; if Maui had been able to get out of his ancestress' body safe and sound, men would have become immortal.[1]

Maui's ancestress is Mother Earth. To enter her body is equivalent to descending *alive* into the depths of the earth, that is, into

Hell. Here, then, we have a descent to the Underworld, such as we find documented, for example, in the myths and sagas of the ancient East and of the Mediterranean world. From one point of view, we may say that all these myths and sagas have an initiatory structure; to descend into Hell alive, confront its monsters and demons, is to undergo an initiatory ordeal. I may add that similar flesh-and-blood descents into Hell are characteristic of heroic initiations, whose goal is the conquest of bodily immortality. Of course, these instances belong to initiatory mythology, and not to ritual properly speaking; but myths are often more valuable than rites for our understanding of religious behavior. For it is the myth which most completely reveals the deep, and often unconscious, desire of the religious man.

In all these contexts, the chthonian Great Mother shows herself pre-eminently as Goddess of Death and Mistress of the Dead; that is, she displays threatening and aggressive aspects. In the funerary mythology of Malekula, a terrifying female figure, named Temes or Le-hev-hev, awaits the dead man's soul at the mouth of a cave or beside a rock. Before her, drawn on the ground, is a labyrinthine design; and when the dead man comes near, the woman obliterates half of the design. If the dead man already knows the labyrinthine design—that is, if he has been initiated— he finds the road easily; if he does not, the woman devours him.[2] As the work of Deacon and Layard has shown, the numerous labyrinthine designs drawn on the ground in Malekula are intended to teach the road to the abode of the dead.[3] In other words, the labyrinth plays the role of a post-mortem initiatory ordeal; it falls in the category of the obstacles that the dead person—or, in other contexts, the Hero—must confront in his journey through the beyond. What I should like to emphasize here is that the labyrinth is presented as a "dangerous passage" into the bowels of Mother Earth, a passage in which the soul runs the risk of being devoured by a female monster. Malekula gives us other mythical figures of the threatening and dangerous female principle; for example, the Crab Woman with two immense claws,[4] or a giant clam (*Tridacna deresa*), which, when it is open, resembles the female sexual organ.[5] These terrifying images of aggressive female sexuality and devouring motherhood bring out still more clearly the initiatory character of descent into the body of the chthonian Great Mother. For Hentze[6] was able to show that a number of South American iconographic motifs represent the mouth of Mother Earth as a *vagina dentata*. The theme of the *vagina dentata* is quite complex, and I do not intend to treat it here. But it is important to note that the ambivalence of the chthonian Great Mother is sometimes expressed, mythically and iconographically, by identifying her mouth with the *vagina dentata*. In initiatory myths and sagas, the Hero's passage through a giantess' belly and his emergence through her mouth are equivalent to a new birth. But the passage is infinitely dangerous.

To realize the difference between this initiatory motif and the pattern that we studied in one of the preceding chapters, we need only remember the situation of the novices shut up in initiatory cabins in the shape of some marine monster; they are supposed to have been swallowed by the monster and to be in its belly, hence they are "dead," digested, and in process of being reborn. One day the monster will disgorge them—that is, they will be born again. But in the group of myths that we are now examining, the Hero makes his way, alive and intact, into a monster or into the belly of a Goddess (who is at once Mother Earth and Goddess of Death); and very often he succeeds in emerging unharmed. According to some variants of the *Kalevala,* the sage Väinämöinen builds himself a boat and, as the text puts it, "begins to row from one end of the bowels to the other." The giantess is finally forced to vomit him up into the sea.[7] Another Finnish myth relates the adventure of the blacksmith Ilmarinen. A girl whom he is courting says that she will marry him on condition that he will walk "along the sparse teeth of the Old Hag of Hiisi." Ilmarinen sets out to find the Hag; when he goes near her, the sorceress swallows him. She tells him to come out through her mouth, but Ilmarinen refuses. "I'll make my own door!" he answers, and with the smith's tools that he has made by magic, he breaks open the Hag's stomach and so comes out. According to another variant, the girl stipulated that Ilmarinen should catch a huge fish. But the fish swallowed him. Refusing to come out either "through his back hole" or "through his mouth," Ilmarinen jumped about in the fish's belly until it burst.[8]

This mythical theme is enormously widespread, especially in Oceania. We need cite only a Polynesian variant. The Hero Nganaoa's boat had been swallowed by a kind of whale, but the hero seized the mast and thrust it into the monster's mouth to keep it open. He then went down into the monster's belly, where he found his two parents, still alive. Nganaoa lit a fire, killed the whale, and emerged through its mouth.[9]

The sea monster's belly, like the body of the chthonian Goddess, represents the bowels of the earth, the realm of the dead, Hell. In the visionary literature of the Middle Ages, Hell is frequently imagined in the form of a huge monster, whose prototype is probably the biblical Leviathan. There is, then, a series of parallel images: the belly of a giantess, of a Goddess, of a sea monster, symbolizing the chthonian womb, cosmic night, the realm of the dead. To enter this gigantic body alive is equivalent to descending into Hell, to confronting the ordeals destined for the dead. The initiatory meaning of this type of descent to the Underworld is clear —he who has been successful in such an exploit no longer fears death; he has conquered a kind of bodily immortality, the goal of all heroic initiations from the time of Gilgamesh.

But there is yet another element that we must take into account. The beyond is also the place of knowledge and of wisdom. The Lord of Hell is omniscient; the dead know the future. In some myths and sagas the Hero descends into Hell to gain wisdom or to learn secret lore. Väinämöinen could not finish a boat that he had created by magic because he lacked three words. To learn them, he sets out in search of a famous wizard, Antero, a giant who for years had lain motionless like a shaman in trance, so that a tree had grown out of his shoulder and birds had made their nests in his beard. Väinämöinen falls into the giant's mouth and is quickly swallowed. But once inside Antero's stomach, he forges himself a magic suit of iron and tells the wizard that he will stay there until he has obtained the three magic words to finish his boat.[10] Now, what Väinämöinen does in flesh and blood the shaman does in trance—that is, his spirit leaves his body and descends into the Underworld. Sometimes this ecstatic journey into the beyond is imagined as entry into the body of a fish or a sea monster. In a Lapp legend, a shaman's son wakes his father, who has been asleep for a long time, with these words: "When will my father come from the bend of the pike's bowels, from the third curve of the entrails?"[11] Why had the shaman undertaken this ecstatic journey if not to obtain secret knowledge, the revelation of mysteries?

Initiatory Symbolism of the Symplegades

But the representation of the beyond as the bowels of Mother Earth or the belly of a gigantic monster is only one among the very many images that figure the Other World as a place that can be reached only with the utmost difficulty. The "clashing rocks," the "dancing reeds," the gates in the shape of jaws, the "two razor-edged restless mountains,"[12] the "two clashing icebergs," the "active door," the "revolving barrier,"[13] the door made of the two halves of the eagle's beak, and many more[14]—all these are images used in myths and sagas to suggest the insurmountable difficulties of passage to the Other World. (The Symplegades were two rocks at the entrance to the Black Sea that clashed together intermittently, but remained apart when Jason and the Argonauts passed through in the *Argo*.) Let us note that these images emphasize not only the danger of the passage—as in the myths of entering a giantess' or a sea monster's body—but especially the impossibility of imagining that the passage could be made by a being of flesh and blood. The Symplegades show us the paradoxical nature of passage into the beyond, or, more precisely, of transfer from this world to a world that is transcendent. For although originally the Other World is the world after death, it finally comes to mean any transcendent state, that is, any mode of being inaccessible to fleshly man and reserved for "spirits" or for man as a spiritual entity.

The paradox of this passage is sometimes expressed in spatial as well as in temporal terms. According to the *Jaiminiya Upanishad Brahmana* (I, 5, 5; I, 35, 7-9; IV, 15, 2-5), the gate of the world of heavenly Light is to be found "where Sky and Earth embrace" and the "Ends of the year" are united.[15] In other words, no human being can go there except "in the spirit." All these mythical images and folklore motifs of the dangerous passage and the paradoxical transfer express the necessity for a change in mode of being to make it possible to attain to the world of spirit. As A. K. Coomaraswamy well put it: "What the formula states literally is that whoever would transfer from this to the Otherworld, or return, must do so through the undimensioned and timeless 'interval' that divides related but contrary forces, between which, if one is to pass at all, it must be 'instantly.' "[16]

Coomaraswamy's interpretation is already a metaphysical exegesis of the symbolism of the Symplegades; it presupposes becoming conscious of the necessity for abolishing contraries; and, as we know, gaining such a consciousness is amply documented in Indian speculation and in mystical literature. But the interest of the Symplegades lies above all in the fact that they constitute a sort of prehistory of mysticism and metaphysics. In short, all these images express the following paradox: to enter the beyond, to attain to a transcendent mode of being, one must acquire the condition of "spirit." It is for this reason that the Symplegades form part of an initiatory scenario. They fall in the class of the ordeals that the Hero—or the dead man's soul—must face in order to enter the Other World.

As we saw, the Other World constantly enlarges its frontiers; it signifies not only the land of the dead but also any enchanted and miraculous realm, and, by extension, the divine world and the transcendent plane. The *vagina dentata* can represent not only passage into Mother Earth, but also the door of Heaven. In a North American tale, this door is alternatively made of the "two halves of the eagle's beak" or of the *vagina dentata* of the Daughter of the King of Heaven.[17] This is but one more demonstration that mythical imagination and philosophical speculation have made particularly good use of the initiatory structure of the Symplegades. The Symplegades become in some sort "guardians of the threshold," homologizable with the monsters and griffins that guard a treasure hidden at the bottom of the sea, or a miraculous fountain from which flows the Water of Youth, or a garden in the midst of which stands the Tree of Life. It is as difficult to enter the Garden of the Hesperides as it is to pass between the clashing rocks or to enter a monster's belly. Each of these exploits constitutes a pre-eminently initiatory ordeal. He who emerges from such an ordeal victorious is qualified to share in a superhuman condition—he is a Hero, omniscient, immortal.

Individual Initiations: North America

The myths, the symbols, and the images that we have just reviewed belong, in large part, to individual initiations; and this, of course, is why we find them documented especially in heroic myths and in stories whose structure is shamanic—that is, in narratives that recount the adventures of a person endowed with extraordinary gifts. As we shall see later, initiations of warriors and shamans are individual; and in their ordeals we can still trace the archetypal scenario revealed by myths. But aside from these initiations, which we might call specialized, since they pre-suppose an exceptional vocation or qualification, there are puberty initiations which are likewise individual. This is the type characteristic of the aboriginal societies of North America. The note peculiar to North American puberty rites is, of course, the obtaining of a tutelary spirit; hence what is involved is a personal quest and personal relations between the novice and his tutelary spirit. This type of puberty initiation is of interest for our investigation from several points of view. Above all, it shows us, more clearly than other initiations, the importance of the novice's religious experience; it is through obtaining his tutelary spirit that the novice receives the revelation of the sacred and changes his existential status. In addition, this type of individual puberty initiation enables us to approach, on one side, the initiations of warriors and shamans and, on the other, the rites for entrance into secret societies. Finally, the North American documents bring out some initiatory motifs which we have already noted elsewhere (in Australia, for example), but which attain their true importance in the shamanic initiations of central and northern Asia; I refer especially to the ritual ascent of trees and sacred poles.

The characteristic element of North American initiations is withdrawal into solitude. Between the ages of ten and sixteen years, the boys isolate themselves in the mountains or the forest. Here there is more than separation from the mother, which is characteristic of all puberty rituals; there is a break with the community of the living. The novice's religious experience is brought on by his immersion in the life of the cosmos and by his ascetic regime; it is not directed by the presence and teaching of instructors. More than in other types of puberty initiations, the novice's introduction to religious life is the result of a personal experience—the dreams and visions provoked by a course of ascetic practices in solitude. The novice fasts, especially for the first four days (an indication of the archaism of the custom), purifies himself by repeated purges, imposes dietary prohibitions on himself, and submits himself to numerous ascetic exercises (e.g., steam bath or bath in icy water, burns, scarifications). He sings and dances through the night, prays at dawn to obtain a tutelary spirit. And it is after these prolonged efforts that he receives the revelation of his spirit. Usually the spirit makes its appearance in animal form, which confirms the cosmic structure of the novice's religious experience. More rarely, the spirit is anthropomorphic (when it proves to be the soul of an ancestor). The novice learns a song by virtue of which he remains connected with his spirit throughout his life. Girls retire into solitude on the occasion of their first menstruation; but for them it is not absolutely necessary to obtain a tutelary spirit.[18]

The same initiatory pattern recurs in the ceremonies for entrance into secret societies (the Dancing Societies) and in shamanic initiations. The distinctive note of all these North American initiations is the belief that the tutelary spirit can be won by an ascetic effort in the wilderness. The ascetic practices pursue the annihilation of the novice's secular personality, in other words, his initiatory death; in many cases, this death is announced by the ecstasy, trance, or pseudo-unconsciousness into which he falls. Like all other initiations, these of North America—whether they are puberty ceremonies or rites for entrance into secret or shamanic societies— aim at the spiritual transmutation of the novice; but it is important to emphasize the cosmic context of their scenarios. The novice's solitude in the wilderness is equivalent to a *personal* discovery of the sacredness of the cosmos and of animal life. All nature is revealed as a hierophany. The passage from secular existence in the community during the nonliturgical summer season to the existence sanctified by meeting with the Gods or spirits is not made without peril. "Possessed" by the Gods or spirits, the novice is in danger of completely losing his psychomental balance. The raging fury of the candidates for the Kwakiutl Cannibal Society is the best example of the danger that accompanies such a spiritual transmutation. We will dwell for a moment on the initiations into the Kwakiutl Dancing Societies; they quite clearly reveal the structure of initiations into North American secret societies. Naturally, I cannot here go into all the details of this extremely complex phenomenon. I shall only mention such aspects of the initiation as can contribute directly to our investigation.[19]

Kwakiutl Dancing Societies

During the winter, that is, during the Sacred Time, when the spirits are believed to return among the living, the social division into clans is abolished, and in its place appears an organization of a spiritual nature, represented by the Dancing Societies. The men abandon their summer names and resume their sacred winter names.[20] During the Winter Ceremonial, the community relives its myths of origin. The dances and pantomimes dramatically reproduce the mythical events which, in the beginning, founded the institutions of the Kwakiutl. The men incarnate the sacred personages, and as a result there is a complete regeneration of society and the cosmos. This movement of universal regeneration is the setting for the initiations of novices. The Dancing Societies are divided into numerous hierarchic grades or Dances, each constituting a closed unit. Some Societies have as many as fifty-three hierarchic degrees, but all members cannot reach the highest degrees. The lower a Dance, the more members it has. The social and economic situation of the candidate—or rather, of his family —plays a role of the first importance. In the *hamatsa* Dance, for example, the members are all chiefs of clans. Then, too, the initiatory ceremony is quite costly, for the candidate has to give valuable presents to the participants. The right to become a member of a Dancing Society is hereditary; consequently the initiation is limited to such boys as are elegible. When the boys reach the age of ten or twelve years, they are initiated into the lower degree. It is these first entrance rites that here concern us.

Listening to the sound of the sacred instruments, the novice falls into trance (the trance is sometimes simulated); this is the sign that he is dying to profane life, that he is possessed by his Spirit. He is either "carried off" into the forest (as in the case of the Cannibal Society), or "ravished" to Heaven (the Dancing Society of the Dluwulaxa or Mitla), or, finally, he remains shut up in the ceremonial house (the Clown Society of Fort Rupert, or the Wikeno Dancing Societies of the warriors and healers). All these carryings off or ravishings find expression in a period of solitude, and it is during this time that the novices are initiated by the spirits. Among the Bella Bella and other tribes, each clan has its own cave, in which the initiating spirit lives; it is in this cave—whose symbolsm is now familar to us—that the initiation takes place.[21] During his seclusion in the forest, the candidate for the Cannibal Society is served by a woman; since he is identified with the God, the woman impersonates the slave. She brings him food and prepares a corpse for him, mummifying it in salt water. The novice hangs it from the roof of his cabin, smokes it, and, tearing strips from it, swallows them without chewing them.[22] This cannibalism is proof of his identification with the God.

The all-important moment comes with the return of the novices from the forest and their entrance into the ceremonial house, for this house is an image of the world (*imago mundi*) and represents the cosmos. To grasp the symbolism of the house, we must remember that, for the Kwakiutl, the universe has three divisions—sky, earth, and Other World. A copper pillar, symbolizing the axis of the world, traverses these three regions at a central point, which is the center of the world. According to the myths, men can mount to Heaven or descend to Hell by climbing up or down a copper ladder; upward, it leads to an opening, the Door to the World

Above. This copper pillar is· represented in the ceremonial house by a cedar pole thirty or thirty-five feet high, the upper half of which projects through a hole in the roof. During the ceremonies the novices sing: "I am at the Center of the World . . . I am at the post of the World! . . ."[23] The house reproduces the cosmos, and in the ceremonial songs it is called "Our World." The ceremonies take place, then, at the center of the visible universe; hence they have a cosmic dimension and value.[24] The pole in the ceremonial house of the Cannibals sometimes bears a human image at its summit, and so is identified not only with the cosmic pillar but also with the cannibal spirit. As we shall see later, the central pole plays quite an important role in North and South American initiations; by climbing it, the novice reaches Heaven. For the moment, and to confine ourselves to the Kwakiutl family, we may note that among the Wikeno the novice is tied to the pole; he struggles to free himself; and the uninitiated, watching from a distance, seeing the pole violently shaken, believe that he is fighting with the cannibal spirit. Among the Bella Bella, the novice climbs the pole; among the Fort Rupert Kwakiutl, he climbs it to the roof of the house, from which he jumps down among the spectators and bites them.[25]

Let us note this fact: the novice's entry into the ceremonial house is equivalent to his symbolic installation at the center of the world. He now inhabits a sacred microcosm—sacred with the sacrality that the world possessed at the moment of creation. In such a sacred space, it is always possible to leave the earth, to transcend it, and enter the world of the Gods. The back part of the ceremonial house is separated from the remainder by a parti-tion, on which the face of the patron spirit is painted. Among the Cannibals, the door in this partition represents a bird's beak. When the novice enters the closed-off part, he is supposed to be swallowed by the Bird.[26] In other words, he flies to Heaven, for bird symbol-ism is always connected with an ascension. The sound of the flutes and other sacred instruments which have such a considerable role in the Kwakiutl and Nootka secret rituals represents the voices of birds.[27] The ascent to Heaven symbolized by the flight of birds is characteristic of archaic culture; and probably the rituals we have just been considering are among the oldest elements of the Kwakiutl religion.

Shut up in the back part of the ceremonial house, the novices continue to be possessed by the spirit of the Society, just as they were when they were ravished to the forest. This possession is equivalent to the death of their individuality, which is dissolved in the supernatural power. At a particular moment the novices, sometimes wearing masks, come out from behind the partition and join in the dances. They imitate the behavior of the Society's spirit by a mimicry that proclaims that they incarnate it. Identified with the spirit, the novice is "out of his mind," and an essential part of the initiation ceremony consists precisely in attempts on the part of the older members of the Society to "tame" him by dances and songs. The novice is progressively cured of the excess of power acquired from the divine presence; he is directed toward a new spiritual equilibrium, helped to establish a new personality, qualitatively different from that which he possessed before encountering the divinity, but nevertheless a properly structured personality, which will replace the psychic tumult of possession. Duly exorcised, he takes his place in one of the lower degrees of the Dancing Society. The ritual prohibitions are, of course, lifted only progressively, toward the end of the Winter Time.

Among the Kwakiutl Dancing Societies, the Cannibal Society is of the greatest interest for the historian of religion. The Kwakiutl has a horror of human flesh. If the novice, sometimes with tremendous difficulty, nevertheless succeeds in becoming a cannibal, it is to give concrete evidence that he is no longer a human being; that he has identified himself with the God. Like his "madness," his cannibalism is proof of his divinization. When he returns to the village after a seclusion of three or four months, he acts like a beast of prey—he jumps from the roof of the house, attacks all those whom he encounters, bites their arms and swallows the morsels of flesh. Four men are barely able to restrain him, and they try to force him into the dancing house. The woman who had accompanied him into the solitude now appears and dances before him naked, holding a corpse in her arms. Finally the novice climbs onto the roof of the ceremonial house, from which he jumps down through the displaced boards, to dance in ecstasy, trembling in every limb. To tame him, the healer (*heliga*) seizes him by the head and drags him to salt water. They go into the water until it reaches their waists. The healer dips the *hamatsa* under water four times. Every time he comes up again he cries *"hap!"* Then they go back to the house. The excitement has left him. He goes home and drinks salt water to cause vomiting. The wild paroxysm is followed by complete prostration, and during the following nights he is silent and depressed at the dances.[28] Like all the other initiations into Kwakiutl secret brotherhoods, initiation into the

Cannibal Society is also the establishment of a new, integrated personality; the novice has to find a *modus vivendi* with the sacred power that he has acquired by incarnating the God.

The initiatory behavior of the Kwakiutl cannibal is of particular interest for the historian of religion; the breakup of his personality, his fury, his taming by the healer, are reminiscent of other religious phenomena, documented in various cultures that have no historical connections. Disintegration of personality and possession are symptoms common to many North American initiations; but when loss of personality and possession occur with exceptional intensity, they are the outstanding syndrome of shamanic vocation. For this reason I shall reserve an analysis of the religious significance of madness and initiatory sicknesses in general for the next chapter, which will deal with shamanism. But the Kwakiutl cannibal exhibits some special traits—for example, his homicidal fury, his behaving like a beast of prey, his "heat," which the healer reduces by baths. Each of these expresses the fact that the human condition has been transcended; that the novice has assimilated such a quantity of sacred power that his secular mode of being has been abolished. And we shall see that similar behavior occurs in other cultures, when the novice, by passing through certain initiatory ordeals, succeeds in transmuting his human existence into a higher. The Scandinavian berserker "heats" himself in his initiatory combat, shares in the sacred frenzy or *furor* (*wut*), behaves at once like a beast of prey and a shaman; not only is he irresistible, he spreads terror all around him. To behave like a beast of prey—wolf, bear, leopard—betokens that one has ceased to be a man, that one incarnates a higher religious force, that one has in some sort become a god. For we must not forget that, on the level of elemental religious experience, the beast of prey represents a higher mode of existence. As we shall see in the next chapter, assimilation of sacred power is expressed in an excessive heating of the body; extreme heat is one of the characteristic marks of magicians, shamans, healers, mystics. In whatever cultural context it appears, the syndrome of magical heat proclaims that the profane human condition has been abolished and that one shares in a transcendent mode of being, that of the Gods.

Men's Secret Societies

This superhuman mode of being is obtained through an increase in magico-religious power. This is why, among the North American aborigines, there are such marked resemblances between puberty initiations and rites for entrance into secret societies or shamanic associations. All of these initiations undertake to conquer a sacred power, and the conquest is proved either by obtaining one or more tutelary spirits, by such exploits as those performed by Indian fakirs, or by unusual behavior, such as cannibalism. Everywhere we decipher the same mystery of death to the secular condition, followed by resurrection to a higher mode of being. In North America, shamanism has influenced the pattern of other initiations. The reason is precisely that the shaman is pre-eminently the example of the man endowed with extraordinary powers—that is, he is in some sort, the exemplary model of all religious men. Very probably we here have the explanation for the origin of secret societies, especially those of men, not only in North America but all over the world. The specialist in the sacred—the medicine man, the shaman, the mystic—has been at once the model and the stimulus for other men to increase their magico-religious powers and their social prestige through repeated initiations.

The morphology of men's secret societies is extremely complex and I cannot here even outline their structures and history.[29] As to their origin, the most generally accepted hypothesis is the one originally suggested by Frobenius and revived by the historico-cultural school.[30] According to it, the male secret societies, or Societies of Masks, were a creation of the matriarchal cycle; their object was to terrify women, primarily by making them believe that the masks were demons and ancestral spirits, to the end of undermining the economic, social, and religious supremacy of woman which has been established by matriarchy. In this form, the hypothesis seems to lack foundation. It is probable that the Societies of Masks played a role in the struggle for male supremacy; but it is hard to believe that the religious phenomenon of the secret society is a result of matriarchy. On the contrary, we observe a perfect continuity between puberty rites and rites for initiation into men's secret societies. Throughout Oceania, for example, both initiations of boys and those requisite for membership in the men's secret societies involve the same ritual of symbolic death through being swallowed by a sea monster, followed by resurrection—which proves that all the ceremonies derive historically from a single center.[31] In West Africa, we find a similar phenomenon; the secret societies derive from the puberty initiations.[32] And it would be easy to lengthen the list of examples.[33]

What, in my view, is original and fundamental in the phenomenon of secret societies is the need for a fuller participation in the
sacred, the desire to live as intensely as possible the sacrality
peculiar to each of the two sexes. This is the reason why initiation
into secret societies so much resembles the initiatory rites of
puberty. We find the same ordeals, the same symbols of death
and resurrection, the same revelation of a traditional and secret
doctrine—and we find them because this initiatory scenario is
the *sine.qua non* for a new and more complete experience of the
sacred. There are, however, some innovations peculiar to the
masked secret societies. The most important of these are the
following: the primary role of secrecy, the cruelty of the initiatory
ordeals, the predominance of the cult of Ancestors (personified
by the masks), and the absence of the Supreme Being in the
ceremonies. We have already had occasion to note the Supreme
Being's progressive loss of importance in Australian puberty rites.
In the secret societies, this phenomenon is general; the place of
the Supreme Being is taken by a demiurgic God, or by the mythical
Ancestor, or by a civilizing Hero. But as we shall soon see, some
initiations into secret societies continue to employ rites and symbols
of celestial ascent, which proves, I think, the importance of the
supreme Celestial Beings whose place, in the course of time, has
been taken by other divine or semidivine figures.

The socioreligious phenomenon of secret male cults and confraternities of masks is especially widespread in Melanesia and
Africa.[34] As an example, I will cite the initiation into the Kuta
secret confraternity of the Ngoye (Ndassa), which is reserved
only for heads of clans.[35] The adepts are beaten with a thong of
panther hide, tied to a horizontal beam about three feet above the
surface of the ground, rubbed with urticaceous leaves, and their
bodies and hair are covered with an ointment made from a plant
that produces terrible itching. We may note in passing that being
beaten or rubbed with nettles is a rite that symbolizes the candidate's initiatory dismemberment, his death at the hands of demons.
We find the same symbolism and the same rites in shamanic
initiations.[36] Another ordeal "consists in making the adept climb
a tree fifteen to twenty feet tall, where he has to drink a medicine."[37]
When the novice returns to the village, he is received by the
women with lamentations; they weep as if he were dying. Among
other Kuta tribes, the novice is severely beaten, which is said to
"kill" his old name so that he may be given another.[38] These rites

need no further comment; as in the puberty initiations, we here have a symbolic death and resurrection, involving an ascent to Heaven and the beginning of a new, consecrated existence.

The Mandja and Banda tribes have a society named *Ngakola*.[39] According to the myth that the novices are told at their initiation, Ngakola lived on earth long ago, in the bush. His body was black and covered with hair. He could kill a man and then bring him to life again, better than before. So he said to the people: "Send me men. I will swallow them and vomit them up renewed." The people obeyed. But Ngakola disgorged only half of the men he had swallowed; so the people killed him. This myth institutes and justifies the rituals of the secret society. A flat sacred stone plays a great part in the initiation ceremonies; according to tradition, this sacred stone was taken from Ngakola's belly. The novice enters a house symbolizing the monster's body. There he hears Ngakola's lugubrious voice, there he undergoes tortures; for he is told that he "has now entered Ngakola's belly," and is being digested. The initiates sing in chorus: "Ngakola, take our entrails; Ngakola, take our livers!"[40] After other ordeals, the initiatory master finally announces that Ngakola, who had swallowed the novice, has vomited him up.

Here we have again what we had already found in Australia—the myth of a semidivine monster who was killed by men because he disgorged only some of the people he had swallowed, and who after his death was made the center of a secret cult whose purpose is initiatory death and resurrection. We also find again the symbolism of death through being swallowed by a monster and entering its belly, a symbolism which plays so large a part in puberty initiations. Let us note once again that rites for entrance into secret societies correspond in every way to tribal initiations: e.g., seclusion, initiatory ordeals and tortures, bestowal of a new name, revelation of a secret doctrine, instruction in a special language. This comes out even more clearly in the description that a Belgian missionary, Léo Bittremieux, has given of the secret society of the Bakhimba, in Mayombe.[41] The initiatory ordeals continue for from two to five years, and the most important is a ceremony of death and resurrection. The novice must be "killed." The performance takes place at night, and the old initiates sing the lament of the mothers and relatives for those who are to die. The candidate is beaten and drinks a narcotic potion called the drink of death, but he also eats calabash seeds, which symbolize intelligence[42]—

a significant detail, for it shows us that initiatory death is the road to wisdom. The candidate is held by the hand, and one of the old men spins him around until he falls to the ground. Then all cry: "Oh, so-and-so is dead!" A native informant adds that "the dead man is rolled along the ground, while the chorus sing a funeral chant: 'He is dead! Ah, he is dead indeed . . . I shall never see him again!' " In the village, his mother, brother, and sister mourn him in the same fashion.[43] Then the initiated relatives of the "dead" men take them on their backs and carry them to a consecrated enclosure called the court of resurrection. There they are laid, stark naked, in a cross-shaped ditch, where they remain until dawn on the day of "commutation" or resurrection, the first day of the native week, which has only four.[44] The novices' heads are then shaved; they are beaten, thrown on the ground, and finally resuscitated by having a few drops of a peppery liquid dropped into their eyes and nostrils. But before their resurrection they have taken an oath of absolute secrecy: "All that I shall see here I will tell to no one, neither woman, man, noninitiate, nor whiteman; otherwise, make me swell up, kill me."[45] The same pattern of initiation is easily recognizable in many other African secret societies.[46]

There is no need of multiplying examples to show, on the one hand, the continuity between puberty rites and initiations into secret societies, and, on the other hand, the constant increase in the severity of the ordeals. Initiatory torture is characteristic of the Melanesian secret societies and of some North American confraternities. The ordeals through which the Mandan novices had to pass, for example, are famous for their cruelty.[47] To understand the meaning of initiatory torture, we must bear in mind that suffering has a ritual value; the torture is supposed to be inflicted by superhuman beings, and its goal is the spiritual transmutation of the initiand. Extreme suffering is likewise an expression of initiatory death. Certain serious illnesses, especially psychomental disorders, are regarded as the sign that superhuman beings have chosen the sick man to be initiated—that is, tortured, dismembered, and "killed," so that he may be resuscitated to a higher existence. As we shall see in the next chapter, initiatory sicknesses are one of the principal syndromes of the shamanic vocation. The tortures of the candidates for secret societies are the homologue of the terrible sufferings that symbolize the mystical death of the future shaman. In both cases, there is a process of spiritual trans-mutation.

Initiatory Motifs Common to Puberty Rites and Secret Societies

So much for the severity of the ordeals. As for the continuity of initiatory motifs, we have already seen how insistently the theme of the swallowing monster recurs, not only in puberty rites and in initiations into secret societies, but also in other mythico-ritual contexts. But there are yet other archetypal motifs that recur in various types of initiations, notably the ritual climbing of trees or sacred poles. We have already encountered examples of this in Australian, African, and North American initiations. The meaning of this climbing rite will become completely clear only when we come to study the initiations and ecstatic techniques of the shamans of northern and central Asia. But the ceremonial climbing of trees and poles is also documented in other cultural zones besides Asia, and in other religious contexts besides shamanism. To confine ourselves to the two American continents, a tree or a sacred pole plays important roles not only in puberty initiations (as, for example, in the north of the Gran Chaco, among the Chamacoco and Vilela tribes, among the Mandan, the Kwakiutl, the Pomo)[48] but also in public festivals (Ge festival of the sun, various festivals among the Tupi, the Plains Indians, the Selish, the Lenape, the Maidu),[49] or in the ceremonies and healing séances of shamans (Yaruro, Araucanian, Maidu).[50] The novice during his initiation, or the shaman in the course of the séance, climbs the tree or the sacred pole; and despite the variety of socioreligious contexts in which it occurs, the ascent always has the same goal—meeting with the Gods or heavenly powers, in order to obtain a blessing (whether a personal consecration, a favor for the community, or the cure of a sick person). In a number of cases, the original meaning of the climb—symbolic ascent to Heaven—seems to have been lost, yet the rite continues to be performed, for the memory of celestial sacrality remains even when the Celestial Beings have been completely forgotten.

Professor Josef Haeckel has shown that the rite and symbolism of the sacred pole were probably brought to South America by waves of hunter-culture peoples from North America; that, consequently, we here have an archaic religious element which, in addition, displays an astonishing similarity to the cosmologies of central and northern Asia.[51] Now in Asia the sacred pole or tree

symbolizes the Cosmic Tree, the *axis mundi,* and they are supposed to stand at the center of the world; by climbing his tree,
the shaman ascends to Heaven. As we saw, the same cosmological
concept and the same meaning of ascent are found among the
Kwakiutl. This raises the whole problem of the historical connections between the North American mythico-ritual complex and the
Asian complex; but I cannot enter into it here.[52] What I should
like to stress is the following fact: ascending to Heaven represents
one of the oldest religious means of personally communicating with
the Gods, and hence of fully participating in the sacred in order to
transcend the human condition. Ascent and flight are proofs par
excellence of the divinization of man. The specialists in the sacred
—medicine men, shamans, mystics—are above all men who are believed to fly up to Heaven, in ecstasy or even in the flesh. This theme
will engage our attention in the next chapter; but we are now in
a position to understand why it is present in certain puberty initiations and in the ceremonies for entrance into secret societies: the
candidate symbolically goes up to Heaven in order to take unto
himself the very source of the sacred, to transmute his ontological
status, and to make himself like the archetype of *homo religiosus,*
the shaman.

The initiatory theme of ascent to Heaven differs radically from
that of the swallowing monster; but although, in all probability,
they originally belonged to different types of culture, we today
often find them together in the same religion; even more, the
two themes sometimes meet during the initiation of a single individual. The reason is not far to seek—the descent to the Underworld and the ascent to Heaven obviously denote different religious
experiences; but the two experiences spectacularly prove that he
who has undergone them has transcended the secular condition of
humanity and that his behavior is purely that of a spirit.

I shall say only a few words about the secret associations of
women. Where we find them to be organizations involving complex
and dramatic entrance rites, we may suspect imitation of certain
external aspects of the male secret societies. Such is the case,
for example, with the secret female cult of the Pangwe, a comparatively recent imitation of the men's societies.[53] It is likewise probable that initiation into the Nyembe association in Gabun has been
influenced by certain rituals peculiar to the men's secret societies.
The initiation is extremely complicated, but it includes a dance in
the course of which one of the directresses, symbolizing a leopard,

attacks and "kills" the novices; finally the other directress likewise "kills" the leopard and frees the novices from its belly.[54] This ritual motif is bound up with hunting and, consequently, properly belongs to men. Among the Mordvins there is a secret women's society whose emblem is a hobbyhorse and whose members are called "horses"; around their necks they wear a purse full of millet, representing the horse's belly.[55] All this symbolism of the horse shows the influence of male military organizations.

But these influences of male religious feeling and symbolism on the morphology of female secret societies must not be allowed to lead us into the error of believing that the entire phenomenon represents something late and hybrid. The influences have been exercised chiefly on the external organization of female societies, and in many cases quite late, after the secrets of some male confraternities were no longer strictly kept. But the phenomenon of the female secret society cannot be reduced to a process of imitation. It is women's particular and peculiar experience which explains their desire to organize themselves in closed associations in order to celebrate the mysteries of conception, of birth, of fecundity, and, in general, of universal fertility. This is clear even in the examples just cited. In the Kuta Lisimba society, which is almost identical with the Nyembe society, at a certain moment the woman directing the ceremony breaks an egg on the roof of the initiatory hut "to ensure the hunters a plentiful harvest of game."[56] Among the Mordvins, the young married women, when they reach the house where the society's ritual banquet is held, are struck three times with whips by the old women, who cry: "Lay an egg!" and the young married women produce a boiled egg from between their breasts.[57] There is no need to go into the complex symbolism of the egg here; but it is obvious that, in these contexts, the egg signifies fertility. Even the lubricious and orgiastic elements, and the crude and obscene language, which are characteristic of female ceremonial gatherings can finally be explained by a ritual goal—ensuring fecundity.[58]

Just as the men's secret societies terrorize women, the women insult, threaten, and even strike the men whom they encounter in the course of their frenzied processions. Such behavior is ritually justified; these are women's mysteries, whose results might be endangered by the presence of men. This is confirmed by the fact that while they are gardening—an activity which is reserved for them alone—Trobriand women have the right to attack and knock down any man who comes too close to their gardens.[59] We have already had occasion to note the tension that exists between groups of girls and young women working together at a specific craft and groups of young men who attack them and try to destroy their instruments.[60] In the final analysis, the tension is always between two different kinds of sacrality, which are the foundations of two different and polar world views—masculine and feminine. It is in this specificity of the female religious experience that we must look to find the primordial motive for the crystallization of secret groups exclusively for women. Now the pre-eminent religious experience of woman is that of the sanctity of life and the mystery of childbearing and universal fecundity. Women's cult associations have as their purpose ensuring full and unhampered participation in this cosmic sacrality; and woman's initiation par excellence is her introduction to the mystery of generation, primordial symbol of spiritual regeneration.

The tension between two kinds of sacrality implies both the antagonism between two magics—feminine and masculine—and their reciprocal attraction. Particularly on the levels of archaic culture, we know that men are fascinated by the "secrets" of women and vice versa. Psychologists have accorded great importance to the fact that primitives are jealous of "women's mysteries," especially of menstruation and the ability to give birth. But they have failed to bring out the complementary phenomenon —women's jealousy of men's magics and lores (e.g., hunting magic, secret lore concerning the Supreme Beings, shamanism and techniques of ascent to Heaven, relations with the dead). If men in their secret rites have made use of symbols and behaviors proper to the condition of woman (e.g., the symbolism of initiatory birth), women too, as we have just seen, have borrowed masculine symbols and rituals. This ambivalent behavior in respect to the mysteries of the opposite sex constitutes a problem of the first importance for the psychologist. But the historian of religion considers only the religious significations of a type of behavior. What he discerns in the antagonism and attraction between two types of sacralities— feminine and masculine—is above all a strong and essentially religious desire to transcend an apparently irreducible existential situation and attain to a total mode of being.

CHAPTER V

Heroic and Shamanic Initiations

᛭

Going Berserk

In a passage that has become famous, the *Ynglingasaga* sets the comrades of Odin before us: "They went without shields, and were mad as dogs or wolves, and bit on their shields, and were as strong as bears or bulls; men they slew, and neither fire nor steel would deal with them; and this is what is called the fury of the berserker."[1] This mythological picture has been rightly identified as a description of real men's societies—the famous *Männerbünde* of the ancient Germanic civilization. The berserkers were, literally, the "warriors in shirts (*serkr*) of bear."[2] This is as much as to say that they were magically identified with the bear. In addition they could sometimes change themselves into wolves and bears. A man became a berserker as the result of an initiation that included specifically martial ordeals. So, for example, Tacitus tells us that among the Chatti the candidate cut neither his hair nor his beard until he had killed an enemy.[3] Among the Taifali, the youth had to bring down a boar or a wolf; among the Heruli, he had to fight unarmed.[4] Through these ordeals, the candidate took to himself a wild-animal mode of being; he became a dreaded warrior in the measure in which he behaved like a beast of prey. He metamorphosed himself into a superman because he succeeded in assimilating the magicoreligious force proper to the carnivora.

The *Volsunga Saga* has preserved the memory of certain ordeals typical of the initiations of berserkers. By treachery, King Siggeir obtains possession of his nine brothers-in-law, the Volsungs.

Chained to a beam, they are all eaten by a she-wolf, except Sigmund, who is saved by a ruse of his sister Signy. Hidden in a hut in the depths of the forest, where Signy brings him food, he awaits the hour of revenge. When her first two sons have reached the age of ten, Signy sends them to Sigmund to be tested. Sigmund finds that they are cowards, and by his advice Signy kills them. As the result of her incestuous relations with her brother, Signy has a third son, Sinfjotli. When he is nearly ten, his mother submits him to a first ordeal: she sews his shirt to his arms through the skin. Siggeir's sons, submitted to the same ordeal, had howled with pain, but Sinfjotli remains imperturbable. His mother then pulls off his shirt, tearing away the skin, and asks him if he feels anything. The boy answers that a Volsung is not troubled by such a trifle. His mother then sends him to Sigmund, who submits him to the same ordeal that Siggeir's two sons had failed to sustain: he orders him to make bread from a sack of flour in which there is a snake. When Sigmund comes home that night, he finds the bread baked and asks Sinfjotli if he did not find anything in the flour. The boy answers that he remembers having seen something, but he paid no attention to it and kneaded everything up together. After this proof of courage Sigmund takes the boy into the forest with him. One day they find two wolfskins hanging from the wall of a hut. The two sons of a king had been transformed into wolves and could only come out of the skins every tenth day. Sigmund and Sinfjotli put on the skins, but cannot get them off. They howl like wolves and understand the wolves' language. They then separate, agreeing that they will not call on each other for help unless they have to deal with more than seven men. One day Sinfjotli is summoned to help and kills all the men who had attacked Sigmund. Another time, Sinfjotli himself is attacked by eleven men, and kills them without summoning Sigmund to help him. Then Sigmund rushes at him and bites him in the throat, but not long afterward finds a way to cure the wound. Finally they return to their cabin to await the moment when they can put off their wolfskins. When the time comes, they throw the skins into the fire. With this episode, Sinfjotli's initiation is completed, and he can avenge the slaying of the Volsungs.[5]

The initiatory themes here are obvious: the test of courage, resistance to physical suffering, followed by magical transformation into a wolf. But the compiler of the *Volsunga Saga* was no longer aware of the original meaning of the transformation. Sigmund and Sinfjotli find the skins by chance and do not know how to put them off. Now transformation into a wolf—that is, the ritual donning of a wolfskin—constituted the essential moment of initiation into a men's secret society. By putting on the skin, the initiand assimilated the behavior of a wolf; in other words, he became a wild-beast warrior, irresistible and invulnerable. "Wolf" was the appellation of the members of the Indo-European military societies.

The scenario of heroic initiations has been traced in other sagas. For example, in the *Saga of Grettir the Strong,* the hero goes down into a funeral barrow which contains a precious treasure and fights successively with a ghost, with twelve berserkers, and with a bear.[6] In the *Saga of Hrolf Kraki,* Böhdvar kills a winged monster and then initiates his young protégé Höttri by giving him a piece of the monster's heart to eat.[7]

Unfortunately, there is not time to dwell on the sociology, the mythology, and the rituals of the Germanic men's associations, which have been so brilliantly studied by Lily Weiser, Otto Höffler, and Georges Dumézil;[8] or on the other Indo-European men's societies, such, for example, as the *mairya* of the Indo-Iranians, which have formed the subject of important works by Stig Wikander and G. Widengren.[9] I will only mention that the behavior of the Indo-European warrior bands offers certain points of resemblance to the secret fraternities of primitive societies. In both alike, the members of the group terrorize women and noninitiates and in some sort exercise a "right of rapine," a custom which, in diluted form, is still found in the popular traditions of Europe and the Caucasus.[10] Rapine, and especially cattle stealing, assimilate the members of the warrior band to carnivora. In the Germanic *Wütende Heer,* or in similar ritual organizations, the barking of dogs (equals wolves) forms part of an indescribable uproar into which all sorts of strange sounds enter, for example, bells and trumpets. These sounds play an important ritual role; they help prepare for the frenzied ecstasy of the members of the group.[11] As we have already seen, in primitive cultures the sound of the bullroarers is believed to be the voice of Supernatural Beings; hence it is the sign of their presence among the initiates. In the Germanic or Japanese men's secret societies the strange sounds, like the masks, attest the presence of the Ancestors, the return of the souls of the dead. The fundamental experience is provoked by the initiates' meeting with the dead, who return to earth more especially about the winter solstice. Winter is also the season when the initiates change into wolves. In other words, during the winter the members of the band are able to transmute their profane condition and attain to a superhuman existence, whether by consorting with the Ancestors or by appropriating the behavior, that is the *magic,* of the carnivora.

The martial ordeal par excellence was the single combat, conducted in such a way that it finally roused the candidate to the "fury of the berserkers." For not military prowess alone was involved. A youth did not become a berserker simply through courage, physical strength, endurance, but as the result of a magico-religious experience that radically changed his mode of being. The young warrior must transmute his humanity by a fit of aggressive and terror-striking fury, which assimilated him to the raging beast of prey. He became "heated" to an extreme degree, flooded by a mysterious, nonhuman, and irresistible force that his fighting effort and vigor summoned from the utmost depths of his being. The ancient Germans called this sacred force *wut,* a term that Adam von Bremen translated by *furor;* it was a sort of demonic frenzy, which filled the warrior's adversary with terror and finally paralyzed him.[12] The Irish *ferg* (literally "anger"), the homeric *menos,* are almost exact equivalents of this same terrifying sacred experience peculiar to heroic combats.[13] J. Vendryès[14] and Marie-Louise Sjoestedt[15] have shown that certain names applied to the Hero in Old Irish refer to "ardor, excitation, turgescence." As Miss Sjoestedt writes, "The Hero is the man in fury, possessed by his own tumultuous and burning energy."[16]

Cuchulainn's Initiation

The saga of the initiation of the young hero Cuchulainn admirably illustrates the eruption of this "tumultuous and burning energy." According to the Old Irish *Tain Bo Cualnge,* Cuchulainn, nephew of Conchobar king of Ulster, one day overheard his master, the druid Cathba, saying: "The little boy that takes arms this day shall be splendid and renowned for deeds of arms . . . but he shall be short-lived and fleeting." Cuchulainn sprang up and, asking his uncle for arms and a chariot, set off for the castle of the three sons of Necht, the worst enemies of the kingdom of Ulster. Although these heroes were supposed to be invincible, the little boy conquered them and cut off their heads. But the exploit heated him to such a degree that a witch warned the king that if precautions were not taken, the boy would kill all the warriors in Ulster. The king decided to send a troop of naked women to meet

Cuchulainn. And the text continues: "Thereupon the young women all arose and marched out . . . and they discovered their nakedness and all their shame to him. The lad hid his face from them and turned his gaze on the chariot, that he might not see the nakedness or the shame of the women. Then the lad was lifted out of the chariot. He was placed in three vats of cold water to extinguish his wrath; and the first vat into which he was put burst its staves and its hoops like the cracking of nuts around him. The next vat into which he went boiled with bubbles as big as fists therein. The third vat into which he went, some men might endure it and others might not. Then the boy's wrath (ferg) went down . . . and his festive garments were put on him."[17]

Although "fictionized," the saga of Cuchulainn constitutes an excellent document for Indo-European military initiations. As Georges Dumézil has well shown, the lad's battle with the three macNechts represents an ancient Indo-European initiatory scenario —the fight with three adversaries or with a three-headed monster.[18] But it is especially Cuchulainn's wrath (ferg), his berserker fury, that is of interest for our investigation. Dumézil[19] had already compared Cuchulainn's initiatory heating, and his subsequent taming by the sight of women's nakedness and cold water, with certain moments in the initiation of the Kwakiutl cannibal. For, as we have seen, the frenetic and homicidal madness of the young Kwakiutl initiate is "treated" by a woman dancing naked before him with a corpse in her arms, and especially by submerging his head in a basin of salt water. Like the heat of the cannibal, the wrath of the young warrior, which manifests itself in extreme heat, is a magicoreligious experience; there is nothing profane or natural in it—it is the syndrome of gaining possession of a sacrality.

Symbolism of Magical Heat

There are reasons for believing that we are here in the presence of a magicoreligious experience that is extremely archaic. For many primitives think of the magicoreligious power as "burning," and express it by terms meaning heat, burn, very hot. It is for the same reason that shamans and medicine men drink salt or highly spiced water and eat aromatic plants—they expect thus to increase their inner heat.[20] That this magical heat corresponds to a real experience is proved by the great resistance to cold displayed both by shamans of the Arctic and Siberia and by Himalayan ascetics. In addition, shamans are held to be "masters over fire"—for example, they swallow burning coals, touch red-hot iron, walk on fire.[21] Similar experiences and conceptions are also documented among more civilized peoples. The Sanskrit term *tapas* finally developed the sense of ascetic effort in general, but its original meaning was extreme heat. It was by becoming heated through asceticism that Prajapati created the universe; he created it by a magic sweat, as in some North American cosmogonies. The *Dhammapada* (387) says that the Buddha is "burning," and Tantric texts assert that the awakening of the kundalini is manifested by a burning.[22] In modern India, the Mohammedans believe that a man in communication with God becomes "burning hot." Anyone who performs miracles is called "boiling." By extension, all kinds of people or acts involving any magicoreligious power are regarded as burning.[23] This sacred power, which causes both the shaman's heat and the heating of the warrior, can be transformed, differentiated, given various colorings, by subsequent efforts. The Indian word *Kratu,* which had begun by denoting the "energy peculiar to the ardent warrior, specifically Indra," and then "victorious force, heroic force and ardor, courage, love of combat," and by extension power and majesty in general, finally came to mean the "force of the pious man, which enables him to follow the prescriptions of the *rta* and to attain happiness."[24] The "wrath" and the heat induced by a violent and excessive access of sacred power are feared by the majority of mankind. The term *shanti,* which in Sanskrit designates tranquillity, peace of soul, freedom from the passions, relief from suffering, derives from the root *sham,* which originally had the meaning of extinguishing the fire, the anger, the fever, in short the heat, provoked by demonic powers.[25]

We are, then, in the presence of a fundamental magico-religious experience, which is universally documented on the archaic levels of culture: access to sacrality is manifested, among other things, by a prodigious increase in heat. There is not space to dwell on this important problem and to show, for example, the intimate relation between the techniques and *mystiques* of fire—a relation shown by the close connections between smiths, shamans, and warriors.[26] I must add only that mastery over fire finds its expression equally in "inner heat" and in insensibility to the temperature of hot coals. From the viewpoint of the history of religion, these different accomplishments show that the human condition has been abolished and that the shaman, the smith, or the warrior participate, each on his own plane, in a higher condition. For this higher condition can be that of a God, that of a spirit, or that of an animal. The respective initiations, though following different paths, pursue the same end —to make the novice die to the human condition and to resuscitate him to a new, a transhuman existence. Naturally, in military initiations the initiatory death is less clearly seen than in shamanic initiations, since the young warrior's principal ordeal consists precisely in vanquishing his adversary. But he emerges from the ordeal victorious only by becoming heated and attaining to the berserker fury—symptoms that express death to the human condition. He who obtains magical heat vividly demonstrates that he belongs to a superhuman world.

Shamanic Initiations

We now come to shamanic initiations. To simplify the exposition, I shall use the term shaman in its most general meaning.[27] We shall, then, be considering not only shamanism in the strict sense, as it has developed principally in northern and central Asia and in North America, but also the various categories of medicine men and wizards who flourish in other primitive societies.

There are three ways of becoming a shaman: first, by spontaneous vocation (the "call" or "election"); second, by hereditary transmission of the shamanic profession; and, third, by personal "quest," or, more rarely, by the will of the clan. But, by whatever method he may have been designated, a shaman is recognized as such only after having received two kinds of instruction. The first is ecstatic (e.g., dreams, visions, trances); the second is traditional (e.g., shamanic techniques, names and functions of the spirits, mythology and genealogy of the clan, secret language).[28] This twofold teaching, imparted by the spirits and the old master shamans, constitutes initiation. Sometimes initiation is public and includes a rich and varied ritual; this is the case, for example, among some Siberian peoples. But the lack of a ritual of this sort in no way implies the lack of an initiation; it is perfectly possible for the initiation to be performed in the candidate's dreams or ecstatic experiences.

It is primarily with the syndrome of the shaman's mystical vocation that we are concerned. In Siberia, the youth who is called to be a shaman attracts attention by his strange behavior; for example, he seeks solitude, becomes absent-minded, loves to roam in the woods or unfrequented places, has visions, and sings in his sleep.[29] In some instances this period of incubation is marked by quite serious symptoms; among the Yakut, the young man sometimes has fits of fury and easily loses consciousness, hides in the forest, feeds on the bark of trees, throws himself into water and fire, cuts himself with knives.[30] The future shamans among the Tungus, as they approach maturity, go through a hysterical or hysteroid crisis, but sometimes their vocation manifests itself at an earlier age—the boy runs away into the mountains and remains there for a week or more, feeding on animals, which he tears to pieces with his teeth. He returns to the village, filthy, bloodstained, his clothes torn and his hair disordered, and it is only after ten or more days have passed that he begins to babble incoherent words.[31]

Even in the case of hereditary shamanism, the future shaman's election is preceded by a change in behavior. The souls of the shaman ancestors of a family choose a young man among their descendants; he becomes absent-minded and moody, delights in solitude, has prophetic visions, and sometimes undergoes attacks that make him unconscious. During these times, the Buriat believe, the young man's soul is carried away by spirits; received in the palace of the gods, it is instructed by his shaman ancestors in the secrets of the profession, the forms and names of the Gods, the worship and names of the spirits. It is only after this first initiation that the youth's soul returns and resumes control of his body.[32]

A man may also become a shaman following an accident or a highly unusual event—for example, among the Buriat, the Soyot, the Eskimos, after being struck by lightning, or falling from a high tree, or successfully undergoing an ordeal that can be homologized with an initiatory ordeal, as in the case of an Eskimo who spent five days in icy water without his clothes becoming wet.[33]

The strange behavior of future shamans has not failed to attract the attention of scholars, and from the middle of the past century several attempts have been made to explain the phenomenon of shamanism as a mental disorder.[34] But the problem was wrongly put. For, on the one hand, it is not true that shamans always are or always have to be neuropathics; on the other hand, those among them who had been ill *became shamans precisely because they had succeeded in becoming cured.* Very often in Siberia, when the shamanic vocation manifests itself as some form of illness or as an epileptic seizure, the initiation is equivalent to a cure. To obtain the gift of shamanizing presupposes precisely the solution of the psychic crisis brought on by the first symptoms of election or call.

But if shamanism cannot simply be identified with a psychopathological phenomenon, it is nevertheless true that the shamanic vocation often implies a crisis so deep that it sometimes borders on madness. And since the youth cannot become a shaman until he has resolved this crisis, it is clear that it plays the role of a *mystical initiation*. The disorder provoked in the future shaman by the agonizing news that he has been chosen by the gods or the spirits is by that very fact valuated as an initiatory sickness. The precariousness of life, the solitude and the suffering, that are revealed by any sickness are, in this particular case, aggravated by the symbolism of initiatory death; for accepting the supernatural election finds expression in the feeling that one has delivered oneself over to the divine or demonic powers, hence that one is destined to imminent death. We may give all these psychopathological crises of the elected the generic name of initiatory sicknesses because their syndrome very closely follows the classic ritual of initiation. The sufferings of the elected man are exactly like the tortures of initiation; just as, in puberty rites or rites for entrance into a secret society, the novice is "killed" by semidivine or demonic Beings, so the future shaman sees in dreams his own body dismembered by demons; he watches them, for example, cutting off his head and tearing out his tongue. The initiatory rituals peculiar to Siberian and central Asian shamanism include a symbolic ascent to Heaven up a tree or pole; in dream or a series of waking dreams, the sick man chosen by the Gods or spirits undertakes his celestial journey to the World Tree. I shall later give some examples of these initiatory ordeals undergone in dream or during the future shaman's period of apparent unconsciousness and madness.

But I should like even now to stress the fact that the psychopathology of the shamanic vocation is not profane; it does not belong to ordinary symptomatology. *It has an initiatory structure and signification;* in short, it reproduces a traditional mystical pattern. The total crisis of the future shaman, sometimes leading to complete disintegration of the personality and to madness, can be valuated not only as an initiatory death but also as a symbolic return to the precosmogonic Chaos, to the amorphous and indescribable state that precedes any cosmogony. Now, as we know, for archaic and traditional cultures, a symbolic return to Chaos is equivalent to preparing a new Creation.[35] It follows that we may interpret the psychic Chaos of the future shaman as a sign that the profane man is being "dissolved" and a new personality being prepared for birth.

Initiatory Ordeals of Siberian Shamans

Let us now find out what Siberian shamans themselves have to tell about the ordeals that they undergo during their initiatory sicknesses. They all maintain that they "die" and lie inanimate for from three to seven days in their yurt or in a solitary place. During this time, they are cut up by demons or by their ancestral spirits; their bones are cleaned, the flesh scraped off, the body fluids thrown away, and the eyes torn from their sockets.[36] According to a Yakut informant, the spirits carry the future shaman to Hell and shut him in a house for three years. Here he undergoes his initiation; the spirits cut off his head (which they set to one side, for the novice must watch his own dismemberment with his own eyes) and hack his body to bits, which are later distributed among the spirits of various sicknesses. It is only on this condition that the future shaman will obtain the power of healing. His bones are then covered with new flesh, and in some cases he is also given new blood.[37] According to another Yakut informant, black "devils" cut up the future shaman's body and throw the pieces in different directions as offerings, then thrust a lance into his head and cut off his jawbone.[38] A Samoyed shaman told Lehtisalo that the spirits attacked him and hacked him to pieces, also cutting off his hands. For seven days and nights he lay unconscious on the ground, while his soul was in Heaven.[39] From a long and eventful autobiography that an Avam-Samoyed shaman confided to A. A. Popov, I will select a few significant episodes. Striken with smallpox, the future shaman remained unconscious for three days, so nearly dead that on the third day he was almost buried. He saw himself go down to Hell, and, after many adventures, was carried to an island, in the middle of which stood a young birch tree which reached up to Heaven. It was the Tree of the Lord of the Earth, and the Lord gave him a branch of it to make himself a drum. Next he came to a mountain. Passing through an opening, he met a naked man plying the bellows at an immense fire on which was a kettle. The man caught him with a hook, cut off his head, and chopped his body to bits and put them all into the kettle. There he boiled the body for three years, and then forged him a head on an anvil. Finally he fished out the bones, which were floating in a river, put them together, and covered them with flesh. During his adventures in the Other World, the future shaman met several semidivine personages, in human or animal form, and each of them revealed doctrines to him or taught him secrets of the healing art. When he awoke in his yurt, among his relatives, he was initiated and could begin to shamanize.[40]

A Tungus shaman relates that, during his initiatory sickness, his shaman ancestors pierced him with arrows until he lost consciousness and fell to the ground; then they cut off his flesh, drew out his bones, and counted them before him; if one had been missing, he could not have become a shaman.[41] According to the Buriat the candidate is tortured by his shaman ancestors, who strike him, cut up his body with a knife, and cook his flesh.[42] A Teleut woman became a shamaness after having a vision in which unknown men cut her body to pieces and boiled it in a pot.[43] According to the traditions of the Altaic shamans, their ancestral spirits open their bellies, eat their flesh, and drink their blood.[44]

These few examples are enough to show that initiatory sicknesses closely follow the fundamental pattern of all initiations: first, torture at the hands of demons or spirits, who play the role of masters of initiation; second, ritual death, experienced by the patient as a descent to Hell or an ascent to Heaven; third, resurrection to a new mode of being—the mode of "consecrated man," that is, a man who can personally communicate with gods, demons, and spirits. The different kinds of suffering undergone by the future shaman are valuated as so many religious experiences; his psychopathological crises are explained as illustrating the carrying off of his soul by demons, or its ecstatic journeys to Hell or Heaven; his physical pains are regarded as arising from the dismemberment of his body. But whatever the nature of his sufferings may be, they have a role in the making of the shaman only to the extent to which he gives them a religious significance and, by the fact, accepts them as ordeals indispensable to his mystical transfiguration. For, as we must not forget, initiatory death is always followed by a resurrection; that is, in terms of psychopathological experience, the crisis is resolved and the sickness cured. The shaman's integration of a new personality is in large part *dependent* on his being cured.

Thus far, I have cited only Siberian examples; but the dismemberment pattern is found almost everywhere. During the initiation of the Araucanian shaman, the master makes the spectators believe that he exchanges the novice's eyes and tongue for others and puts a stick through his abdomen.[45] Among the River Patwin, the candidate for the Kuksu society is supposed to have his navel pierced by a lance and an arrow from Kuksu's own hands; he dies

and is resuscitated by a shaman.[46] Among the Sudanese of the
Nuba Mountains, the first initiatory consecration is called "head,"
because "the novice's head is opened so that the spirit can enter."[47]
At Malekula, the initiation of the medicine man includes, among
other things, the novice's dismemberment: the master cuts off his
arms, feet, and head, and then puts them back in place.[48] Among
the Dyaks, the *manangs* say that they cut off the candidate's
head, remove the brain, and wash it, thus giving him a clearer
mind.[49] Finally, as we shall soon see, cutting up the body and
exchange of viscera are essential rites in some initiations of Australian medicine men. Initiatory cutting up of shamans and medicine men would deserve a long comparative investigation; for
their resemblance to the myth and ritual of Osiris, on the one hand,
and the ritual dismemberment of the Hindu *meriah,* on the other,
are disconcerting and have not yet been explained.[50]

One of the specific characteristics of shamanic initiations, aside
from the candidate's dismemberment, is his reduction to the state
of a skeleton. We find this motif not only in the accounts of the
crises and sicknesses of those who have been chosen by the spirits
to become shamans but also in the experiences of those who have
acquired their shamanic powers through their own efforts, after a
long and arduous quest. Thus, for example, among the Ammasilik
Eskimos, the apprentice spends long hours in his snow hut, meditat-
ing. At a certain moment, he falls "dead," and remains lifeless for
three days and nights; during this period an enormous polar bear
devours all his flesh and reduces him to a skeleton.[51] It is only after
this mystical experience that the apprentice receives the gift of
shamanizing. The *angakuts* of the Iglulik Eskimos are able in
thought to strip their bodies of flesh and blood and to contemplate
their own skeletons for long periods.[52] I may add that visualizing
one's own death at the hands of demons and final reduction to the
state of a skeleton are favorite meditations in Indo-Tibetan and
Mongolian Buddhism.[53] Finally, we may note that the skeleton is
quite often represented on the Siberian shaman's costume.[54]

We are here in the presence of a very ancient religious idea,
which belongs to the hunter culture. Bone symbolizes the final root
of animal life, the mold from which the flesh continually arises.
It is from the bone that men and animals are reborn; for a time,
they maintain themselves in an existence of the flesh; then they die,
and their "life" is reduced to the essence concentrated in the
skeleton, from which they will be born again.[55] Reduced to skeletons, the future shamans undergo the mystical death that enables

them to return to the inexhaustible fount of cosmic life. They are not born again; they are "revivified"; that is, the skeleton is brought back to life by being given new flesh.[56] This is a religious idea that is wholly different from the conception of the tillers of the soil; these see the earth as the ultimate source of life, hence they assimilate the human body to the seed that must be buried in the soil before it can germinate. For, as we saw, in the initiatory rituals of many agricultural peoples the neophytes are symbolically buried, or undergo reversion to the embryonic state in the womb of Mother Earth. The initiatory scenario of the Asiatic shamans does not involve a return to the earth (e.g., symbolic burial, being swallowed by a monster), but the annihilation of the flesh and hence the reduction of life to its ultimate and indestructible essence.

Public Rites of Shamanic Initiations

Among the public initiation ceremonies of Siberian shamans, those of the Buriat are among the most interesting. The principal rite includes an ascent. A strong birch is set up in the yurt, with its roots on the hearth and its crown projecting through the smoke hole. This birch is called *udeshi burkhan,* "the guardian of the door," for it opens the door of Heaven to the shaman. It will always remain in his tent, serving as distinguishing mark of a shaman's residence. On the day of his consecration, the candidate climbs the birch to the top (in some traditions, he carries a sword in one hand) and, emerging through the smoke hole, shouts to summon the aid of the gods. After this, the master shaman (called "father shaman"), the apprentice, and the entire audience go in procession to a place far from the village, where, on the eve of the ceremony, a large number of birches had been set in the ground. The procession halts by a particular birch, a goat is sacrificed, and the candidate, stripped to the waist, has his head, eyes, and ears anointed with its blood, while other shamans play their drums. The father shaman now climbs a birch and cuts nine notches in the top of its trunk. The candidate then climbs it, followed by the other shamans. As they climb they all fall—or pretend to fall—into ecstasy. According to Potanin, the candidate has to climb nine birches, which, like the nine notches cut by the father shaman, symbolize the nine heavens.[57]

As Uno Harva has well seen, the Buriat shaman's initiation is strangely reminiscent of certain ceremonies in the Mithraic mysteries. For example, the candidate's purification by the blood of a goat resembles the *taurobolium,* the chief rite of the mysteries of

Mithra, and his climbing the birch suggests the Mithraic mystes' climbing a ladder with seven rungs, which, according to Celsus, represented the seven planetary heavens.[58] Antique Near Eastern influences can be observed almost everywhere in central Asia and Siberia, and very probably the Buriat shaman's initiatory rite should be classed among examples of such influences. But it should be noted that the symbolism of the World Tree and the rite of initiatory climbing the birch in central and northern Asia are earlier than the cultural elements brought from Mesopotamia and Iran. If the conception—which is so characteristic for central Asia and Siberia—of seven, nine, or sixteen heavens finally derives from the Babylonian idea of seven planetary heavens, the symbolism of the World Tree as *axis mundi* is not specifically Babylonian. This symbolism occurs almost everywhere, and in strata of culture where Mesopotamian influences cannot reasonably be suspected.[59]

What we should note in the initiatory rite of the Buriat shaman is that the candidate is believed to go to Heaven for his consecration. To ascend to Heaven by the aid of a tree or a pole is also the essential rite in the séances of the Altaic shamans.[60] The birch or the pole is assimilated to the tree or pillar which stands at the center of the world and which connects the three cosmic zones— earth, Heaven, and Hell. The shaman can also reach the center of the world by beating his drum. For as the Samoyed shaman's dream showed us, the body of the drum is supposed to be made from a branch taken from the cosmic tree. Listening to the sound of his drum, the shaman falls into ecstasy, in which he flies to the tree, that is, to the center of the world.[61] As we saw in the last chapter, the ritual climbing of a tree or pole plays an important part in the initiatory rites and religious ceremonies of many South and North American peoples; we may now add that it is peculiar especially to shamanic initiations. The initiation of the Araucanian *machi* includes the ritual climbing of a tree, or a tree trunk stripped of its bark, to a platform where the novice addresses a prayer to the God.[62] The Carib *pujai* undertakes his ecstatic ascent to Heaven by climbing onto a platform hung from the roof of the hut by a number of cords twisted together; as they unwind, they whirl the platform around faster and faster.[63]

Techniques of Ecstasy

The examples just cited enable us to distinguish the essential notes of shamanic initiations and, consequently, to understand the significance of shamanism for the general history of religion. The shaman or the medicine man can be defined as a specialist in the sacred, that is, an individual who participates in the sacred more completely, or more truly, than other men. Whether he is chosen by Superhuman Beings or himself seeks to draw their attention and obtain their favors, the shaman is an individual who succeeds in having mystical experiences. In the sphere of shamanism in the strict sense, the mystical experience is expressed in the shaman's trance, real or feigned. The shaman is pre-eminently an ecstatic. Now on the plane of primitive religions ecstasy signifies the soul's flight to Heaven, or its wanderings about the earth, or, finally, its descent to the subterranean world, among the dead. The shaman undertakes these ecstatic journeys for four reasons: first, to meet the God of Heaven face to face and bring him an offering from the community; second, to seek the soul of a sick man, which has supposedly wandered away from his body or been carried off by demons; third, to guide the soul of a dead man to its new abode; fourth, to add to his knowledge by frequenting higher beings.[64]

But the body's abandonment by the soul during ecstasy is equivalent to a temporary death. The shaman is, therefore, the man who can die, and then return to life, many times. This accounts for the many ordeals and teachings required in every shamanic initiation. Through his initiation, the shaman learns not only the technique of dying and returning to life but also what he must do when his soul abandons his body—and, first of all, how to orient himself in the unknown regions which he enters during his ecstasy. He learns to explore the new planes of existence disclosed by his ecstatic experiences. He knows the road to the center of the world, the hole in the sky through which he can fly up to the highest Heaven, or the aperture in the earth through which he can descend to Hell. He is forewarned of the obstacles that he will meet on his journeys, and knows how to overcome them. In short, he knows the roads that lead to Heaven and Hell. All this he learned during his training in solitude or under the guidance of the master shamans.

Because of his ability to leave his body with impunity, the shaman can, if he so wishes, act in the manner of a spirit; e.g., he flies through the air, he becomes invisible, he perceives things at great distances, he mounts to Heaven or descends to Hell, sees souls and can capture them, and is incombustible. The exhibition of certain fakirlike accomplishments during the séances, especially the so-called fire tricks, is intended to convince the spectators that the shaman has assimilated the mode of being of spirits. The powers of turning themselves into animals, of killing at a distance, or of foretelling the future are also among the powers of spirits; by exhibiting them, the shaman proclaims that he shares in the spirit condition. The desire to behave in the manner of a spirit signifies above all the desire to assume a superhuman condition; in short, to enjoy the freedom, the power, and the knowledge of the Supernatural Beings, whether Gods or spirits. The shaman obtains this transcendent condition by submitting to an initiatory scenario considerably more complex and dramatic than the patterns of initiation which we examined in the preceding chapters.

In summary, the important moments of a shamanic initiation are these five: first, torture and violent dismemberment of the body; second, scraping away of the flesh until the body is reduced to a skeleton; third, substitution of viscera and renewal of the blood; fourth, a period spent in Hell, during which the future shaman is taught by the souls of dead shamans and by "demons"; fifth, an ascent to Heaven to obtain consecration from the God of Heaven.

Initiations of Australian Medicine Men

Now it is disconcerting to note that this peculiarly Siberian and central Asian pattern of initiation is found again, almost to the letter, in Australia. (I refer to the pattern as a whole, and not only to certain initiatory motifs that are found everywhere, such as ascent to Heaven, descent to Hell, dismemberment of the body.) The Siberian-Australian parallelism confronts the historian of religion with the problem of the possible dissemination of shamanism from a single center. But before entering upon this difficult question, we must see what is the traditional pattern of the initiation of Australian medicine men. Thanks to A. P. Elkin's book, *Aboriginal Men of High Degree*,[65] the subject can now be set forth with reasonable clarity in brief compass.

Just as in the case of northern Asiatic or American shamanism, in Australia too one becomes a shaman in three ways: by inheriting the profession, by call or election, by personal quest. But whatever way he has taken, a candidate is not recognized as a medicine man until he has been accepted by a certain number of medicine men or been taught by some of them, and, above all, after a more or less laborious initiation. In the majority of instances, the initiation consists in an ecstatic experience, during which the candidate undergoes certain operations performed by mythical Beings, and undertakes ascents to Heaven or descents to the subterranean world. The initiatory ritual is also, as Elkin puts it, "a re-enactment of what has occurred in the past, generally to a cult-hero. If this is not always clear, at least Supernatural Beings, dream-time or sky Heroes, or spirits of the dead, are regarded as the operators, that is the masters of the craft."[66] The candidate is "killed" by one of these Supernatural Beings, who then perform certain surgical operations on the lifeless body: the spirit or the dream-time Hero "removes his 'insides' " and "substitutes new ones together with some magical substances";[67] cuts him open "from his neck to his groin"; removes his shoulder and thigh bones, and sometimes also his frontal bone; and "inserts magical substances before drying and putting them back."[68]

To cite some examples: among the Warburton Ranges tribes the postulant enters a cave and two totemic Heroes (the wildcat and the emu) kill him, open his body, remove the organs, and replace them by magical substances. They also remove the scapula and tibia and, before restoring them, stuff them with the same magical substances.[69] Among the Arunta, the candidate goes to sleep in front of the mouth of a cave. A spirit named Iruntarinia kills him by a lance thrust that enters his neck from behind and comes out through his mouth. The spirit then carries him into the cave, removes his viscera, and gives him new ones.[70] A famous medicine man of the Unmatjera tribe told Spencer and Gillen of the essential moments of his initiation. One day an old doctor "killed" him by throwing crystals at him with a spear thrower. "The old man then cut out all of his insides, intestines, liver, heart, lungs—everything in fact, and left him lying all night long on the ground. In the morning the old man came and looked at him and placed some more *atnongara* stones [i.e., small crystals] inside his body and in his arms and legs, and covered over his face with leaves. Then he sang over him until his body was all swollen up. When this was so he provided him with a complete set of new inside parts, placed a lot more *atnongara* stones in him, and patted him on the head, which caused him to jump up alive."[71]

R. and C. Berndt have collected valuable information regarding the making of the medicine man among the tribes of the Western Desert of South Australia. Mourned as dead, because everyone knows that he will be "cut into pieces," the postulant goes to a water hole. There two medicine men cover his eyes and throw him into the jaws of the Serpent, which swallows him. The postulant remains in the Serpent's belly for an indefinite time. Finally the medicine men bring two kangaroo rats as an offering to the Serpent, whereupon the Serpent ejects the postulant, throwing him high into the air. He falls "alongside a certain rock-hole," and the medicine men set out in search of him, but he has been reduced to the size of an infant. (The initiatory theme of regression to the embryonic in the monster's belly, homologous with the maternal womb, is apparent here.) One of the medicine men takes the baby in his arms and "they fly back to the camp."

After this consecration, which is mystical because performed by a Supernatural Being, the initiation proper begins, in which the old masters play the principal role. Set in a circle of fire, the baby-postulant rapidly grows and recovers his adult size. He declares that he knows the Serpent well, that they are even friends, for he stayed in its belly for some time. Then comes a period of seclusion, during which the postulant meditates and converses with the spirits. One day the medicine men take him to the bush and smear his body with red ocher. "He is made to lie full-length on his back before fires, and is said to be a dead man. The head-doctor proceeds to break his neck and his wrists, and to dislocate the joints at the elbows, the upper thighs, the knees and ankles." The masters stuff his body with shells, and also put shells into his ears and jaws, so that the postulant will be able to hear and understand spirits, birds, and strangers. His stomach too is stuffed with shells, so that he will have a "renewed life and become invulnerable to attack by any weapon." Then he is "sung" by the medicine men, and revives. All return to the camp, where the new doctor is tested: the medicine men throw their lances at him; but because of the shells with which he is stuffed, he is not harmed.[72]

This example represents a highly elaborate initiation. We can recognize two principal initiatory themes in it: (1) being swallowed by a monster, and (2) bodily dismemberment—of which only the second is peculiar to the initiations of medicine men. What we really have here is two initiations, the first performed by a Supernatural Being, the second by the doctors. But although he undergoes a return to the womb, the postulant does not die in the Serpent's belly, for he is able to remember his sojourn there. The real initiatory putting to death is performed by the old doctors, and in the manner reserved for medicine men: dismemberment of the body, change of organs, introduction of magical substances.

For the initiatory operations proper always include the renewal of the organs and viscera, the cleaning of the bones, and the insertion of magical substances—quartz crystals or pearl shell, or "spirit snakes." Quartz is connected with the "sky world and with the rainbow"; pearl shell is similarly "connected with the rainbow serpent," that is, in sum, still with the sky.[73] This sky symbolism goes along with ecstatic ascents to Heaven; for in many regions the candidate is believed to visit the sky, whether by his own power (for example, by climbing a rope) or carried by a snake. In the sky he converses with the Supernatural Beings and mythical Heroes. Other initiations involve a descent to the realm of the dead: for example, the future medicine man goes to sleep by the burying ground, or enters a cave, or is transported underground or to the bottom of a lake.[74] Among some tribes, the initiation also includes the novice's being "roasted" in or at a fire.[75] Finally, the candidate is resuscitated by the same Supernatural Beings who had killed him, and he is now "a man of Power."[76] During and after his initiation he meets with spirits, Heroes of the mythical Times, and souls of the dead—and in a certain sense they all instruct him in the secrets of the medicine man's profession. Naturally, the training proper is concluded under the direction of the older masters.

In short, the candidate becomes a medicine man through a ritual of initiatory death, followed by a resurrection to a new and superhuman condition. But the initiatory death of the Australian medicine man, like that of the Siberian shaman, has two specific notes not found elsewhere in combination: first, a series of operations performed on the candidate's body (opening of the abdomen, renewal of the organs, washing and drying the bones, insertion of magical substances); second, an ascent to Heaven, sometimes followed by other ecstatic journeys into the Other World. The revelations concerning the secret techniques of the medicine men are obtained in trance, in dream, or in the waking state, before, during, or after the initiatory ritual proper.

Asiatic Influences in Australia

Elkin compares the initiatory pattern of the Australian medicine man to a mummification ritual documented in eastern Australia, and which seems to have been introduced by way of the Torres Strait islands, where a certain type of mummification was practiced until quite recently.[77] Melanesian influences on Australian culture are incontestable. But Elkin is inclined to believe that these Melanesian influences brought ideas and techniques that originally belonged to other, higher cultures. If he does not insist upon the final Egyptian origin of the ritual of mummification, he compares, and rightly, the parapsychological powers of the Australian medicine men with the feats of Indian and Tibetan yogis. For walking on fire, using the magic cord, the power of disappearing and reappearing, "fast traveling," and so on, are just as popular among Australian medicine men as they are among yogis and fakirs. "It is possible," Elkin writes, "that there is some historical connection between the Yoga and occult practices of India and Tibet and the practices and psychic powers of Aboriginal men of high degree. Hinduism spread to the East Indies. Yoga is a cult in Bali, and some of the remarkable feats of the Australian medicine men are paralleled by their fellow-professionals in Papua."[78]

If Elkin's conjecture should prove to be well founded, we should have, in Australia, a situation comparable to that which we have already noted in central Asia and Siberia; just as central and north Asian shamanism seems to have been profoundly affected by elements of culture coming from Mesopotamia, Iran, India, and China, so the corpus of rites, beliefs, and occult techniques of the Australian medicine men may have taken its present form primarily under Indian influence. But this is by no means to say that these two forms of shamanism—Australian and north Asian— should be regarded as the result of influences received from higher religions. Such influences have certainly modified the mystical ideologies and techniques of shamanism, but they did not *create* them.

The problem of the origin and dissemination of shamanism is certainly extremely complicated, and I cannot enter upon it here.[79] But I must at least mention a few of the most important points. First, it should be said that the specifically shamanic techniques and ideologies—for example, ascending to Heaven by means of a tree, or "magic flight"—are documented almost all over the world, and it seems difficult to explain them by Mesopotamian or Indian influences. Equally widespread are the beliefs concerning an *axis mundi* at the center of the universe, a point that makes possible communication between the three cosmic zones. Next, we must bear in mind that the fundamental characteristic of shamanism is ecstasy, interpreted as the soul forsaking the body. Now no one has yet shown that the ecstatic experience is the creation of a particular historical civilization or a particular cultural cycle. In all probability the ecstatic experience, in its many aspects, is coexistent with the human condition, in the sense that it is an integral part of what is called man's gaining consciousness of his specific mode of being in the world. Shamanism is not only a technique of ecstasy; its theology and its philosophy finally depend on the *spiritual value* that is accorded to ecstasy.

What is the meaning of all these shamanic myths of ascent to Heaven and magical flight, or of the power to become invisible and incombustible? They all express a break with the universe of daily life. The twofold purpose of this break is obvious: it is the transcendence and the freedom that are obtained, for example, through ascent, flight, invisibility, incombustibility of the body. I need hardly add that the terms transcendence and freedom are not documented on the archaic levels of culture. But the experience is there, and that is what is important. The desire for absolute freedom—that is, the desire to break the bonds that keep him tied to earth, and to free himself from his limitations—is one of man's essential nostalgias. And the break from plane to plane effected by flight or ascent similarly signifies an act of transcendence; flight proves that one has transcended the human condition, has risen above it, by transmuting it through an excess of spirituality. Indeed, all the myths, the rites, and the legends that we have just reviewed can be translated as the longing to see the human body act after the manner of a spirit, to transmute man's corporal modality into the spirit's modality.[80]

The history of religion shows that such a desire to behave like a spirit is a universal phenomenon; it is not confined to any particular moment in the history of humanity. In the archaic religions, the shaman and the medicine man play the role of the mystics in developed religions; hence they constitute an exemplary model for the rest of the community precisely because they have *realized* transcendence and freedom, and have, by that fact, become like spirits and other Supernatural Beings. And there is good reason to believe that the desire to resemble Supernatural Beings has tormented man from the beginning of his history.

The problem of shamanism goes beyond the sphere of our investigation, and I have had to limit myself to presenting only some aspects of this extremely complex religious phenomenon, namely, its initiatory ideology and rituals. Here again we have seen the importance of the theme of mystical death and rebirth. But we have also observed the presence of certain notes that are almost peculiar to shamanic initiation: dismemberment of the body, reduction to a skeleton, renewal of the internal organs; the great importance accorded to mystic ascents and to descents into the world underground; finally, the outstanding role of memory. Shamans and medicine men are men who remember their ecstatic experiences. Some shamans even claim that they can remember their previous existences.[81] We observe, then, a marked deepening of the experience of initiatory death and at the same time a strengthening of memory and, in general, of all the psychomental faculties. The shaman stands out by the fact that he has succeeded in integrating into consciousness a considerable number of experiences that, for the profane world, are reserved for dreams, madness, or post-mortem states. The shamans and mystics of primitive societies are considered—and rightly—to be superior beings; their magicoreligious powers also find expression in an extension of their mental capacities. Hence the shaman becomes the exemplar and model for all those who seek to acquire power. The shaman is the man who *knows* and *remembers,* that is, who understands the mysteries of life and death; in short, who shares in the spirit condition. He is not solely an ecstatic but also a contemplative, a thinker. In later civilizations the philosopher will be recruited among these beings, to whom the mysteries of existence represent a passionate interest and who are drawn, by vocation, to know the inner life.

CHAPTER VI

Patterns of Initiation in Higher Religions

What I have set myself to accomplish in this last chapter may seem rash, not to say foolhardy. Not because certain traditional patterns of initiation are not still clearly discernible in the higher religions, but because to study them would require more elaborate treatment than is possible in a single chapter. The religions to which we now come are infinitely more complex than primitive religions. As it happens—except for those of India—they are no longer living religions; and we cannot always be sure that we rightly understand the few documents that they have left to us. The reader hardly needs to be reminded that initiation is first and foremost a secret rite. If we know something about initiations in primitive societies, it is because a few white men have contrived to be initiated and because a few natives have given us some information. Even so, we are far from apprehending the deeper dimensions of primitive initiations.

What can we reliably report concerning the rites of Eleusis or the Greco-Oriental mysteries? In regard to their secret ceremonies, we have practically no direct testimony at all. In general, our information on the subject of initiation in antiquity is fragmentary and secondhand; it is even frankly partisan when it has come to us from Christian writers. If, nevertheless, scholars have been able to discuss antique initiations, it is precisely because they have believed that they could reconstruct certain initiatory patterns—in the last analysis, because they were already acquainted with the phenomenon of initiation, either as it is still to be observed in the

103

primitive and Asiatic worlds or as it was understood at certain periods in the history of Christianity. From the methodological point of view, the reconstruction of an initiatory scenario on the basis of a few fragmentary documents and with the aid of ingenious comparisons is a perfectly valid procedure. But if we can hope to reconstruct the initiatory pattern of the Greco-Oriental mysteries, it would be dangerous to conclude that, by so doing, we should also have deciphered the *religious experiences* of the initiates. The question whether the content of such religious experiences is still accessible to modern scholars, limited, as we have seen, to a lamentably scanty documentation, can be argued endlessly. Whatever side he may take in this methodological controversy, every scholar agrees that we cannot hope for valid results except at the price of a long and most meticulous labor of exegesis. Such a labor is not possible here. So, for the most part, we shall have to content ourselves with approximations.

India

I shall begin with India, for there a large number of archaic religious forms have been preserved alongside more recent ideas and beliefs. We had occasion earlier to examine the *upanayana,* the puberty rite that is obligatory for the three highest castes and through which the novice is born into *brahman,* thus becoming *dvi-ja,* "twice-born." We also examined the *diksha,* the initiatory rite which must be performed by anyone who is about to offer the *soma* sacrifice, and which essentially consists in the sacrificer's symbolic transformation into an embryo. Finally, we reviewed another initiatory rite of return to the womb—the *hiranyagarbha,* involving the mystical birth of the postulant from Mother Earth. Both the *diksha* and the *hiranyagarbha* are initiations that give the postulant access to the deepest zones of sacrality. But India has several other initiations of the same type, that is, which pursue a more complete participation in the sacred, or a radical change in the initiand's existential status. It is this class of initiations which especially concerns us now—initiations that accomplish passage from the profane to a transcendent state. From the morphological point of view, we could consider these initiations to be the Indian counterpart of initiations into secret societies in the primitive world, and, in particular, of shamanic initiations. Of course, this does not mean that the two contents can be homologized; but only that we are dealing with highly specialized initiations, to which only a comparatively small number of individuals submit them-selves, in the hope of transmuting their mode of being.

Sometimes the pattern of an archaic initiation is preserved almost entire, although the experience of initiatory death is given new values. The most illuminating examples of continuing and at the same time revaluating an archaic pattern are found in Indo-Tibetan Tantrism. Tantrism is pre-eminently the expression of the indigenous spirituality, the reaction of the not fully Hinduized popular strata. Hence it naturally makes use of archaic, pre-Aryan religious categories. Thus, for example, we find the characteristic motifs of shamanic initiations in the myths, rites, and folklore of the Tantric *siddhas,* especially Matsyendranath and Gorakhnath, figures who particularly struck the popular imagination. According to some legends, Gorakhnath initiated Matsyendranath's two sons in the following way: he killed them, washed their entrails "after the fashion of washerwomen," hung their skins from the branches of a tree, and then resuscitated them.[1] This scenario is curiously re-miniscent of one of the motifs peculiar to the initiations of Siberian shamans and Australian medicine men. And Queen Mayanamati, who was also initiated by Gorakhnath, behaved like a shaman: she was incombustible, floated on water, could cross a bridge made of a hair, walked on the edge of a razor, descended to Hell, fought with the God of Death and recovered her husband's soul.[2]

All these are folklore motifs whose closest counterpart is found in the oral literature of the central Asian and Siberian shamans.[3] But these motifs also have analogues in the rites of Tantrism. To give only one example: in the Indo-Tibetan rite called *tchoed* (*gtchöd*), the novice offers his own flesh for the demons to eat. By the power of his meditation, he conjures up a Goddess holding a sword, who decapitates him and cuts his body to pieces; then he sees demons and wild beasts fling themselves on the fragments of his flesh and devour them. In another Tantric meditation, the novice imagines that he is being stripped of his flesh and finally sees himself as a "huge, white, shining skeleton."[4] We have come upon this same initiatory theme in Siberian and Eskimo shamanism. But in the case of the Indo-Tibetan *tchoed,* we have a new valuation of the traditional theme of dismemberment and reduction to a skeleton—the novice submits himself to an initiatory ordeal by stimulating his imagination to conjure up a terrifying vision, which, however, he masters by the power of his thought. He knows that what is before him is a creation of his own mind; that the Goddess and the demons are as unreal as is his own body and, with it, the entire cosmos. For the novice is a Mahayana Buddhist; he knows that the world is "void," in other words, ontologically unreal.

This initiatory meditation is at the same time a post-mortem experience, hence a descent to Hell—but through it the novice realizes the emptiness of all posthumous experience, so that he will feel no more fear at the moment of death and will thus escape being reborn on earth. The traditional experience of bodily dismemberment—brought on, in the shamanic world, by suitable rites, by initiatory sicknesses, or by dreams and visions—is no longer interpreted as a mystical death, indispensable for resurrection into a new mode of being; it now serves as an instrument of knowledge; by virtue of it, the novice understands what is meant by the universal void, and thereby draws closer to final deliverance.[5]

But to gain the best possible view of the process of revaluating a traditional initiatory theme, our best course will be to consider the various techniques that together go to make up Yoga. Not only does the outward aspect of Yoga practice suggest the behavior of a novice during his initiatory training; for the yogi forsakes the company of men, withdraws into solitude, submits to a course of ascetic practices that are sometimes extremely severe, and puts himself under the oral teaching of a master, a teaching that is pre-eminently secret, communicated "from mouth to ear," as the Hindu texts put it. In addition to all this, the corpus of Yoga practices reproduces an initiatory pattern. Like every other initiation, Yoga ends by radically changing the existential status of him who submits himself to its rules. By virtue of Yoga, the ascetic abolishes the human condition (in Indian terms, the unenlightened life, the existence doomed to suffering) and gains an unconditioned mode of being—what the Indians call deliverance, freedom, moksha, mukti, nirvana. But to annihilate the profane human condition in order to gain absolute freedom means to die to this conditioned mode of being and to be reborn into another, a mode of being that is transcendent, unconditioned.

The symbolism of initiatory death is clearly discernible in the various psychophysiological techniques peculiar to Yoga. If we watch a yogi while he is practicing Yoga, we get the impression that he is trying in every way to do exactly the opposite of what is done "in the world," that is, what men do as men, prisoners of their own ignorance. We see that, instead of constantly moving, the yogi immobilizes himself in an absolutely static posture, a posture which is called *asana* and which makes him like a stone or a plant. To the agitated and unrhythmical breathing of the man who lives in the world, he opposes *pranayama*, rhythmical reduction of the tempo of respiration, and dreams of finally achieving complete suspension of breath. To the chaotic flux of psychomental life, he replies by fixing his thought on a single point (*ekagrata*). In short, he does the opposite of what life obliges man to do—and he does this in order to free himself from the multifarious conditionings that constitute the whole of profane existence, and to make his way at last to an unconditioned plane, a plane of absolute freedom. But he cannot reach such a situation, comparable to that of the Gods, except by dying to unenlightened life, to profane existence.

In the case of Yoga, we are dealing with a complex of beliefs, ideas, and ascetic and contemplative techniques whose object is to transmute, and hence to abolish, the human condition. Now we must take good note that this long and difficult ascetic training proceeds along the well-known lines of a pattern of initiation; in the last analysis, Yoga practice "kills" the normal (that is, the metaphysically "ignorant") man, prey to illusions, and engenders a new man, deconditioned and free. Obviously, the final goal of Yoga cannot be homologized with the ends pursued by the various shamanic initiations or initiations into secret societies which we analyzed in the last two chapters. For if there are yogis whose aim is mystical union with the Deity, the true yogi strives above all to obtain perfect spiritual autonomy. But what is of interest to our investigation is the fact that all these various goals, pursued by mystics or magicians, shamans or yogis, require ascetic training and spiritual exercises which, in their very structure, display the classic pattern of initiation—the neophyte's transmutation through a mystical death.

This becomes even more evident if we examine certain yogic meditations. We have just seen in what sense the symbolism of mystical death was revaluated by the Tantric *tchoed*. Knowledge of post-mortem states can also be obtained through an exercise described in the *Shiva-samhita*: by a particular meditation, the yogi anticipates the process of reabsorption which occurs after death. And since the yogic *sadhana* also has a cosmic context, the same meditation also reveals the process by which the cosmos is periodically reabsorbed.[6]

Another traditional initiatory theme taken over and revaluated by Yoga and Buddhism is that of the "new body" in which the initiate is reborn. The Buddha himself says that he has shown his disciples the methods that, starting from the body of flesh, produce another body, formed from an "intellectual substance" (*rupim manomayam*).[7] And Hathayogis, Tantrics, and alchemists seek, through their respective techniques, to obtain a "divine body" (*divya deha*), which is absolutely spiritual (*cinmaya*), or to change the natural body, which is raw, "unripe" (*apakva*), into a body that is perfect, "ripe" (*pakva*).[8] In short, we find in India, though charged with other values, the same primordial images that we have found in traditional initiations—dismemberment of the body, death and resurrection, generation and new birth, obtaining a new, supernatural body. However different the ends pursued by the Indian sage, magician, or mystic, they all hope to realize them through corporal and psychomental techniques whose object is abolishing the human condition. Furthermore the process of man's deliverance or divinization can always be homologized with the essential moments of an initiation, and it is never more clearly expressed than in the traditional imagery and terminology of initiations.

Traces of Puberty Rites in Ancient Greece

If we now turn to the Mediterranean religions, we again find the three great categories of initiations—puberty rites, secret confraternities, and mystical initiations. But we do not find all three of them in the same historical period. When Greece and Rome make their entrance into history, their puberty rites appear to have lost the religious aura which, to judge from myth and legend, they possessed during the protohistorical period. To confine ourselves to Greece: in the historic period puberty rites appear in the diluted form of a civic education that included, among other things, a nondramatic introduction of boys into the religious life of the city. Yet the mythological personages and scenarios that regulate this series of civic ceremonies still preserve the memory of a more archaic state of things, which is not without resemblances to the atmosphere in which puberty rites are performed among primitive peoples. Thus, for example, it has been shown that the legendary figure of Theseus, and the rites connected with his name, can be more easily explained if we regard them as dependent upon an initiatory scenario. Many episodes in the saga of Theseus are in fact initiatory ordeals—for example, his ritual descent into the sea[9] (an ordeal equivalent to a journey to the beyond) and precisely to the undersea palace of the Nereids (themselves the very type of the fairies who protect young men); or, again, his entering the labyrinth and fighting the monster, a typical theme of heroic initiations; or finally, his carrying off Ariadne, one of the many epiphanies of Aphrodite, which means that Theseus completes his initiation by a hierogamy. According to H. Jeanmaire, the ceremonies constituting the *Theseia* stemmed from archaic rituals which, at an earlier period, marked the return of the boys to the city, after their initiatory period in the bush.[10]

It has also been shown that an ancient puberty scenario survived in the famous Spartan discipline of Lycurgus, which, among other things, included the toughening of the body and the art of hiding (*krypteia*). This custom in every way resembled the archaic initiatory ordeals. The adolescent was sent away to the mountains, naked, and had to live for a whole year on what he could steal, being careful to let no one see him; any novice who let himself be seen was punished.[11] In other words, the Lacedemonian youth led the life of a wolf for a whole year. In addition there are similarities between the *krypteia* and lycanthropy. To change into a wolf, or to behave like a wolf ritually, are typical characteristics of the martial and shamanic initiations. We are here in the presence of archaic beliefs and rites which long survived both in northern and southern Europe.

It would be easy to extend our list of the survivals of initiatory figures and scenarios in Greek myths and legends. The mythical Curetes[12] still show traces of their function as masters of initiation: they bring up boys in the bush, teaching them the archaic techniques of hunting and gathering wild fruits, of dancing and music. So too certain moments in the story of Achilles can be interpreted as initiatory ordeals: he was brought up by the centaurs, that is, he was initiated in the bush by masters in animal disguise or manifesting themselves under animal aspects; he passed through fire and water, classic initiatory ordeals, and he even lived for a time among girls, dressed as a girl, a custom characteristic of certain primitive puberty initiations.

Eleusis and the Hellenistic Mysteries

It would be possible to show that ancient themes from puberty initiations survived in the same way in Iran or Rome.[13] But the time has come for us to approach initiations that were still alive in historical times, so that we see in what way, and to what an extent, an ancient scenario can be revaluated in a highly developed society. The Eleusinian mysteries, the rites of Dionysus, Orphism, are exceedingly complex phenomena, whose importance in the religious and cultural history of Greece is considerable.[14] We shall here be concerned only with their initiatory rites. Now, as I said earlier, it is on this particular subject that we are least well documented. Nevertheless, we are able to reconstruct their patterns. The Eleusinian mysteries,[15] like the Dionysiac ceremonies, were founded on a divine myth; hence the succession of rites reactualized the primordial event narrated in the myth, and the participants in the rites were progressively introduced into the divine presence. To give an example: on the evening of their arrival at Eleusis, the initiands broke off their dances and rejoicings when they were told that Kore had been carried away. Torch in hand, crying and lamenting, they wandered everywhere, searching for Kore. Suddenly a herald announced that Helios had revealed where Kore was; and again all was gaiety, music, dancing. The myth of Demeter and Kore became contemporary once more; the rape of Kore, Demeter's laments, take place *here and now,* and it is by virtue of this nearness of the Goddesses, and finally of their *presence,* that the initiate (mystes) will have the unforgettable experience of initiation.

For, as Aristotle already noted (Frag. 15), the mystes did not learn anything new; he already knew the myth, and he was not taught any really secret doctrine; but he performed ritual gestures and saw sacred objects. The initiation proper was performed in the place of initiation (telesterion) at Eleusis. It began with purifications. Then, his head covered by a cloth, the mystes was led into the telesterion and seated on a chair spread with an animal skin. For everything after this, we are reduced to conjecture. Clement of Alexandria (*Protrepticus,* II, 21) has preserved the sacred formula of the mysteries: "I fasted, I drank the *kykeon,* I took out of the chest, having done the act I put again into the basket, and from the basket again into the chest." We understand the first two parts of the rite—the fast and the drinking of the *kykeon,* which was a mixture of flour, water and mint that, according to the myth, Queen Metanira had offered to Demeter, exhausted by her long search for Kore.

For the rest of the sacred formula handed down by Clement, numerous interpretations have been proposed, which there is not space to discuss here.[16] Some form of initiatory death, that is, a symbolic descent to Hell, is not improbable, for the play on words between "initiation" (*teleisthai*) and "dying" (*teleutan*) was quite popular in Greece.[17] "To die is to be initiated," Plato said. If, as seems likely, the mystical chest represented the nether world, the mystes, by opening it, symbolically descended to Hell. What we must note is that after this mysterious handling of the sacred objects, the mystes was born anew. We learn from Hippolytus that, at the culminating moment, the hierophant announced: "She who is Magnificent has given birth to a sacred child, Brimo (has engendered) Brimos."[18] Finally, the second degree of initiation included the *epopteia;* the mystes became the *epoptes,* "he who sees." We know that the torches were put out, a curtain raised, and the hierophant appeared with a box. He opened it and took out a ripe ear of grain. According to Walter Otto, "there can be no doubt of the miraculous nature of the event. The ear of wheat growing and maturing with a supernatural suddenness is just as much a part of the mysteries of Demeter as the vine growing in a few hours is part of the revels of Dionysus. . . . We find exactly the same plant miracles in the nature festivals of primitive peoples."[19] Soon afterward the sacred marriage between the hierophant and the priestess of Demeter took place.

It would be naïve to suppose that this brief treatment could convey the essentials of a mystery which, for over a thousand years, dominated the religious life of Greece and which, for at least a century, has given rise to impassioned controversies among scholars. The Eleusinian mysteries—like Dionysianism and Orphism in general—confront the investigator with countless problems, especially in regard to their origin and, hence, their antiquity. For in each of these cases we have to do with extremely archaic rites and beliefs. None of these initiatory cults can be regarded as a creation of the Greek mind. Their roots go deep into prehistory. Cretan, Asiatic, and Thracian traditions were taken over, enriched, and incorporated into a new religious horizon. It was through Athens that Eleusis became a Panhellenic religious center; but the mysteries of Demeter and Kore had been celebrated at Eleusis for centuries. The Eleusinian initiation descends directly from an agricultural ritual centered around the death and resurrection of a divinity controlling the fertility of the fields. The bull-roarer, which figured in the Orphic-Dionysiac ceremonies, is a religious object characteristic of primitive hunter cultures.[20] The myths and rites illustrating the dismemberment of Dionysus and of Orpheus—or Osiris—are strangely reminiscent of the Australian and Siberian data described in the preceding chapter. The myths and rites of Eleusis have their counterpart in the religions of certain tropical cultures whose structure is agricultural and matriarchal.[21] The fact that such elements of archaic religious practice recur in the most central position in the Greek and the Greco-Oriental mysteries proves not only their extraordinary vitality but also their importance for the religious life of humanity. Undoubtedly we here have religious experiences that are at once primordial and exemplary.

For the purpose of our investigation, one thing is particularly of interest—that these experiences are brought on by rites which, both in the Greco-Oriental and the primitive worlds, are initiatory, that is, pursue the novice's spiritual transmutation. At Eleusis, as in the Orphic-Dionysiac ceremonies, as in the Greco-Oriental mysteries of the Hellenistic period, the mystes submits himself to initiation in order to transcend the human condition and to obtain a higher, superhuman mode of being. The initiatory rites reactualize an origin myth, which relates the adventures, death, and resurrection of a Divinity. We know very little about these secret rites, yet we know that the most important of them concerned the death and mystical resurrection of the initiand.

On the occasion of his initiation into the mysteries of Isis, Apuleius suffered a "voluntary death" (*ad instar voluntariae mortis*) and "approached the realm of death" to obtain his "spiritual birthday" (*natalem sacrum*).[22] The exemplary model for these rites was the myth of Osiris. It is probable that in the mystery of the Phrygian Great Mother—and perhaps elsewhere too—the mystes was symbolically buried in a tomb.[23] According to Firmicus Maternus, he was regarded as *moriturus,* "about to die."[24] This mystical death was followed by a new, spiritual birth. In the Phrygian rite, Sallustius records, the new initiates "received nourishment of milk as if they were being reborn."[25] And in the text which is known under the title of the *Liturgy of Mithra,* but which is pervaded with Hermetic Gnosticism, we read: "Today, having been born again by thee, out of so many myriads rendered immortal . . ." or "Born again for rebirth of that life-giving birth . . ."[26]

Everywhere there is this spiritual regeneration, a palingenesis, which found its expression in the radical change in the mystes' existential status. By virtue of his initiation, the neophyte attained to another mode of being; he became equal to the Gods, was one with the Gods. Apotheosis, deification, demortalizing (*apathana-*

tismos) are concepts familiar to all the Hellenistic mysteries.[27] Indeed, for antiquity in general, the divinization of man was not an extravagant dream. "Know, then, that you are a God," Cicero wrote.[28] And in a Hermetic text we read: "I know thee, Hermes, and thou knowest me: I am thou and thou art I."[29] Similar expressions are found in Christian writings. As Clement of Alexandria says, the true (Christian) Gnostic "has already become God."[30] And for Lactantius, the chaste man will end by becoming *consimilis Deo,* "identical in all respects with God."[31]

The ontological transmutation of the initiate was proved above all through his existence after death. The Homeric *Hymn to Demeter,* Pindar, and Sophocles already praise the bliss of initiates in the Other World, and pity those who die without having been initiated.[32] In the Hellenistic period the idea that he who had been initiated into the mysteries enjoyed a privileged spiritual situation, both during life and after death, had become increasingly widespread. Those who submitted to initiation, then, sought thereby to obtain a superhuman ontological status, more or less divine, and to ensure their survival after death, if not their immortality. And, as we have just seen, the mysteries employ the classic pattern: mystical death of the initiand, followed by a new, spiritual birth.

For the history of religion, the particular importance of the Greco-Oriental mysteries lies in the fact that they illustrate the need for a personal religious experience engaging man's entire existence, that is, to use Christian terminology, as including his "salvation" in eternity. Such a personal religious experience could not flourish in the framework of the public cults, whose principal function was to ensure the sanctification of communal life and the continuance of the State. In the great historical civilizations in which the mysteries proliferated, we no longer find the situation characteristic of primitive cultures; there, as we have noted more than once, the initiations of the youth were at the same time an occasion for the complete regeneration not only of the collectivity but also of the cosmos. In the Hellenistic period we find an entirely different situation; the immense success of the mysteries illustrates the break between the religious elites and the religion of the State, a break that Christianity will widen and, at least for a time, make complete.[33]

But for our present investigation the interest of the mysteries lies in the fact that they demonstrate the perennial significance of the traditional patterns of initiation and their capacity for being indefinitely reanimated and enriched with new values. In the Hellenistic world we find the same state of things that we observed in India; an archaic pattern can be taken over and utilized for many various spiritual ends, from mystical union with the Deity to the magical conquest of immortality or the achievement of final deliverance, *nirvana*. It is as if initiation and its patterns were indissolubly linked with the very structure of spiritual life; as if initiation were an indispensable process in every attempt at total regeneration, in every effort to transcend man's natural condition and attain to a sanctified mode of being. Equally significant is the fact that the imagery of the mysteries finally permeated an immense philosophical and spiritualistic literature, particularly in late antiquity. Homologizing philosophy to initiation had been a common motif even from the beginnings of Pythagoreanism and Platonism. But the maieutic procedure (from the root *maia,* "midwife") by which Socrates sought to "deliver" a new man had its prototype in archaic societies, in the work of the masters of initiation; they too delivered neophytes, that is, helped them to be born to spiritual life. Toward the end of antiquity the motif of initiatory delivery was accompanied by the theme of spiritual paternity, a theme already documented for Brahmanism and late Buddhism. (See pp. 53 ff.) St. Paul has "spiritual sons," sons whom he has engendered by faith.

But this is only a beginning. Though abstaining from revealing the secrets of the various Hellenistic mysteries, many philosophers and theosophists propounded allegorical interpretations of the initiatory rites. The majority of these interpretations referred the rites of the mysteries to the successive stages through which the human soul must pass in its ascent to God. Any acquaintance with the works of Iamblichus, Proclus, Synesius, Olympiodorus, as of many other Neoplatonists or theosophists of the last centuries of antiquity, suffices to show how completely they assimilated the mystery initiations to a psychodrama through which the soul can free itself from matter, attain regeneration, and take its flight to its true home, the intelligible world. In making this assimilation these writers were continuing a process of spiritual revaluation that had already found expression in the mysteries of Eleusis. There too, at a certain moment in history, an agricultural ritual had been charged with new religious values. Though preserving its primitive agricultural structure, the mystery no longer referred to the fertility of the soil and the prosperity of the community, but to the spiritual destiny of each individual mystes. The late commentators were innovators only in the sense that they read their own spiritual situations, determined by the profound crisis of their times, into the ancient rites.

Hence it is doubtful if this enormous mass of hermeneutic writing is of any service in an attempt to discover the original meaning of the Eleusinian, Orphic, or Hellenistic mysteries. But if these allegorical interpretations cannot put us in possession of historical realities, they are nevertheless of considerable value. For such interpretations characterize the entire history of later syncretistic spirituality. It was here that the countless Gnosticisms, both Christian and heterodox, of the first centuries of our era found their ideologies, their symbols, their key images. The touching drama of the human soul blinded and wounded by forgetfulness of its true self was set forth by Gnostic writers with the help of scenarios that finally derived from philosophical exegesis of the mysteries. It was through these syncretistic Gnosticisms that the interpretation of the Hellenistic mysteries as a ritually guided experience of the regeneration of the soul spread through Europe and into Asia. Certain aspects of this mysteriosophy survived even quite late into the Middle Ages. Finally the entire doctrine took on new life, in literary and philosophical circles, through the rediscovery of Neoplatonism in the Italy of the Renaissance.

Christianity and Initiation

From the end of the nineteenth century until about thirty years ago, a number of scholars were convinced that they could explain the origins of Christianity by a more or less direct influence from the Greco-Oriental mysteries. Recent researches have not supported these theories. On the contrary, it has even been suggested that the renaissance of the mysteries in the first centuries of our era may well be related to the rise and spread of Christianity; that certain mysteries may well have reinterpreted their ancient rites in the light of the new religious values contributed by Christianity.

It does not lie within our province to discuss all the aspects of this problem.[34] However, we must make it clear that the presence of one or another initiatory theme in primitive Christianity does not necessarily imply the influence of the mystery religions. Such a theme could have been taken directly from one of the esoteric Jewish sects, especially the Essenes, concerning whom the Dead Sea manuscripts have now added sensationally to our knowledge.[35] Indeed, it is not even necessary to suppose that an initiatory theme was "borrowed" by Christianity from some other religion. As we have said, initiation is coexistent with any new revaluation of spiritual life. Hence there are two different problems involved, which it would be dangerous to confuse. The first raises the question of the initiatory elements (scenarios, ideology, terminology) in primitive Christianity. The second concerns the possible historical relations between Christianity and the mystery religions.

Let us begin by defining in what sense it is possible to speak of initiatory elements in primitive Christianity. Obviously, Christian baptism was from the first equivalent to an initiation. Baptism introduced the convert to a new religious community and made him worthy of eternal life. It is known that between 150 B.C. and A.D. 300 there was a strong baptist movement in Palestine and Syria. The Essenes too practiced ritual baths or baptisms. As among the Christians, it was an initiatory rite; but, unlike the Christians, the Essenes repeated their ritual baths periodically. Hence it would be useless to seek a parallel to Christian baptism in the lustration rites of the mysteries or other ceremonies of pagan antiquity. Not only the Essenes but other Jewish movements were familiar with it. But baptism could become a sacrament for the earliest Christians precisely because it had been instituted by Christ. In other words, the sacramental value of baptism derived from the fact that the Christians saw Jesus as the Messiah, the Son of God.

All this is already indicated by St. Paul (I Corinthians 10) and developed in St. John's Gospel: baptism is a free *gift* of God which makes possible a new birth from water and the Spirit (John 1: 5). As we shall soon see, the symbolism of baptism is much enriched after the third century. We shall then find borrowings from the language and imagery of the mysteries. But none of these borrowings occurs in primitive Christianity.

Another cult act whose structure is initiatory is the Eucharist, instituted by Jesus at the Last Supper. Through the Eucharist the Christian shares in the body and blood of the Lord. Ritual banquets were frequent in the mysteries, but the historical precedents for the Last Supper are not to be sought so far away. The Qumran texts have shown that the Essenes regarded meals taken in common as an anticipation of the Messianic Banquet. As Krister Stendhal points out, this idea is also found in the Gospels: ". . . Many will come from east and west and sit at table with Abraham, Isaac and Jacob in the Kingdom of Heaven" (Matthew 8: 2). But here there is a new idea: the Christians regarded Jesus as already risen from the dead and raised to Heaven, whereas the Essenes awaited the resurrection of the Teacher of Righteousness as priestly Messiah together with the anointed of Israel. Even more important is the fact that, for the Christians, the Eucharist depended on a historical person and a historical event (Jesus and the Last Supper), but we do not find in the Qumran texts any redemptory significance accorded to a historical person.[36]

Thus we see in what sense primitive Christianity contained initiatory elements. On the one hand, baptism and the Eucharist sanctified the believer by radically changing his existential status. On the other hand, the sacraments separated him from the mass of the "profane" and made him part of a community of the elect. The initiatory organization of the community was already highly developed among the Essenes. Just as the Christians called themselves saints and "the chosen," the Essenes regarded themselves as initiates. Both were conscious that the virtue of their initiation set them apart from the rest of society.

The Qumran texts help us better to understand the historical context of the message of Jesus and of the development of the earliest Christian communities. We realize to what an extent primitive Christianity was bound up with the history of Israel and the hopes of the Jewish people. But even so, it is impossible not to realize all that distinguishes Christianity from the Essenes and in general from all other contemporary esoteric cults. Above all, there is the feeling of joy and newness. As has been pointed out, the terms designating newness and joy are characteristic of primitive Christian language.[37] The *newness* of Christianity is constituted by the historicity of Jesus; and the *joy* springs from certainty of his resurrection. For the earliest Christian communities, the resurrection of Jesus *could not be* identified with the periodic death and resurrection of the God of the mysteries. Like Christ's life, suffering, and death, his resurrection had occurred in history, "in the days of Pontius Pilate." The resurrection was an irreversible event; it was not repeated yearly, like the resurrection of Adonis, for example. It was not an allegory of the sanctity of cosmic life, as was the case with the so-called vegetation Gods, nor an initiatory scenario, as in the mysteries. It was a "sign" that formed part of the Messianic expectation of the Jewish people, and as such it had its place in the religious history of Israel, for the resurrection of the dead was an accompaniment of the coming of the Time. The resurrection of

Jesus proclaimed that the last age (the *eschaton*) had begun. As St. Paul says, Jesus was resurrected as "the firstborn from the dead" (Colossians 1: 18). This explains the belief which we find recorded in the Gospels, that many resurrections followed that of Jesus: "The graves were opened; and many bodies of the saints which slept arose" (Matthew 27: 52). For the earliest Christians, the resurrection established a new era of history—the validation of Jesus as Messiah, and hence the spiritual transmutation of man and the total renewal of the world. This, of course, constituted a "mystery," but a mystery that was to be "proclaimed upon the housetops." And initiation into the Christian mystery was open to all.

In short, the initiatory elements in primitive Christianity simply demonstrate once again that initiation is an inseparable element in any revaluation of the religious life. It is impossible to attain to a higher mode of being, it is impossible to participate in a new irruption of sanctity into the world or into history, except by dying to profane, unenlightened existence and being reborn to a new, regenerated life. In view of the "inevitability" of initiation, it is surprising that we find so little trace of initiatory scenarios and terminology in primitive Christianity. St. Paul never uses *telete,* a specific technical term of the mysteries. It is true that he uses *mysterion,* but in the sense given it in the Septuagint, that is, "secret."[38] In the New Testament, *mysterion* does not refer to a cult act, as it does in the ancient religions. For St. Paul, the mystery is God's secret, that is, his decision to save man through his Son, Jesus Christ. The reference, then, is basically to the mystery of redemption. But redemption is an idea that is incomprehensible except in the context of the Biblical tradition; it is only in that tradition that man, originally the son of God, had lost this privileged station by his sin.[39]

Jesus speaks of the "mysteries of the kingdom of Heaven" (Matthew 13: 11; Mark 4: 11; Luke 8: 10), but the expression is only the counterpart of the "king's secret" of the Old Testament (Tobit 12: 7). In this sense, the mysteries concern the kingdom that Jesus opens to believers. The mysteries of the kingdom of heaven are the "secret counsels" that a king communicates only to his familiars (Judith 2: 2) and hides from others in the form of parables so that "they seeing see not; and hearing they hear not" (Matthew 13: 13). In conclusion, although Jesus' message also has an initiatory structure—and has it precisely because initiation is an integral part of any new religious revelation—there is no reason to

suppose that primitive Christianity was influenced by the Hellenistic mysteries.

But with the spread of Christianity into all the provinces of the
Roman Empire, especially after its final triumph under Constantine,
there is a gradual change in perspective. The more that Christianity
becomes a universalistic religion, the more its historicity recedes into
the background. This does not mean that the Church abandons the
historicity of Christ, as was done by certain Christian heresies and
by Gnosticism. But by becoming paradigmatic for the entire
inhabited world, the Christian message tended more and more to
be couched in ecumenical terms. Primitive Christianity was bound
up with a local history, that of Israel. From a certain point of view,
any local history is in danger of provincialism. When a local history
becomes sacred and at the same time exemplary, that is, a paradigm
for the salvation of all humanity, it demands expression in a
universally understandable language. But the only universal religious language is the language of symbols. The Christian writers
will increasingly turn to symbols to make the mysteries of the
Gospel intelligible. But the Roman Empire had two universalistic
spiritual movements, that is, movements not confined within the
frontiers of a local culture: the mysteries and philosophy. Victorious Christianity borrowed from both the former and the latter.
Hence we find a threefold process of enrichment of primitive
Christianity: (1) by archaic symbols which will be rediscovered
and revalued by being given new Christological meanings; (2) by
borrowing from the imagery and initiatory themes of the mysteries;
(3) by the assimilation of Greek philosophy.

For our purpose, all that is pertinent is the incorporation of
initiatory motifs into victorious Christianity. But we must refer in
passing to the Church Fathers' use of archaic and universally disseminated symbols. For example, we find the symbols of the Cosmic
Tree and of the center of the world incorporated into the symbolism
of the Cross. The Cross is described as a "tree rising from earth to
Heaven," as "the Tree of Life planted on Calvary," the tree that
"springing from the depths of the Earth, rose to Heaven and
sanctifies the uttermost bounds of the universe."[40] In other words,
in order to convey the mystery of universal redemption through the
Cross, Christian writers used not only the symbols of the Old
Testament and the ancient Near East (reference to the Tree of
Life) but also the archaic symbols of the Cosmic Tree set at the
center of the world and ensuring communication between Heaven

and earth. The Cross was the visible sign of the redemption accomplished by Jesus Christ; hence it must replace the ancient symbols of elevation to Heaven. And since the redemption extended to the whole of humanity, the Cross had to be set at the center of the world, that it might sanctify the entire universe.

As for baptism, the Fathers emphasize its initiatory function more and more plastically by multiplying images of death and resurrection. The baptismal font is compared to both the tomb and the womb; it is the tomb in which the catechumen buries his earthly life and the womb in which the life eternal is born.[41] The homologization of prenatal existence both to immersion in the water of baptism and to initiatory death is clearly expressed in a Syrian liturgy: "And so, O Father, Jesus lived, through thy will and the will of the Holy Ghost, in three earthly dwellings: in the womb of the flesh, in the womb of the baptismal water, and in the somber caverns of the underworld."[42] It could be said that in this case there was an effort to reconsecrate an archaic initiatory theme by linking it directly with the life and death of Jesus.

But from the third century, and especially after the fourth, borrowings from the language and imagery of the mysteries become frequent. The initiatory motifs of Neoplatonism had already entered the writing of the Fathers by their assimilation of Greek philosophical terminology. Addressing the pagans, Clement of Alexandria uses the language of the mysteries: "O truly sacred mysteries! O pure light! In the blaze of the torches I have a vision of heaven and of God. I become holy by initiation."[43]

By the fourth century, the constitution of the *arcana disciplina,* the "secret teaching," is complete; in other words, the idea that the Christian mysteries are to be guarded from the uninitiated finally triumphs. As Father Hugo Rahner expresses it, "The mysteries of baptism and of the sacrificial altar were surrounded with a ritual of awe and secrecy, and soon the iconostasis concealed the holy of holies from the eyes of the noninitiate: these became . . . 'mysteries that make men freeze with awe.' 'This is known to the initiates' is a phrase running through all the Greek sermons, and as late a writer as the Pseudo-Areopagite warns the Christian initiate who has experienced the divine mystagogy to keep silence: 'Take care that you do not reveal the holy of holies, preserve the mysteries of the hidden God so that the profane may not partake of them and in your sacred illuminations speak of the sacred only to saints.' "[44]

What we find, in short, is a sublimation of the initiatory themes of the mysteries. This process was possible because it formed part of a larger movement—the Christianization of the religious and cultural traditions of the ancient world. As is well known, Christianity in its triumph had finally appropriated not only Greek philosophy, but the essentials of Roman juridical institutions, and the Oriental ideology of the Sovereign Cosmocrator, but also the whole immemorial heritage of Gods and Heroes, of popular rites and customs, especially the cults of the dead and fertility rituals. This wholesale assimilation was due to the very dialectics of Christianity. As a universalistic religion, Christianity was obliged to homologize and find a common denominator for all the religious and cultural "provincialisms" of the known world. This grandiose unification could be accomplished only by translating into Christian terms all the forms, figures, and values that were to be homologized.

For our purpose it is important to note that, together with Neoplatonic philosophy, the first values to be accepted by Christianity were the initiatory themes and the imagery of the mysteries. Christianity took the place of the mysteries, as it took the place of the other religious forms of antiquity. The Christian initiation could not coexist with initiations into the mysteries. Otherwise the religion that sought to preserve at least the historicity of Christ would have been in grave danger of becoming indistinguishably confused with the countless syncretistic Gnosticisms and religions. The intolerance of Christianity in its hour of triumph is the most striking proof that no confusion with the Hellenistic mysteries was possible. For the fact is that even Christianity, a revealed religion which did not originally imply any secret rite, which had proclaimed and propagated itself in the broad light of day and for all men, came in the end to borrow from the liturgies and the vocabulary of the Hellenistic mysteries. Morphologically speaking, Christianity too comprises an initiatory pattern—if only by the fact that baptism symbolizes the catechumen's mystical death and resurrection in Christ. It would be needless to insist on the radical differences in religious content that separate the Christian *mysterion* from the Hellenistic mysteries; for, as the result of a succession of profound and thoroughly documented studies, those differences are today clear. But in estimating the role and the importance of initiation in the religious life of humanity, it is not without interest to record the fact that certain initiatory themes were taken over and revaluated by Christianity.

Survival of Initiatory Motifs in Christian Europe

The final triumph of Christianity put an end to the mysteries and to the initiatory Gnosis. The spiritual regeneration previously sought in initiations into the mysteries was now obtained through the Christian sacraments. But certain patterns of initiation, more or less Christianized, continued to survive for many centuries. We here touch the circumference of a problem of some magnitude, which has not yet been adequately studied—the survival and successive transformations of initiatory scenarios in Christian Europe from the Middle Ages down to modern times. Since we cannot go into the problem in its entirety, let us content ourselves with taking a bird's-eye view of it. To begin with, it is important to observe in what forms Europe has preserved the various types of initiations that we have studied in these chapters; for they did not always survive as *rites* properly speaking, but more especially in the form of folk customs, of games, and of literary motifs. In general, the initiations which succeeded in preserving their ritual reality are puberty ceremonies. Throughout almost all of rural Europe, and down to the end of the nineteenth century, the ceremonies marking the passage from one age class to the next still reproduced certain themes characteristic of traditional puberty initiations. The incorporation of the boys into the group of youths always implied a "transition rite" and a certain number of initiatory ordeals. If the symbolism of death and resurrection is in most cases almost forgotten, the initiatory structure of the ordeals has been fairly well preserved. It has further been shown that the initiatory constitution of men's secret societies of pre-Christian times was continued in the more or less military organizations of the youth, in their symbols and secret traditions, their entrance rites, their peculiar dances (for example the sword dance and others), and even their costumes.[45] So too we can glimpse an ancient initiatory pattern in the ceremonial of the artisans' guilds, especially in the Middle Ages. The apprentice had to spend a certain period of time with his master. He learned the "secrets of the profession," the traditions of the corporation, the symbolism of his trade. Apprenticeship included a certain number of trials, and the novice's promotion to active membership in the corporation was accompanied by a vow of secrecy. Traces of ancient initiatory scenarios are still discernible in the rites peculiar to masons and blacksmiths, especially in Eastern Europe.[46]

These few examples illustrate the different modes of survival of initiatory rites in Christian Europe; for, whatever the degree to which they were desacralized, all these ceremonies can still be regarded as rites: they involve ordeals, special teaching, and, above all, secrecy. Beside this group of survivals, we must cite a certain number of popular customs, which were very probably derived from pre-Christian initiatory scenarios, but whose original meaning has been forgotten in the course of time, and which, furthermore, underwent strong ecclesiastical pressure for their Christianization. Among these popular customs of a complexion suggesting the mysteries, first place must go to the masquerades and dramatic ceremonies that accompany the Christian winter festivals, which take place between Christmas and Carnival.

But there are also cases in which certain initiatory patterns have been preserved in strictly closed milieux, leading an almost clandestine existence. Alchemy deserves special mention. It is important not only because it has preserved and transmitted the Hermetic doctrines of late antiquity but also for the role that it played in the history of Western culture. Now it is significant that in the work of the alchemists (*opus alchymicum*) we find the ancient pattern of initiatory torture, death, and resurrection; but this time it is applied on an entirely different plane of experience—that of experimentation with mineral substance. To transmute it, the alchemists treat matter as the Gods—and, consequently, the initiands—were treated in the Hellenistic mysteries: the mineral substances suffer, die, and are reborn to another mode of being, that is, are transmuted. Zosimus, one of the most important alchemists of the Hellenistic period, relates a vision that he had in a dream: a personage named Ion reveals to him that he (Ion) has been pierced by a sword, cut to pieces, beheaded, flayed, burned in fire, and that he suffered all this "in order that he could change his body into spirit." On awakening, Zosimus wonders if all that he saw in his dream was not related to a certain alchemical process.[47] In Ion's torture and cutting to pieces it is easy to recognize the pattern characteristic of shamanic initiations. But now it is not the postulant who suffers the initiatory torture, but a mineral substance, and it does so in order to change its modality, to be transmuted.

In the course of the *opus alchymicum,* we come upon other initiatory motifs; thus, for example, the phase named *nigredo* corresponds to the "death" of the mineral substances, to their dissolution or putrefaction, in short to their reduction to the *prime matter*. In some texts by late Western alchemists the reduction of substances to the prime matter is homologized with a return to the womb. All these phases of the *opus alchymicum* seem to indicate not only the stages of a process of transmutation of the mineral substances but also the inner experiences of the alchemist himself. There is a synchronism between the alchemical operations and the alchemist's mysterious experiences, which end by effecting his complete regeneration. As Gichtel said in regard to the operation *albedo*: "with this regeneration we receive not only a new soul, but a new body. . . ."[48]

All this would demand development and a detailed examination which space does not permit. But at least these few remarks were necessary to show that, through alchemy, certain initiatory patterns of archaic structure survived in Europe even down to the dawn of modern time—nay, more, that the alchemists employed these initiatory processes in order to realize their grandiose dream of mineral transmutation, that is, of the "perfecting" of metals through their spiritualization, through their final transformation into gold; for gold was the only perfect metal, the only one that, on the level of mineral existence, corresponded to the divine perfection. From a Christian point of view, we could say that the alchemists were striving to deliver nature from the consequence of the "fall," in short, to save it. In setting about this ambitious task of cosmic soteriology, the alchemists employed the classic scenario of all traditional initiation—death and resurrection of the mineral substances in order to regenerate them.

Patterns of Initiation and Literary Themes

It is probable that during the Middle Ages other types of initiations were performed in small closed circles. We find symbols and allusions to initiatory rites in the trials of the Knights Templars or of other so-called heretics and even in the trials of witches. But these initiations, in so far as they were still really practiced, affected only restricted circles surrounded by the deepest secrecy. We witness, if not the total disappearance of initiations, at least their almost final eclipse. All the more interesting, then, I think, is the presence of a considerable number of initiatory motifs in the literature that, from the twelfth century, grew up around the *"Matière de Bretagne,"* especially in the romance giving a leading role to Arthur, the Fisher King, Percival, and other Heroes pursuing the

Grail quest. The Celtic origin of the motifs of the Arthurian cycle appears to be accepted today by the majority of scholars. George Lyman Kittredge, Arthur Brown, Roger Sherman Loomis,[49] to cite only some American scholars, have abundantly demonstrated the continuity between the themes and figures of Celtic mythology —as still to be seen in Welsh and Irish tales—and the Arthurian personages. Now it is important to note that most of these scenarios are initiatory; there is always a long and eventful quest for marvelous objects, a quest which, among other things, implies the Heroes' entering the other world. To what extent this Matter of Britain contained not only remnants of Celtic mythology but also the memory of real rites it is difficult to decide. In the rules for admission into the company led by Arthur, we can decipher certain ordeals for entrance into a secret society of the *Männerbund* type.

But for our purpose, it is the proliferation of initiatory symbols and motifs in the Arthurian romances which is significant. In the Grail Castle, Percival has to spend the night in a chapel in which lies a dead knight; thunder rolls, and he sees a black hand extinguishing the only lighted candle.[50] This is the very type of the initiatory night watch. The ordeals that the Heroes undergo are innumerable—they have to cross a bridge that sinks under water or is made of a sharp sword or is guarded by lions and monsters. In addition, the gates to castles are guarded by animated automatons, fairies, or demons. All these scenarios suggest passage to the beyond, the perilous descents to Hell; and when such journeys are undertaken by living beings, they always form part of an initiation. By assuming the risks of such a descent to Hell, the Hero pursues the conquest of immortality or some other equally extraordinary end. The countless ordeals undergone by the personages of the Arthurian cycle fall in the same category; at the end of their quest, the Heroes cure the king's mysterious malady and thereby regenerate the "Waste Land," or even themselves attain sovereignty. Now it is well known that the function of sovereignty is generally bound up with an initiatory ritual.

All this literature with its abundance of initiatory motifs and scenarios[51] is most valuable for our purpose because of its popular success. The fact that people listened with delight to romantic tales in which initiatory clichés occurred to satiety proves, I think, that such adventures provided the answer to a profound need in medieval man. It was only his imagination which was fed by these initiatory scenarios; but the life of the imagination, like the life of a dream, is as important for the whole psyche of the human being as is daily life. We here touch upon a problem that is beyond the competence of the historian of religion, for it belongs by right to psychology. But I must touch upon it, in order that we may understand what happened to the majority of initiatory patterns when they had lost their ritual reality; they became what, for example, we find them to be in the Arthurian romances—literary motifs. This is as much as to say that they now deliver their spiritual message on a different plane of human experience, by addressing themselves directly to the imagination. Something similar had taken place, and long before, with fairy tales. Paul Saintyves attempted to show that a certain category of fairy tales is initiatory in structure (and, he added, in origin). Other folklorists have taken up the same thesis, and recently the Dutch Germanist Jan de Vries has brought out the initiatory elements in sagas and fairy tales.[52] Whatever side one may take in this controversy on the origin and meaning of fairy tales, it is impossible to deny that the ordeals and adventures of their heroes and heroines are almost always translatable into initiatory terms. Now this to me seems of the utmost importance: from the time—which it is so difficult to determine—when fairy tales took shape as such, men, both primitive and civilized alike, have listened to them with a pleasure susceptible of indefinite repetition. This amounts to saying that initiatory scenarios—even camouflaged, as they are in fairy tales—are the expression of a psychodrama that answers a deep need in the human being. Every man wants to experience certain perilous situations, to confront exceptional ordeals, to make his way into the Other World—and he experiences all this, on the level of his imaginative life, by hearing or reading fairy tales, or, on the level of his dream life, by dreaming.

Another phenomenon that, though apparently chiefly literary, also probably comprised an initiatory organization is the *Fedeli d'Amore*.[53] Representatives of the movement are documented in the thirteenth century in Provence and Italy as well as in France and Belgium. The *Fedeli d'Amore* constituted a secret and spiritual militia, devoted to the cult of the "One Woman" and to initiation into the mystery of "Love." They all used a "hidden language" (*parlar cruz*) so that their doctrine should not be accessible to *"la gente grosa,"* to use the expression of one of the most famous *Fedeli,* Francesco da Barberino (1264-1348). Another *fedele d'amore,* Jacques de Baisieux, in his poem *C'est des fiez d'amours,* lays it down that the *fedele* "must not reveal Love's counsels, but hide them with care."[54] That initiation through Love was spiritual in nature is clear from Jacques de Baisieux's interpretation of the word *amor*:

> *A* senefie en sa partie
> *Sans,* et *mor* senefie *mort*;
> Or l'assemblons, s'aurons *sans mort.*[55]

"Woman" symbolizes the transcendent intellect, Wisdom. Love of a woman awakens the adept from the lethargy into which the Christian world had fallen because of the spiritual unworthiness of the pope. In the writings of the *Fedeli d'Amore* we find allusions to a "widow who is no widow"; this is *Madonna Intelligenza,* who was left a widow because her husband, the pope, died to spiritual life by devoting himself entirely to things temporal.

Strictly speaking, this is not a heretical movement, but simply a secret group that no longer accorded the pope the status of spiritual leader of Christianity. We know nothing of their initiation rites; but they must have had such rites, for the *Fedeli d'Amore* constituted a militia and held secret meetings. But they are chiefly important because they illustrate a phenomenon that will become more marked later—the communication of a secret spiritual message through literature. Dante is the most famous example of this tendency—which already anticipates the modern world—to consider art, and especially literature, the paradigmatic method of communicating a theology, a metaphysics, and even a soteriology.

These few remarks help us to understand what initiatory patterns have become in the modern world—meaning by the term "modern world" the various categories of individuals who no longer have any religious experience properly speaking and who live a desacralized existence in a desacralized world. An attentive analysis of their behavior, beliefs, and ideals could reveal a whole camouflaged mythology and fragments of a forgotten or degraded religion. Nor is this surprising, for it was as *homo religiosus* that man first became conscious of his own mode of being. Whether he wants to or not, the nonreligious man of modern times continues the behavior patterns, the beliefs, and the language of *homo religiosus*—though at the same time he desacralizes them, empties them of their original meanings. It could be shown, for example, that the festivals and celebrations of a nonreligious, or ostensibly nonreligious society, its public ceremonies, spectacles, sports competitions, youth organizations, propaganda by pictures and slogans, literature for mass popular consumption—all still preserve the structure of myths, of symbols, of rites, although they have been emptied of their religious content.[56] But there is yet more: the imaginative activity and the dream experiences of modern man continue to be pervaded by religious symbols, figures, and themes. As some psychologists delight in repeating, the unconscious is religious.[57] From one point of view it could be said that in the man of desacralized societies, religion has become "unconscious"; it lies buried in the deepest strata of his being; but this by no means implies that it does not continue to perform an essential function in the economy of the psyche.

To return to patterns of initiation: we can still recognize them, together with other structures of religious experience, in the imaginative and dream life of modern man. But we recognize them too in certain types of real ordeals that he undergoes—in the spiritual crises, the solitude and despair through which every human being must pass in order to attain to a responsible, genuine, and creative life. Even if the initiatory character of these ordeals is not apprehended as such, it remains true nonetheless that man becomes *himself* only after having solved a series of desperately difficult and even dangerous situations; that is, after having undergone "tortures" and "death," followed by an awakening to another life, qualitatively different because regenerated. If we look closely, we see that every human life is made up of a series of ordeals, of "deaths," and of "resurrections." It is true that in the case of modern man, since there is no longer any religious experience fully and consciously assumed, initiation no longer performs an ontological function; it no longer includes a radical change in the initiand's mode of being, or his salvation. The initiatory scenarios function only on the vital and psychological planes. Nevertheless, they continue to function, and that is why I said that the process of initiation seems to be co-existent with any and every human condition.

Concluding Remarks

We have reached the end of our investigation; let us cast a backward look over the road that we have traveled. We have seen that the various types of initiations can be classed in two categories: first, puberty rites, by virtue of which adolescents gain access to the sacred, to knowledge, and to sexuality—by which, in short, they become *human beings*; second, specialized initiations, which certain individuals undergo in order to transcend their human condition and become protégés of the Supernatural Beings or even their equals. We also saw that, though it can avail itself of certain patterns that are in some sort its peculiar property, this second category of initiations generally employs the patterns typical of puberty rites. Since we cannot here present the geographical distribution[58] of these two categories of initiations, nor outline their respective histories, we shall confine ourselves to reviewing certain conclusions that follow from our investigation.

1. Although puberty rites among primitives are generally associated with the bull-roarer and circumcision, *this is not always the case*. From this we may conclude that initiation constitutes an autonomous and unique phenomenon, which can exist—and in fact does exist—without the corporal mutilations and the dramatic rites that are habitually associated with it.

2. Puberty initiations have an immense dissemination and are documented for the most archaic peoples—Australians, Fuegians, Californians, Bushmen, Hottentots, among others. However, there are primitive societies in which puberty rites apparently do not exist or are extremely rudimentary; such, for example, is the case with certain Arctic and north Asian peoples. But the religious life of these peoples is dominated by shamanism, and, as we have seen, one becomes a shaman by means of a long and sometimes dramatic initiation. Similarly, although in our day puberty rites have almost disappeared in Polynesia, secret societies flourish there; and these always employ initiatory scenarios. It follows that, in one way or another, initiatory rites are universally disseminated in the primitive world, whether in the form of age-grading ceremonies, of rites for entrance into secret societies, or, finally, of initiatory ordeals requisite for the realization of a mystical vocation.

3. In the eyes of those who perform them, initiations are believed to have been revealed by Divine or Supernatural Beings. Hence the initiatory ceremony is an imitation of the Gods; by performing it, one lives the sacred primordial Time again and the neophytes, together with all the initiates, participate in the presence of the Gods or mythical Ancestors. Initiation, then, is a recapitulation of the sacred history of the world and the tribe. On the occasion of the age-grading of adolescents, the entire society is plunged back into the mythical Times of origin and therefore emerges regenerated.

4. Initiatory scenarios differ markedly; we need only compare

the simplicity of the Kurnai initiation with similar Australian or Melanesian ceremonies. Some types of puberty initiations are organically related to certain cultures; we had occasion to show the structural connection between one or another initiatory motif and hunting or agricultural societies. Like every other cultural fact, the phenomenon of initiation is also a historical fact. In other words, the concrete expressions of initiation are related both to the structure of the respective society and to its history. On the other hand, initiation implies an existential experience—the experience of ritual death and the revelation of the sacred; that is, it exhibits a dimension that is metacultural and transhistorical. This is why the same initiatory patterns continue to be active in culturally heterogeneous societies. Certain scenarios of the Greco-Oriental mysteries are already documented in cultures as primitive as those of the Australians or the Africans.

5. For the reader's convenience, we may here again mention the initiatory patterns that are distinguished by their frequency and their wide dissemination: (a) the simplest patterns, comprising only the neophyte's separation from his mother and his introduction to the sacred; (b) the most dramatic pattern, comprising circumcision, ordeals, tortures, that is, a symbolic death followed by resurrection; (c) the pattern in which the idea of death is replaced by the idea of a new gestation followed by a new birth, and in which the initiation is expressed principally in embryological and gynecological terms; (d) the pattern whose essential element is individual withdrawal into the wilderness and the quest for a protecting spirit; (e) the pattern peculiar to heroic initiations, in which the emphasis falls on victory gained by magical methods (e.g., metamorphosis into a wild beast, frenzy, etc.); (f) the pattern characteristic of the initiations of shamans and other specialists in the sacred, comprising both a descent to Hell and an ascension to Heaven (essential themes: dismemberment of the body and renewal of the viscera, climbing trees); (g) the pattern that we may call "paradoxical," because its principal feature is ordeals that are inconceivable on the level of human experience (ordeals of the Symplegades type). It is true that these Symplegades ordeals are in some sort a part of all the foregoing patterns (except, of course, the first); yet it is justifiable to speak of a paradoxical pattern, since this pattern is capable of being detached from the ritual complex and, as a symbol, fulfilling an important function in myths and folklores: particularly the function of revealing the structures of ultimate reality and of spirit.

6. As we saw, several patterns of initiation can coexist in the same culture. Such a plurality of patterns can be explained historically by the successive influences that have in the course of time been exercised on the culture. But consideration must also be given to the metacultural character of initiation; the same initiatory patterns are found in the dreams and the imaginative life both of modern man and of the primitive. To repeat: we are dealing with an existential experience that is basic in the human condition. This is why it is always possible to revive archaic patterns of initiation in highly evolved societies.

7. We cannot say that there is "evolution" when one pattern gives place to another, nor that a pattern derives genetically from the one that preceded it, nor, finally, that some particular pattern is superior to all others. Each represents a creation that is self-sufficient. Nevertheless, this fact is to be noted: the dramatic intensity of initiatory scenarios increases in more complex cultures; elaborate rites, masks, and cruel or terrifying ordeals make their appearance in similar cultures. The purpose of all these innovations is to make the experience of ritual death more intense.

8. We find initiatory death already justified in archaic cultures by an origin myth that can be summarized as follows: a Supernatural Being had attempted to renew men by killing them in order to bring them to life again "changed"; for one reason or another, men slew this Supernatural Being, but they later celebrated secret rites inspired by this drama; more precisely, the violent death of the Supernatural Being became the central mystery, reactualized on the occasion of each new initiation. Initiatory death is thus the repetition of the death of the Supernatural Being, the founder of the mystery. Since the primordial drama is repeated during initiation, the participants in an initiation also imitate the fate of the Supernatural Being: his death by violence. By virtue of this ritual anticipation, death, too, is itself sanctified, that is, is charged with a religious value. Death is valuated as an essential moment in the existence of the Supernatural Being. By dying ritually, the initiate shares in the supernatural condition of the founder of the mystery. Through this valuation, death and initiation become interchangeable. And this, in sum, amounts to saying that concrete death is finally assimilated to a transition rite toward a higher condition. Initiatory death becomes the *sine qua non* for all spiritual regeneration and, finally, for the survival of the soul and even for its immortality. And one of the most important consequences that the rites and ideology of initiation have had in the history of humanity

is that this religious valuation of ritual death finally led to conquest of the fear of *real* death, and to belief in the possibility of a purely spiritual survival for the human being.

It must never be forgotten that initiatory death simultaneously signifies the end of the "natural," noncultural man, and passage to a new modality of existence—that of a being "born to spirit," that is, a being that does not live solely in an immediate reality. Thus initiatory death forms an integral part of the mystical process by which the novice becomes *another,* fashioned in accordance with the model revealed by the Gods or the mythical Ancestors. This is as much as to say that one becomes truly a man in proportion as one ceases to be a natural man and resembles a Supernatural Being.

The interest of initiation for an understanding of archaic mentality lies predominantly in its showing us that the true man—the spiritual man—is not *given,* is not the result of a natural process. He is "made" by the old masters, in accordance with the models revealed by the Divine Beings and preserved in the myths. These old masters constitute the spiritual elites of archaic societies. It is they who know, who know the world of spirit, the truly human world. Their function is to reveal the deep meaning of existence to the new generations and to help them assume the responsibility of being truly men and hence of participating in culture. But since for archaic societies "culture" is the sum of the values received from Supernatural Beings, the function of initiation may be reduced to this: to each new generation, it reveals a world open to the transhuman, a world that, in our philosophical terminology, we should call transcendental.

Epilogue

As we saw, modern man no longer has any initiation of the traditional type. Certain initiatory themes survive in Christianity; but the various Christian denominations no longer regard them as possessing the values of initiation. The rituals, imagery, and terminology borrowed from the mysteries of late antiquity have lost their initiatory aura; for fifteen centuries they have formed an integral part of the symbolism and ceremonial of the Church.

This is not to say that there have not existed, and do not still exist, small groups seeking to revive the "esoteric" meaning of the institutions of the Catholic Church. The attempt of the writer J. K. Huysmans is the best known, but his is not the only one. These efforts have met with almost no response outside of the restricted circles of writers and amateur occultists. It is true that for the past thirty years or so Catholic authorities have shown much interest in images, symbols, and myths. But this is due primarily to the revival of the liturgical movement, to the renewed interest in Greek patrology, and to the increasing importance accorded to mystical experience. None of these trends was initiated by an esoteric group. On the contrary, the Roman Church quite visibly has the same desire to live in history and to prepare its adherents to face the problems of contemporary history as the Protestant churches have. If many Catholic priests are far more interested in the study of symbols today than Catholic priests in general were thirty years ago, it is not in the sense in which Huysmans and his friends were interested, but in order the better to understand the difficulties and crises of their parishioners. It is for the same reason that psychoanalysis is increasingly studied, and applied, by the clergy of various Christian denominations.

To be sure, we find today a considerable number of occult sects, secret societies, pseudo-initiatory groups, hermetistic or neospiritualistic movements, and the like. The Theosophical Society, Anthroposophy, Neo-Vedantism, Neo-Buddhism are merely the best-known expressions of a cultural phenomenon found almost everywhere in the Western world. It is no new phenomenon. Interest in occultism, accompanied by a tendency to form more or less secret societies or groups, already appears in Europe in the sixteenth century and reaches its height in the eighteenth. The only secret movement that exhibits a certain ideological consistency, that already has a history, and that enjoys social and political prestige is Freemasonry. The other self-styled initiatory organizations are for the most part recent and hybrid improvisations. Their interest is chiefly sociological and psychological; they illustrate the disorientation of a part of the modern world, the desire to find a substitute for religious faith. They also illustrate the indomitable inclination toward the mysteries, the occult, the beyond—an inclination that is an integral part of the human being and that is found in all ages on all levels of culture, especially in periods of crisis.

Not all the secret and esoteric organizations of the modern world include entrance rites or initiation ceremonies. Initiation is usually reduced to instruction obtained from a book. (The number of initiatory books and periodicals published throughout the world is amazing.) As for occult groups requiring a formal initiation, what little is known about them shows that their "rites" are either sheer inventions or are inspired by certain books supposed to contain precious revelations concerning the initiations of antiquity. These so-called initiation rites frequently betoken a deplorable spiritual poverty. The fact that those who practice them can regard them as infallible means of attaining to supreme gnosis shows to what a degree modern man has lost all sense of traditional initiation. But the success of these enterprises likewise proves man's profound need for initiation, that is, for regeneration, for participation in the life of spirit. From one point of view, the pseudo-initiatory sects and groups perform a positive function, since they help modern man to find a spiritual meaning for his drastically desacralized existence. A psychologist would even say that the extreme spuriousness of these pretended initiation rites is of little significance, the important fact being that the deep psyche of the participant regains a certain equilibrium through them.

The majority of the pseudo-occult groups are hopelessly sterile. No important cultural creation whatever can be credited to them. On the contrary, the few modern works in which initiatory themes are discernible—James Joyce's *Ulysses,* T. S. Eliot's *The Waste Land*—were created by writers and artists who make no claim to have been initiated and who belong to no occult circle.

And so we come back to the problem on which we touched earlier—that initiatory themes remain alive chiefly in modern man's unconscious. This is confirmed not only by the initiatory symbolism of certain artistic creations—poems, novels, works of plastic art, films—but also by their public reception. Such a massive and spontaneous acceptance proves, it seems to us, that in the depth of his being modern man is still capable of being affected by initiatory scenarios or messages. Initiatory motifs are even to be found in the terminology used to interpret these works. For example, such and such a book or film will be said to rediscover the myths and ordeals of the Hero in quest of immortality, to touch upon the mystery of the redemption of the world, to reveal the secrets of regeneration through woman or love, and so on.

It is not surprising that critics are increasingly attracted by the religious implications, and especially by the initiatory symbolism, of modern literary works. Literature plays an important part in contemporary civilization. Reading itself, as a distraction and escape from the historical present, constitutes one of the characteristic traits of modern man. Hence it is only natural that modern man should seek to satisfy his suppressed or inadequately satisfied religious needs by reading certain books that, though apparently "secular," in fact contain mythological figures camouflaged as contemporary characters and offer initiatory scenarios in the guise of everyday happenings.

The genuineness of this half-conscious or unconscious desire to share in the ordeals that regenerate and finally save a Hero is proved, among other things, by the presence of initiatory themes in the dreams and imaginative activity of modern man. C. G. Jung has stressed the fact that the process that he terms individuation, and that, in his view, constitutes the ultimate goal of human life, is accomplished through a series of ordeals of initiatory type.

As we said before, initiation lies at the core of any genuine human life. And this is true for two reasons. The first is that any genuine human life implies profound crises, ordeals, suffering, loss and reconquest of self, "death and resurrection." The second is that, whatever degree of fulfillment it may have brought him, at a certain moment every man sees his life as a failure. This vision does not arise from a moral judgment made on his past, but from an obscure feeling that he has missed his vocation; that he has betrayed the best that was in him. In such moments of total crisis, only one hope seems to offer any issue—the hope of beginning life over again. This means, in short, that the man undergoing such a crisis dreams of new, regenerated life, fully realized and significant. This is something other and far more than the obscure desire of every human soul to renew itself periodically, as the cosmos is renewed. The hope and dream of these moments of total crisis are to obtain a definitive and total *renovatio,* a renewal capable of transmuting life. Such a renewal is the result of every genuine religious conversion.

But genuine and definitive conversions are comparatively rare in modern societies. To us, this makes it all the more significant that even nonreligious men sometimes, in the depths of their being, feel the desire for this kind of spiritual transformation, which, in other cultures, constitutes the very goal of initiation. It does not fall to us to determine to what extent traditional initiations fulfilled their promises. The important fact is that they proclaimed their intention, and professed to possess the means, of transmuting human life. The nostalgia for an initiatory renewal which sporadically arises from the inmost depths of modern nonreligious man hence seems to us highly significant. It would appear to represent the modern formulation of man's eternal longing to find a positive meaning in death, to accept death as a transition rite to a higher mode of being. If we can say that initiation constitutes a specific dimension of human existence, this is true above all because it is only in initiation that death is given a positive value. Death prepares the new, purely spiritual birth, access to a mode of being not subject to the destroying action of Time.

Notes

☸

FOREWORD

1. *Le Chamanisme et les techniques archaïques de l'extase* (Paris, 1951); *Le Yoga. Immortalité et liberté* (Paris, 1955), of which an English translation, *Yoga: Immortality and Freedom,* will be published in the fall of 1958 (New York, Bollingen Series No. LVI); and *Forgerons et alchimistes* (Paris, 1956).

INTRODUCTION

1. Cf. A. van Gennep, *Les Rites de passage* (Paris, 1909).

CHAPTER I. INITIATION MYSTERIES IN PRIMITIVE RELIGIONS

1. Cf. A. van Gennep, *Les Rites de passage* (Paris, 1909) and H. Webster, *Primitive Secret Societies: A Study in Early Politics and Religion* (New York, 1908).

2. "A class cannot initiate its own young men, but both classes cooperate in this ceremony. On the other hand, in those tribes which have no longer any class organisation in a vigorous state, it is the local organisation by its assembled initiated men which conducts the ceremonies. Such a case is that of the Kurnai and the Chepara tribes." A. W. Howitt, *The Native Tribes of South-East Australia* (London, 1904), p. 512.

3. Webster, *Primitive Secret Societies*, p. 139, note 2.

4. Howitt, *Native Tribes*, pp. 516 ff.

5. As among many Australian tribes, the pole plays an important ritual role: it is allowed to fall in the direction in which it has been decided to perform the ceremony; cf. R. H. Mathews, "The Bora or Initiation Ceremonies of the Kamilaroi Tribe," *Journal of the Royal*

Anthropological Institute, XXIV (1895), 411-427; XXV (1896), 318-339, especially 327.

6. *Ibid.,* XXIV, 422.

7. *Ibid.,* XXV, 325.

8. *Ibid.,* XXIV, 414 ff.

9. *Ibid.,* XXIV, 418.

10. P. E. Worms, "Djamar, the Creator," *Anthropos,* 45 (1950), 650-651 and note 80. This is a type of religious behavior common to all peoples of archaic culture. In Australia, when the initiate takes part in religious ceremonies, "it is realized both by himself and all present that hé is no longer himself: he is the great 'dream-time' hero whose role he is re-enacting, even if only for a few minutes." A. P. Elkin, *Aboriginal Men of High Degree* (Sidney, 1946), p. 13. Cf. also our *The Myth of the Eternal Return,* trans. Willard R. Trask (New York, 1954), pp. 32 ff.

11. B. Spencer and F. J. Gillen, *The Arunta* (London, 1927), I, 188.

12. Howitt, *Native Tribes,* p. 626.

13. *Ibid.,* p. 526. Among the Wotjobaluk, too, the novice is "roasted" at the fire; cf. *ibid.,* p. 615. Fire plays an important role in the initiation ceremonies of other Australian tribes; cf. B. Spencer and F. J. Gillen, *The Northern Tribes of Central Australia* (London, 1904), pp. 389 ff., and *The Arunta,* I, 295 ff.; W. L. Warner, *A Black Civilisation* (New York, 1937), p. 325; F. Speiser, "Ueber Initiationen in Australien und Neuguinea," *Verhandlungen der Naturforschenden Gesellschaft in Basel* (1929), pp. 216–18; G. Róheim, *The Eternal Ones of the Dream* (New York, 1945), pp. 113 ff. "Ritual roasting" is also documented in some initiations of medicine men; cf. Elkin, *Aboriginal Men,* pp. 91 (among the Kattang-speaking people), 129 (among the Maitakudi).

14. Howitt, *Native Tribes,* pp. 525 ff. As a Cape York informant expresses it, the novices are "stolen from the mother." D. F. Thomson, "The Hero Cult, Initiation and Totemism on Cape York," *Journal of the Royal Anthropological Institute,* LXIII (1933), 474.

15. Howitt, *Native Tribes,* p. 530.

16. *Ibid.,* pp. 584 ff.

17. R. H. Mathews, "The Burbung of the Wiradjuri Tribes," *Journal of the Royal Anthropological Institute,* XXV (1896), 295-318; XXVI (1897), 272–285, especially I, 307 ff., and II, 272 ff.

18. We may note in passing that Mungan-Ngaua's disappearance into the sky is equivalent to his transformation into a remote and inactive god, a rather frequent phenomenon in the case of the Creator Gods of primitive religions. Cf. our *Traité d'histoire des religions* (Paris, 1949), pp. 53 ff.

19. Howitt, *Native Tribes,* pp. 628 ff.

20. This is the opinion of W. Schmidt, *Der Ursprung der Gottesidee,* III (Münster, 1931), 621-623. This simplicity of initiation, that is, the

absence of any ritual mutilation (e.g., knocking out the incisor, circumcision), is also characteristic of some Northern Territory tribes. See the descriptions of initiation ceremonies among the Melville Islanders, the peoples of Port Essington, the Kakadu, and the Larakias in B. Spencer, *Native Tribes of the Northern Territory* (London, 1914), pp. 91 ff., 115 ff., 121 ff., 153 ff. Speiser is of the opinion that the initiations documented in the Northern Territory, and especially the Melville Islanders' initiation, represent the original and hence the most ancient form of Australian initiations. (Cf. "Ueber Initiationen," pp. 59-71, 247; Speiser puts the Kurnai initiation immediately after the Northern Territory type, *ibid.*, p. 249.) Speiser's classification is not completely convincing, for the Northern Territory, and especially Melville Island, have been subjected to strong Melanesian influences. See below, p. 149 n. 36.

21. The route followed by the procession from the camp to the mountains represents the path connecting the two circles of the sacred ground; cf. Howitt, *Native Tribes*, p. 536.

22. *Ibid.*, p. 543.

23. Spencer and Gillen, *The Arunta*, I, 187. The dramatic and choreographic recapitulation of the primordial events is a theme common to all Australian initiations. Cf. also Thomson, "The Hero Cult," pp. 488 and *passim;* R. Piddington, "Karadjeri Initiation," *Oceania*, III, (1932-33), 70 ff.

24. Howitt, *Native Tribes*, p. 557.

25. *Ibid.*, p. 559.

26. *Ibid.*, pp. 527-562.

27. *Ibid.*, pp. 585 ff.

28. R. H. Mathews, "The Burbung of the Wiradjuri Tribes," *Journal of the Royal Anthropological Institute*, XXV (1896), 311.

29. *Ibid.*, p. 297.

30. A. L. P. Cameron, "On Some Tribes of New South Wales," *Journal of the Royal Anthropological Institute*, XIX (1885), 344 ff. 357-358; cf. also Howitt, *Native Tribes*, 588-589. Similar myth and ritual are found among the Euahlayi; cf. K. L. Parker, *The Euahlayi Tribe* (London, 1905), pp. 62-64.

31. Howitt, *Native Tribes*, p. 596.

32. Spencer and Gillen, *Northern Tribes of Central Australia*, pp. 343, 347, 366.

33. Howitt, *Native Tribes*, p. 502. See other examples in our *Le Chamanisme et les techniques archaïques de l'extase* (Paris, 1951), pp. 134 ff.

34. Howitt, *Native Tribes*, pp. 587-588.

35. *Ibid.*, p. 654.

36. *Ibid.*, p. 674. Cf. the prohibition against drinking during the daytime imposed on the initiands of Cape York. Thomson "The Hero Cult," p. 483.

37. Among the Yamana, the Halakwulup, and the Selknam, the initiands are obliged to drink through a bird bone. Cf. J. Haeckel, "Jugendweihe und Männerfest auf Feuerland. Ein Beitrag zu ihrer kulturhistorischen Stellung," *Mitteilungen der Osterreichischen Gesellschaft für Anthropologie, Ethnologie und Prähistorie,* LXXIII-LXXVII, (1947), pp. 91, 114.

38. "Before they reach their destination the young men are forced to go through high grass and reeds, and made to climb small trees to test their physical strength and power." J. Nilles, "The Kuman of the Chimbu Region, Central Highlands, New Guinea," *Oceania,* XXI (1950), 37.

39. Haeckel, "Jugendweihe"; cf. Schmidt, *Ursprung,* II (1929), 949.

40. Schmidt, *Ursprung,* V (1935), 78; VI (1937), 132.

41. Howitt, *Native Tribes,* p. 563. Another ritual prohibition is that against touching the body with the fingers; the neophyte is obliged to use a scratching stick; cf. Thomson, "The Hero Cult," p. 483. The same custom is found among the Fuegians; cf. Schmidt, *Ursprung,* VI, 132-133.

42. Piddington, "Karadjeri Initiation," p. 67.

43. N. B. Tindale, "Initiation among the Pitjandjara Natives of the Mann and Tomkinson Ranges in South Australia," *Oceania,* VI, (1935), 222-223.

44. Spencer and Gillen, *Northern Tribes of Central Australia,* p. 365; Warner, *Black Civilisation,* pp. 260-285; Piddington, "Karadjeri Initiation," p. 67; Róheim, *Eternal Ones,* p. 13.

45. Cf., for example, Tindale, "Initiation," p. 220.

46. C. P. Mountford, *Brown Men and Red Sand* (Melbourne, 1948), p. 33.

47. Spencer and Gillen, *The Arunta,* I, 175 ff. For the Pitjandjara, cf. Tindale, "Initiation," p. 213.

48. Howitt, *Native Tribes,* p. 609. Among the Arunta the novices, after subincision, embrace the sacred pole (Spencer and Gillen, *Northern Tribes of Central Australia,* p. 342). Now, among some Arunta clans—for example, the Achilpa—the sacred pole (*kauwa-auwa*) is a symbol of the *axis mundi.* (Cf. Spencer and Gillen, *The Arunta,* I, 378 ff.) On the ritual function and cosmological signification of the sacred pole of the Achilpa, see E. de Martino, "Angoscia territoriale e riscatto culturale nel mito Achilpa delle origini," *Studi e Materiali di Storia delle Religioni,* XXII (1951-52), 51-66.

49. Howitt, *Native Tribes,* p. 631.

50. R. H. Mathews, "The Burbung," XXVI (1897), 277.

51. Piddington, "Karadjeri Initiation," p. 79.

52. Howitt, *Native Tribes,* pp. 581-582. A. P. Elkin gives the following details concerning the magic cord of the medicine men of

southeastern Australia: "This cord becomes a means of performing marvellous feats, such as sending fire from the medicine-man's inside, like an electric wire. But even more interesting is the use made of the cord to travel up to the sky or to the tops of trees or through space. At the display at initiation time, in a time of ceremonial excitement, the doctor lies on his back under a tree, sends his cord up and climbs upon it to a nest on the top of the tree, then across to other trees, and at sunset, down to the tree again." Elkin, *Aboriginal Men*, p. 64. On the rites and symbolism of ascension, see below, Chapters IV and V.

53. See some examples in our *Le Chamanisme*, pp. 125 ff., 134 ff.

Chapter II. The Initiatory Ordeals

1. See the list of tribes which, though they practice circumcision, know nothing of subincision in F. Speiser, "Ueber Initiationen in Australien und Neuguinea," pp. 82-84, and in A. E. Jensen, *Beschneidung und Reifezeremonien bei Naturvölkern* (Stuttgart, 1933), p. 105.

2. Cf. F. Graebner, "Kulturkreise in Ozeanien," *Zeitschrift für Ethnologie* (1905), p. 764; Speiser, "Ueber Initiationen," p. 197.

3. W. Schmidt, "Die Stellung der Aranda," *Zeitschrift für Ethnologie* (1908), pp. 866 ff., especially pp. 898-900; F. Speiser, "Ueber die Beschneidung in der Südsee," *Acta Tropica* (1944), I, 27. Speiser believes that circumcision is an Austronesian cultural element, disseminated from Indonesia to Melanesia and Australia.

4. Cf. Jensen, *Beschneidung*, pp. 21 ff., 73 (Africa), 115-128 (North and South America).

5. B. Spencer and F. J. Gillen, *The Arunta* (London, 1927), I, 202 ff.; cf. also their *The Northern Tribes of Central Australia* (London, 1904), pp. 334 ff., 342 ff. The bull-roarer represents the mythology of the supernatural Being Djamar; swinging the bull-roarer makes Djamar present. Cf. P. E. Worms, "Djamar, the Creator," *Anthropos*, XLV (1950), 657.

6. C. Strehlow, *Die Aranda- und Loritja-Stämme in Zentralaustralien* (Frankfurt on the Main, 1920), IV, 24 ff.

7. N. B. Tindale, "Initiation Among the Pitjandjara Natives of the Mann and Tomkinson Ranges in South Australia," *Oceania*, VI (1935), 218-219.

8. R. Piddington, "Karadjeri Initiation," *Oceania*, III (1932-33), 71 ff.

9. H. Basedow, *The Australian Aboriginal* (Adelaide, 1925), pp. 241 ff.

10. Spencer and Gillen, *Northern Tribes of Central Australia*, p. 501.

11. On bull-roarers in Australia, cf. O. Zerries, *Das Schwirrholz. Untersuchung über die Verbreitung und Bedeutung des Schwirrens im Kult* (Stuttgart, 1942), pp. 84-125.

12. *Ibid.*, pp. 176 ff., 193, etc.; W. Schmidt, *Der Ursprung der Gottesidee*, IV (Münster, 1931), 61, 86, 200.

13. On the dissemination of this motif, see Zerries, *Das Schwirrholz*, pp. 188 ff. For the bull-roarer in Thrace and ancient Greece, cf. R. Pettazzoni, *I Misteri* (Bologna, 1924), pp. 19-34.

14. We may add that if the bull-roarer is always connected with initiation, the reverse is not true; initiation does not necessarily imply the bull-roarer. In Australia there are initiations without bull-roarers. (Cf. Speiser, "Ueber Initiationen," p. 156.) It follows that originally the puberty initiation could be performed without the ritual presence of bull-roarers (Speiser, "Ueber die Beschneidung," p. 15; Zerries, *Das Schwirrholz*, p. 183). Probably the bull-roarer was brought to Australia by waves of Melanesian culture; cf. Speiser, "Kulturgeschichtliche Betrachtungen über die Initiationen in der Südsee," *Bulletin der Schweizerischen Gesellschaft für Anthropologie und Ethnologie*, XXII (1945-46), 50 ff. The bull-roarer has different significations in different primitive religions; among the Arunta and the Loritja, it is the secret body of the mythical Ancestors; in Africa, the Malay Peninsula, New Guinea, and elsewhere, the sound of the bull-roarers represents the voice of the Ancestors (Zerries, *Das Schwirrholz*, p. 184); among the Pomo, it symbolizes the voice of the dead, who periodically return to earth at the time of initiations (*ibid.*, p. 186).

15. Hermann Baumann had already suggested this conclusion for the African hunter culture (cf. *Schöpfung und Urzeit der Menschen im Mythos der afrikanischen Völker* [Berlin, 1936], pp. 377, 384), and Otto Zerries has established it for other cultures (*Das Schwirrholz*, pp. 182 ff).

16. H. Straube, *Die Tierverkleidungen der afrikanischen Naturvölker* (Wiesbaden, 1955), pp. 8 ff. and *passim*. Among some African tribes the bull-roarer is called lion or leopard (cf. Zerries, *Das Schwirrholz*, p. 178), which illuminates the sequence of mythical Beings in animal form–bull-roarer–circumcision–mystical death–initiation.

17. Straube, *Die Tierverkleidungen*, pp. 198 ff.

18. Zerries, *Das Schwirrholz*, pp. 194, 231.

19. Cf. examples in Jensen, *Beschneidung*, p. 130.

20. Junod, cited *ibid.*, p. 55.

21. See examples, *ibid.*, pp. 27, 104, etc.

22. J. Winthuis, *Das Zweigeschlechterwesen* (Leipzig, 1928), pp. 39 ff. and *passim*.

23. Cf. H. Baumann, *Das doppelte Geschlecht. Ethnologische Studien zur Bisexualität in Ritus und Mythos* (Berlin, 1955), p. 212. For other bisexual divine figures in northern Australia, see A. Lommel, *Die Unambal* (Hamburg, 1952), pp. 10 ff.

24. Cf. our "La Terre-Mère et les hiérogamies cosmiques," *Eranos-Jahrbuch*, XXII (1954), pp. 78 ff.

25. W. E. Roth, *Ethnological Studies among the North-West-Central*

Queensland Aborigines (Brisbane and London, 1897), p. 180. H.
Klaatsch records similar beliefs among the Niol-Niol, a Northwest
Australian people; cf. Baumann, *Das doppelte Geschlecht*, p. 214, note
15.

26. R. M. Berndt, *Kunapipi* (Melbourne, 1951), p. 16.
27. Cf. M. F. Ashley-Montagu, *Coming into Being among the
Australian Aborigines, A Study of the Procreative Beliefs of the Native
Tribes of Australia* (New York, 1938), *passim;* A. P. Elkin, *The Aus-
tralian Aborigines* (Sydney, 1938), p. 158, note 1, and his review of
Ashley-Montagu's book in *Oceania,* VIII (1938), 376-380; Phyllis M.
Kaberry, *Aboriginal Woman, Sacred and Profane* (Philadelphia, 1939),
p. 43. It should be added that some ethnologists deny that the Austral-
ians aborigines do not know the real cause of conception; cf. W. L.
Warner, *A Black Civilisation* (New York, 1937), pp. 23-24, 595;
D. F. Thompson, "Fatherhood in the Wik-Monkam Tribe," *American
Anthropologist,* n.s., XXXVIII (1936), 374-393; Géza Róheim, "The
Nescience of the Aranda," *British Journal of Medical Psychology,* XVII
(1938), 343-560; R. M. Berndt and C. H. Berndt, *Sexual Behavior
in Western Arnhem Land* (New York, 1951), pp. 80 ff. But see also
M. F. Ashley-Montagu, "Nescience, Science, and Psycho-Analysis,"
Psychiatry, IV (1941), pp. 45-60.

28. Baumann, *Das doppelte Geschlecht,* p. 57; Jensen, *Beschneidung,* pp. 33 (Africa), 129 ff. (novices dressed as girls and costumes
burned at the conclusion of the initiation).

29. W. Ellis, *Polynesian Researches,* 2nd ed. (London, 1831), I, 324;
W. E. Mühlmann, *Arioi und Mamaia* (Wiesbaden, 1955), pp. 43 ff.,
77.

30. W. Schmidt, "Die geheime Jünglingsweihe der Karesau-In-
sulaner, Deutsch-Neu-Guinea," *Anthropos,* II (1907), 1029-1056.

31. P. Wirz, *Die Marind-Anim* (Hamburg, 1922 ff.), II, 3, pp. 43
ff; Baumann, *Das doppelte Geschlecht,* p. 228.

32. A. C. Haddon, "The Secular and Ceremonial Dances of Torres
Straits," *International Archiv für Ethnologie,* VI (1893), 131 ff.,
140 ff.

33. A. W. Howitt, *The Native Tribes of South-East Australia* (London, 1904), pp. 658 ff. The ceremony is fairly widespread in Australia;
cf. Piddington, "Karadjeri Initiation," p. 71; C. P. Mountford, *Brown
Men and Red Sand* (Melbourne, 1948), p. 32; G. Róheim, *The Eternal
Ones of the Dream* (New York, 1945), p. 218, etc.; Berndt, *Kunapipi,*
p. 36 (opening a vein in the arm is equivalent to reopening the urethral
incision).

34. Piddington, "Karadjeri Initiation," p. 72; Howitt, *Native Tribes,*
p. 676 (Itchumundi); Warner, *A Black Civilisation,* pp. 274 ff.; D.
Bates, *The Passing of the Aborigines* (New York, 1939), pp. 41 ff.;
144 ff.; Róheim, *The Eternal Ones,* pp. 227 ff., 230 ff.

35. Margaret Mead, "The Mountain Arapesh," *American Museum of Natural History, Anthropological Papers,* II (1940), 348 ff.

36. Albert Anfinger, "Einige ethnographische Notizen zur Beschneidung in Neuguinea," *Ethnos,* VI (1941), 37 ff. The same custom is followed in Wogeo, one of the Schouten Islands in the territory of New Guinea: "Women are automatically cleaned by the process of menstruation, but men, in order to guard against disease, have periodically to incise the penis and allow a quantity of blood to flow. This operation is often referred to as men's menstruation." I. Hogbin, *Oceania,* V (1935), 330; cited by Ashley-Montagu, *Coming into Being,* p. 303.

37. Alphons Schäfer, "Zur Initiation im Wagi-Tal," *Anthropos,* XXXIII (1938), 421 ff.

38. J. Nilles, "The Kuman of the Chimbu Region, Central Highlands, New Guinea," *Oceania,* XXI (1950), 37.

39. Ashley-Montagu, *Coming into Being,* pp. 302 ff.

40. Cf., for example, Tindale, "Initiation among the Pitjandara," p. 208; Róheim, *The Eternal Ones,* pp. 229 ff. See also B. Bettelheim, *Symbolic Wounds: Puberty Rites and the Envious Male* (Glencoe, Ill., 1954), pp. 173 ff. On the cultural chronology of Australia, cf. D. S. Davidson, *The Chronological Aspects of Certain Australian Social Institutions* (Philadelphia, 1928), "Archaeological Problems in Northern Australia," *Journal of the Royal Anthropological Institute,* LXV (1934), 145-184, and "North-Western Australia and the Question of Influences from the East Indies," *Journal of the American Oriental Society,* LVIII (1938), 61-80; F. D. McCarthy, "The Prehistoric Cultures of Australia," *Oceania* XIX (1949), 305-319; and "The Oceanic and Indonesian Affiliations of Australian Aboriginal Cultures," *Journal of the Polynesian Society,* LXII (1953), 243-261.

41. Cf. Speiser, "Ueber Initiationen," especially pp. 219-223, 247 ff.; Baumann, *Das doppelte Geschlecht,* pp. 216 ff.

42. Cf. Howitt, *Native Tribes,* pp. 592, 603, 657, etc.; R. H. Mathews, "The Burbung of the Wiradjuri Tribes," *Journal of the Royal Anthropological Institute,* XXV (1896), 310; Schmidt, *Ursprung,* III, 1062-1080 (tribes of southeastern Australia); H. Webster, *Primitive Secret Societies: A Study in Early Politics and Religion* (New York, 1908), pp. 40-41 (Australia, Melanesia); Jensen, *Beschneidung,* pp. 26, 39, 100 ff. (Africa, Melanesia).

43. Schmidt, *Ursprung,* VI, 458 ff. But is should be added that, according to Gusinde, the revelations concerning the Supreme Being are not made directly but by allusion, and that in the Yamana initiations the principal role is played by the Earth Spirit (*Erdgeist*) Yetaita; cf. M. Gusinde, *Die Yamana* (Mödling, 1937), pp. 940 ff. Cf. also p. 29 ff.

44. R. Lowie, in his review of Gusinde's book, holds that the Yamana puberty ceremony was originally only for boys. Cf. *American Anthropologist* (1938), pp. 499 ff.

45. W. Koppers, *Primitive Man and his World Picture* (London, 1952), p. 140. In addition to this popular account of Fuegian initiations, the reader can profitably consult Gusinde's monographs *Die Selknam* (Mödling, 1951), and *Die Yamana* (Vienna, 1937); Vol. I of the *Handbook of South American Indians*, Bulletin 143, Bureau of American Ethnology (Washington, 1945); and J. Haeckel's article, "Jugendweihe und Männerfest auf Feuerland. Ein Beitrag zu ihrer kulturhistorischen Stellung" (*Mitteilungen der Oesterreichischen Gesellschaft für Anthropologie, Ethnologie und Prähistorie*, LXIII-LXXVII (1947), 84-114.

46. Koppers, *Primitive Man*, pp. 140 ff.

47. Gusinde, *Die Yamana*, pp. 942 ff.; Haekel, "Jugendweihe," p. 89.

48. Haekel, "Jugendweihe," p. 100.

49. Similar secret male festivals also exist among the Yamana and the Selknam; cf. *ibid.*, p. 94.

50. The same ceremony is found among the Yamana. Similar myths are documented among other South American tribes; see A. Métraux, "A Myth of the Chamacoco Indians and its Social Significance," *Journal of American Folklore*, LVI (1943), 113-119. Cf. the historico-cultural analysis of this mythico-ritual complex of the "terrorization of women," in Haekel, "Jugendweihe," pp. 106 ff.

51. Webster, *Primitive Secret Societies*, p. 24.

52. G. Landtman, *The Kiwai-Papuans of British New-Guinea* (London, 1927), p. 96.

53. H. Ward, cited in Jensen, *Beschneidung*, p. 31; A. Bastian, *Die deutsche Expedition an der Loango-küste* (Jena, 1875), II, 18.

54. Jensen, *Beschneidung*, p. 39.

55. L. Frobenius, *Masken und Geheimbünde Afrikas* (Halle, 1898), p. 145.

56. K. Weule, cited in Jensen, *Beschneidung*, 57.

57. O. D. Tauern, *Patasiva und Patalima* (Leipzig, 1918), pp. 145 ff.; Jensen, *Beschneidung*, p. 78.

58. G. Tessmann, *Die Pangwe* (Berlin, 1913), II, 39-94; summary in Jensen, *Beschneidung*, pp. 33-35.

59. E. Torday and T. A. Joyce, *Les Bushongo* (Brussels, 1910), pp. 82 ff. A month later the third and last *Dina* (ordeal) takes place, consisting in climbing a tree. *Ibid.*, pp. 84-85.

60. The Men's House is a characteristic feature of the Melanesian cultural complex, but the institution is found elsewhere in the world and always in connection with puberty rites. Cf. Webster, *Primitive Secret Societies*, Chapter I, "The Men's House," pp. 1-19; H. Schurtz, *Altersklassen und Männerbünde* (Berlin, 1902), pp. 202-317. See also E. Schlesier, *Die Erscheinungsformen des Männerhauses und des Klubwesen in Mikronesien* (The Hague, 1953).

61. J. Holmes, "Initiation Ceremonies of Natives of the Papuan

Gulf," *Journal of the Royal Anthropological Institute,* XXXII (1902), 418-425.

62. A. Riesenfeld, *The Megalithic Culture of Melanesia* (Leiden, 1950), p. 591; cf. pp. 593 ff. for an analysis of the megalithic elements in the Nanga ceremony.

63. L. Fison, "The Nanga, or Sacred Stone Enclosure of Wainimaia, Fiji," *Journal of the Royal Anthropological Institute,* XIV (1885), 22; see especially pp. 19-26. A. B. Joske, "The Nanga of Viti Levu," *International Archiv für Ethnologie,* II (1889), 254-271, gives a similar description, with some variants (e.g., pp. 264-265, one of the instructors shouts to the novices that they are responsible for the death of the men lying in the enclosure). Cf. also B. Thomson, *The Fijians* (London, 1908), pp. 148-157.

64. Cf. A. Slawik, "Kultische Geheimbünde der Japaner und Germanen," *Wiener Beiträge zur Kulturgeschichte und Linguistik,* IV (1936), 675-764, 739 ff.

65. Jensen, *Beschneidung,* p. 53.

66. See some African examples, *ibid.,* p. 29.

67. *Ibid.,* p. 36.

68. *Ibid.,* p. 94.

69. For example, at Ceram; Zerries, *Das Schwirrholz,* p. 44. On this motif, see our "Mystère et régénération spirituelle," *Eranos-Jahrbuch,* XXIII (1955), 89, note 41.

70. Webster, *Primitive Secret Societies,* p. 103.

71. A. R. Radcliffe-Brown, "The Rainbow-Serpent Myth in South-East Australia," *Oceania,* I (1930), 344.

72. Schurtz, *Altersklassen,* p. 224.

73. H. Nevermann, *Masken und Geheimbünde Melanesien* (Leipzig, 1933), pp. 24, 40, 56.

74. Jensen, *Beschneidung,* p. 83.

75. *Ibid.,* pp. 87 (the Kai), 89 (the Jabim). Among the Karesau, the candidates are isolated in two cabins, and they are said to be in the spirit's belly; cf. Schmidt, "Die geheime Jünglingsweihe," pp. 1032 ff.

76. F. E. Williams, "The Pairama Ceremony in the Purari Delta, Papua," *Journal of the Royal Anthropological Institute,* LIII (1923), 363 ff.; Speiser, "Ueber Initiationen," pp. 120 ff.; Nevermann, *Masken,* pp. 51 ff.

77. R. Thurnwald, "Primitive Initiations- und Wiedergeburtsriten," *Eranos-Jahrbuch,* VII (1940), 393.

78. On this cosmological symbolism in initiation ceremonies, see Chapter III.

79. Cf. Webster, *Primitive Secret Societies,* p. 42, note 2.

80. Cannibals, too, do not use their fingers (cf., e.g., Jensen, *Beschneidung,* p. 143), because they consider themselves to be ghosts.

81. *Ibid.,* pp. 60-61.

82. E.g., the island of Mailu; cf. *ibid., 92.*

83. *Ibid.* This use of a little stick during the initiation period is a custom documented in more archaic cultures than those just mentioned; it exists among the Fuegians and the Californians; cf. Schmidt, *Ursprung,* VI, 132 ff.

84. In the Congo, initiates are called *nganga,* "the knowing ones," and noninitiates *vanga,* "the unenlightened." Webster, *Primitive Secret Societies,* p. 175.

85. Cf., for example, Spencer and Gillen, *The Arunta,* I, 178 ff.; A. Lommel, "Notes on the Sexual Behaviour and Initiation, Wunambal Tribe, North Western Australia," *Oceania,* XX (1949-50), 159; Mountford, *Brown Men,* pp. 33-34. Among the Euahlayi, the young man is initiated into the mystery of Gayandi, and the bull-roarer is revealed to him, only after he has taken part in five *Boorahs;* cf. K. L. Parker, *The Euahlayi Tribe* (London, 1905), p. 81.

86. Howitt, *Native Tribes,* pp. 662 ff.

87. Tindale, "Initiation among the Pitjandara," p. 223.

CHAPTER III. FROM TRIBAL RITES TO SECRET CULTS

1. B. Spencer, *Native Tribes of the Northern Territory of Australia* (London, 1914), p. 326; B. Spencer and F. J. Gillen, *The Arunta* (London, 1927), II, 481; W. E. Roth, *Ethnological Studies among the North-West-Central Queensland Aborigines* (Brisbane and London, 1897), p. 184; K. L. Parker, *The Euahlayi Tribe* (London, 1905), pp. 56-57; W. L. Warner, *A Black Civilisation* (New York, 1937), pp. 75-76. Cf. also W. Schmidt, *Der Ursprung der Gottesidee* (Münster, 1931), III, 706-709 (Kulin), 988-990 (Euahlayi).

2. For example, among the tribes of southern South America; cf. J. Haeckel, "Jungendweihe und Männerfest auf Feuerland. Ein Beitrag zu ihrer kulturhistorischen Stellung," *Mitteilungen der Oesterreichische Gesellschaft für Anthropologie, Ethnologie und Prähistorie,* LXIII-LXXVII (1947), 132 ff.

3. Cf. Frazer, *Balder the Beautiful* (London, 1913), I, 22-100; E. S. Hartland, *Primitive Paternity* (London, 1910), I, 91-98; W. E. Peuckert, *Geheimkulte* (Heidelberg, 1951), pp. 256-257.

4. Cf. Frazer, *Balder,* pp. 56, 59-61, 66.

5. Cf. H. Ploss and M. Bartels, *Das Weib in der Natur- und Völkerkunde* (Leipzig, 1908), I, 454-502; W. Schmidt and W. Koppers, *Völker und Kulturen* (Regensburg, 1924), I, 273-275 (diffusion of the custom).

6. R. M. Berndt and C. H. Berndt, *The First Australians* (New York, 1954), p. 54.

7. R. M. Berndt and C. H. Berndt, *Sexual Behaviour in Western Arnhem Land* (New York, 1951), pp. 89-91.

8. See the list of peoples in Peuckert, *Geheimkulte*, p. 258.

9. Ploss and Bartels, *Das Weib*, I, 464 ff.

10. E. Gasparini, *Nozze, società e abitazione degli antichi Slavi* (Venice, 1954), Appendix I and II, p. 14.

11. Cf. our "Mystère et régénération spirituelle," *Eranos-Jahrbuch,* XXIII (1955), 79.

12. W. Schmidt, *Das Mutterrecht* (Vienna, 1955), p. 131.

13. Cf. our *Traité d'histoire des religions* (Paris, 1949), p. 270.

14. Frazer, *Balder*, I, 76 ff.

15. Schmidt, *Das Mutterrecht*, p. 132.

16. H. Ling-Roth, "The Native of Borneo," *Journal of the Royal Anthropological Institute*, XXIII (1893), 41 ff.; H. Baumann, *Das doppelte Geschlecht. Ethnologische Studien zur Bisexualität in Ritus und Mythos* (Berlin, 1955), p. 62.

17. Baumann, *Das doppelte Geschlecht*, pp. 62-63.

18. R. P. Heckel, "Miscellanea," *Anthropos*, XXX (1935), 875; Gasparini, *Nozze*, p. 27. Graded stages of initiation are also found among the tribes of northwestern Australia: "With sexual maturity the girl may take part in the women's secret corroborees. After she has a child, she may assist at the rites carried out for her female relatives. Later she gradually learns the songs that are *daragu* (=sacred) and *gunbu* (=taboo) to the men, and in old age, she directs proceedings and becomes responsible for the handing on of her knowledge to the generation of women below her." Phyllis M. Kaberry, *Aboriginal Woman, Sacred and Profane*, (Philadelphia, 1939), p. 237.

19. Our "Mystère et régénération," p. 81, after R. Wolfram, "Weiberbünde," *Zeitschrift für Volkskunde*, XLII (1933), 143 ff. Childbirth already constitutes a mystery among some Australian tribes. Phyllis Kaberry had more difficulty in collecting secret childbirth songs than she had in obtaining information from men in regard to the initiation of boys; cf. *Aboriginal Woman*, pp. 241 ff.

20. Our "Mystère et régénération," p. 82; R. Wolfram, "Weiberbünde," p. 144.

21. Our *Images et symboles* (Paris, 1952), pp. 120 ff.; cf. also R. Wolfram, *Schwerttanz und Männerbund* (Cassel, 1935 ff), p. 172.

22. R. Heine-Geldern, "Südostasiens," in G. Buschan, *Illustrierte Völkerkunde* (Stuttgart, 1923), II, 841; Gasparini, *Nozze*, pp. 18 ff.

23. Cf. A. Slawik, "Kultische Geheimbünde der Japaner und Germanen," *Wiener Beiträge zur Kulturgeschichte und Linguistik*, IV (1936), 737 ff.; Peuckert, *Geheimkulte*, p. 253.

24. D. Zelenin, *Russische (ostslawische) Volkskunde* (Berlin, 1927), pp. 337 ff.; Gasparini, *Nozze*, pp. 22-33; our *"Mystère et régénération,"* pp. 80 ff.

25. T. Volkov, "Rites et usages nuptiaux en Ucraïne," *L'Anthropologie* (1891, 1892), summarized in Gasparini, *Nozze*, pp. 42 ff.

26. R. M. Berndt, *Kunapipi* (Melbourne, 1951), p. 34.

27. The mystical foundresses of the ceremony, the Wauwalak Sisters, are "as much alive spiritually today as ever they were." Berndt, *Kunapipi*, p. 33.

28. The theme of the myth follows a well-known pattern: (1) a Supernatural Being kills men (to initiate them); (2) (not understanding the meaning of this initiatory death) men avenge themselves by slaying him; (3) but afterward they institute secret ceremonies related to this primordial drama; (4) the Supernatural Being is made present at these ceremonies through an image or a sacred object supposed to represent his body or his voice.

29. *Ibid.*, p. 36.

30. *Ibid.*, p. 37.

31. *Ibid.*, p. 41.

32. *Ibid.*, p. 38. The elder Sister was smeared with afterbirth blood; the younger Sister's efforts in dancing before the Serpent had brought on her menstrual flow (*ibid.*, p. 23).

33. *Ibid.*, p. 14. The cabin in which the two Sisters took refuge— and which plays a part in the two other rituals dependent on this myth, *djunggawon* and *njurlmack*—likewise represents the Mother's womb.

34. *Ibid.*, p. 45.

35. *Ibid.*, p. 53.

36. A. P. Elkin, Preface to Berndt's book, *ibid.*, p. xxii; W. Schmidt, "Mythologie und Religion in Nord Australien," *Anthropos*, XLVIII (1953), 898-924.

37. "Then we had nothing: no sacred objects, no sacred ceremonies, the women had everything." Berndt, *Kunapipi*, p. 8, cf. pp. 55, 58, 59. As we have seen, similar traditions are documented among the Selknam and among some tribes of the Amazon basin; cf. Chapter II, note 50 (p. 145), and Métraux's article cited therein, especially pp. 117-118.

38. Cf., for example, Berndt, *Kunapipi*, pp. 24 ff.

39. Cf. H. Lommel, in C. Hentze, *Tod, Auferstehung, Weltordnung* (Zurich, 1955), p. 128. For the ceremony as it is performed today, see Mrs. Sinclair Stevenson, *The Rites of the Twice-Born* (Oxford, 1920), pp. 27 ff.

40. For an analysis of this motif in Buddhist philosophy, cf. our *Images et symboles*, pp. 100 ff.

41. R. Thurnwald, "Primitive Initiations- und Wiedergeburtstriten," *Eranos-Jahrbuch*, VII (1940), 390, citing G. Wagner, "Reifeweihen bei den Bantu-Stammen Kavirondos und ihre heutige Bedeutung," Archiv für Anthropologie, n.s., XXV (1939), 85-100.

42. On the *diksha*, see the texts collected by S. Lévi, *La Doctrine du sacrifice dans les Brahmanas* (Paris, 1898), pp. 103 ff. Cf. also our

Le Yoga. Immortalité et liberté (Paris, 1954), pp. 118, 374; H. Lommel, in Hentze, *Tod*, pp. 115 ff.

43. In Hentze, *Tod*, p. 127.

44. Cf. our "Kosmogonische mythen und magische Heilung," *Paideuma*, VI (1956), 194-204.

45. Cf. *Shatapatha Brahmana*, III, 2, 1, 18 ff. In the *Maitrayani-Samhita* (III, 6, 8), the union is between Yajña and Dakshina. Cf. also Lommel, in Hentze, *Tod*, pp. 114 ff.

46. M. Canney, "The Skin of Rebirth," *Man*, XCI (July, 1939), 104-105; W. S. Routledge and K. Routledge, *With a Prehistoric People* (London, 1910), pp. 151-153. Cf. also our "Mystère et régénération, pp. 66-67.

47. Cf. T. Zachariae, "Scheingeburt," *Zeitschrift der Vereins für Volkskunde*, XX (1910), 141 ff.; also in his *Kleine Schriften* (Bonn and Leipzig, 1920), pp. 266 ff. W. Crooke, *Things Indian, Being Discursive Notes on Various Subjects Connected with India* (London, 1906), pp. 500 ff.; Sir J. G. Frazer, *Totemism and Exogamy* (London, 1910), I, 32; IV, 208 ff.; Lommel, in Hentze, *Tod*, pp. 121 ff., and H. Hoffmann, *ibid.*, pp. 139 ff.

48. Cf. Hentze, *Tod*, pp. 148 and *passim*.

49. *Ibid.*, p. 145; P. Wirz, *Totenkult auf Bali* (Stuttgart, 1928), Fig. 27.

50. See some references in R. Briffault, *The Mothers* (London, 1927), I, 471 ff. For south India, cf. H. Whitehead, *The Village Gods of South India*, 2nd ed. (Madras, 1921), pp. 37 ff., 55, 64, 98, etc.; G. Oppert, *On the Original Inhabitants of Bharatavarsa or India* (Westminster, 1893), pp. 24, 274 ff., 461 ff.; our *Le Yoga*, pp. 346 ff.

51. The legend is already attested in the *Rig-Veda* (VII, 33, 13) and became widely disseminated; for the other Vedic sources, cf. L. Sieg, *Sagenstoffe des Rigveda* (Stuttgart, 1902), pp. 105 ff. For the south Indian variants, see Oppert, *Original Inhabitants*, pp. 67 ff. Cf. also P. Thieme, "Ueber einige Benennungen des Nachkommen," *Zeitschrift für Vergleichende Sprachforschung*, LXVI (1939), 141 ff. ("Topf als Name des Bastards").

52. G. van der Leeuw, "Das sogenannte Hockerbegräbnis und der ägyptische *Tjknu*," *Studi e Materiali di Storia delle religioni*, XIV (1938), 150-167; Hentze, *Tod*, pp. 150 ff.

53. H. Maspero, "Les procédés de 'nourrir le Principe vital' dans la religion taoïste, *Journal Asiatique* (1937), p. 198. On "embryonic respiration" in Taoism, cf. our *Le Yoga*, pp. 71 ff. 395 ff.

54. Liu Hua-yang, *Huei-ming-king*, cited in R. Stein, "Jardins en miniature d'Extrême-Orient," *Bulletin de l'Ecole Française d'Extrême Orient*, XLII (1943), 97.

55. On this motif, cf. our *Forgerons et alchimistes* (Paris, 1956), p. 159.

56. *Ibid.*, p. 160.

57. Stein, "Jardins en miniature," p. 44.

58. Cf. our "Kosmogonische Mythen," *passim.*

CHAPTER IV. INDIVIDUAL INITIATIONS AND SECRET SOCIETIES

1. Cf. our "Mystère et régénération spirituelle," *Eranos-Jahrbuch,* XXIII (1955), p. 90, after W. D. Westervelt, *Legends of Ma-ui the Demi-god* (Honolulu, 1910), pp. 128 ff.; J. F. Stimson, *The Legends of Maui and Tahaki* (Honolulu, 1937), pp. 46 ff.

2. J. Layard, *Stone Men of Malekula* (London, 1942), pp. 225 ff., 649 ff.; and "The Making of Man in Malekula," *Eranos-Jahrbuch,* XVI (1949).

3. A. B. Deacon, "Geometrical Drawings from Malekula and Other Islands of the New Hebrides," *Journal of the Royal Anthropological Institute,* LXVI (1934), 132 ff., and *Malekula: A Vanishing People of the New Hebrides* (London, 1934), especially pp. 552 ff.; J. Layard, "Totenfahrt auf Malekula," (*Eranos-Jahrbuch,* IV [1937], 242-291), and *Stone Men of Malekula,* pp. 340 ff., 649 ff. Cf. also W. F. Jackson Knight, *Cumaean Gates: A Reference of the Sixth Aeneid to Initiation Pattern* (Oxford, 1936), p. 19.

4. Layard, *Stone Men of Malekula,* pp. 730, 221.

5. Layard, "The Making of Man in Malekula," p. 228 and Pl. II.

6. C. Hentze, *Tod, Auferstehung, Weltordnung* (Zurich, 1955), pp. 79 ff., 90 ff. Cf. also W. Krickeberg, "Ostasien-Amerika," *Sinologica,* II (1950), 195-233, especially 228 ff.

7. Cf. our "Mystère et régénération," pp. 90 ff., citing M. Haavio, *Väinämöinen, Eternal Sage* (FF Communications, No. 144 [Helsinki, 1952]), pp. 117 ff.

8. Haavio, *Väinämöinen,* pp. 114 ff.

9. Our "Mystère et régénération," p. 92; cf. L. Rademacher, "Walfischmythen," *Archiv für Religionswissenschaft,* IX (1906), 246 ff.; F. Graebner, *Das Weltbild der Primitiven* (Munich, 1924), pp. 62 ff.

10. Haavio, *Väinämöinen,* pp. 106 ff.; our "Mystère et régénération," p. 95

11. Haavio, *Väinämöinen,* p. 124.

12. On the motif of the "clashing rocks," see A. B. Cook, *Zeus* (Cambridge, 1940), III, 2, pp. 975-1016 (Appendix P: "Floating Islands"); K. von Spiess, "Der Schuss nach dem Vogel," *Jahrbuch für Historische Volkskunde,* V-VI (1937), 204-235, and "Die Hasenjagd," *ibid.,* pp. 243-267. The expression "two razor-edged restless mountains" is attested in the *Suparnadhyaya* (25, 5; reading, with Coomaraswamy, *parvatah asthirah*); cf. A. K. Coomaraswamy, "Symplegades," *Studies and Essays in the History of Science and Learning Offered in Homage to George Sarton* (New York, 1947), p. 470, note 11.

13. On the theme of the "active door" in Celtic mythology, cf. A. C.

Brown, *Iwain* (Boston, 1903), pp. 80 ff. On the "revolving barrier," cf. *ibid.*, and G. L. Kittredge, *A Study of Sir Gawain and the Green Knight* (Cambridge, Mass., 1916), pp. 244 ff. Cf. also Coomaraswamy, "Symplegades," pp. 479 ff.

14. Some South American tribes picture the door of Heaven or of the (subterranean) Other World as a jaguar's jaws; cf. Krickeberg, "Ostasien-Amerika," p. 201. The architectural motif of the door in the form of a monster's jaws is quite widespread in Central America; *ibid.*, p. 232, and C. Hentze's studies, especially *Objets rituels, croyances et dieux de la Chine antique et de l'Amérique* (Anvers, 1936), *Die Sakralbronzen und ihre Bedeutung in den frühchinesischen Kulturen* (Anvers, 1941), and *Bronzegerät, Kultbauten, Religion im ältesten China der Shangzeit* (Anvers, 1951). Cf. also his *Tod*, p. 90 and Figs. 76, 77, 106, on the Symplegades in the form of a *vagina dentata* in South American ceramics. On the Symplegades in South American mythology and folklore, cf. Coomaraswamy, "Symplegades," p. 475.

15. Coomaraswamy, "Symplegades," p. 470. On this motif, see also Coomaraswamy, "Svayamatrnna: Janua Coeli," *Zalmoxis*, II (1939), 3-51.

16. Coomaraswamy, "Symplegades," p. 486. Cf. Also our *Le Chamanisme et les techniques archaïques de l'extase* (Paris, 1951), pp. 419 ff.

17. Cf. Coomaraswamy, "Symplegades," p. 475.

18. The bibliography is too extensive to be given here. The documentation down to *ca.* 1908 is utilized by Sir J. G. Frazer, *Totemism and Exogamy* (London, 1910), III, 370-456. For a general study, see J. Haeckel, "Schutzgeistsuche und Jugendweihe im westlichen Nordamerika," *Ethnos*, XII (1947), 106-122.

19. Among the numerous works by Franz Boas which are fundamental for our investigation are "The Social Organization and the Secret Societies of the Kwakiutl Indians," *Annual Report of the Smithsonian Institution, 1894-95* (Washington 1897), pp. 311-738; "Ethnology of the Kwakiutl," *35th Annual Report of the Bureau of American Ethnology, 1913-1914* (Washington, 1921), pp. 43-1481; *The Religion of the Kwakiutl Indians*, Columbia University Contributions to Anthropology, X (2 vols., New York, 1930). Cf. also P. Drucker, "Kwakiutl Dancing Societies," *Anthropological Records*, University of California Publications, II (Berkeley and Los Angeles, 1940), 201-230; J. Haeckel, "Initiationen und Geheimbünde an der Nordwestküste Nordamerikas," *Mitteilungen der Anthropologische Gesellschaft in Wien*, LXXXIII (1954), 176-190; W. Müller, *Weltbild und Kult der Kwakiutl-Indianer* (Wiesbaden, 1955).

20. "It is clear that with the change of name the whole social structure, which is based on the names, must break down. Instead of being grouped in clans, the Indians are now grouped according to the spirits which have initiated them." Boas, "Secret Societies," p. 418.

21. Drucker, "Kwakiutl Dancing Societies," p. 210, note 24; Müller, *Weltbild und Kult*, p. 72.

22. Boas, "Secret Societies," pp. 440 ff.; Müller, *Weltbild und Kult*, 72.

23. Boas, "Secret Societies," p. 457. On the cosmological symbolism of the ceremonial house, cf. Müller, *Weltbild und Kult*, pp. 17 ff.

24. Müller, *Welbild und Kult*, p. 20.

25. Haeckel, "Initiationen und Geheimbünde," p. 170.

26. Cf. Boas, "Secret Societies," Pl. 29; Haeckel, "Initiationen und Geheimbünde," p. 169.

27. Haeckel, "Initiationen und Geheimbünde," p. 189.

28. Boas, "Secret Societies," pp. 441-443, 524 ff.; and "Ethnology of the Kwakiutl," pp. 1172 ff. The Bella Coolas also have a Cannibal Society; initiation into it resembles that of the Kwakiutl; cf. Boas, "Secret Societies," pp. 649-650; and "The Mythology of Bella Coola Indians," *Memoirs of the American Museum of Natural History*, I, 2 (1900), 118–120. For the initiation rituals of other secret societies among the Indians of northwestern America, cf. Frazer, *Totemism and Exogamy*, III, 449-512, 527-550; and Haeckel, "Initiationen und Geheimbünde," *passim*.

29. General studies are H. Schurtz, *Altersklassen und Männerbünde* (Berlin, 1902), pp. 318-437; H. Webster, *Primitive Secret Societies: A Study in Early Politics and Religion* (New York, 1908), pp. 74-190; *Semaine d'ethnologie religieuse. Compte-rendu analytique de la III* session* (Enghien and Moedling, 1923), pp. 329-456. Cf. also W. E. Peuckert, *Geheimkulte* (Heidelberg, 1951).

30. L. Frobenius, "Die Masken und Geheimbünde Afrikas," *Abhandlungen d. Kaiserl. Leopold-Carolin. Deutsch. Akademie d. Naturforscher*, LXXIV (1899), 1-266; cf. *Semaine d'ethnologie religieuse*, pp. 335 ff.; W. Schmidt, *Das Mutterrecht* (Vienna, 1955), pp. 171 ff.

31. E. M. Loeb, "Tribal Initiation and Secret Societies," *University of California Publications in American Archaeology and Ethnology*, XXV, 3 (Berkeley, 1929), 262.

32. A. E. Jensen, *Beschneidung und Reifezeremonien bei Naturvölkern* (Stuttgart, 1933), p. 79.

33. Cf. Webster, *Primitive Secret Societies*, p. 176, note 2; F. Speiser, "Ueber Initiationen in Australien und Neuguinea," *Verhandlungen der Naturforschenden Gesellschaft in Basel* (1929), pp. 256 ff.; Jensen, *Beschneidung*, p. 99; A. van Gennep, *Les Rites de passage* (Paris, 1909), pp. 126 ff.

34. Melanesia: H. Codrington, *The Melanesians* (Oxford, 1891), pp. 69-115; R. Parkinsons, *Dreissig Jahre in der Südsee* (Stuttgart, 1907), pp. 565-680; W. H. R. Rivers, *The History of Melanesian Society* (Cambridge, 1914), II, 205-233, 592-593; H. Nevermann, *Masken und Geheimbünde Melanesiens* (Berlin and Leipzig, 1933);

H. Kroll, "Der Iniet. Das Wesen eines melanesischen Geheimbundes," *Zeitschrift für Ethnologie*, LXX (1937), 180-220. Africa: Frobenius, "Masken und Geheimbünde Afrikas"; E. Johanssen, *Mysterien eines Bantu-Volkes* (Leipzig, 1925); E. Hildebrandt, *Die Geheimbünde Westafrikas* (Leipzig, 1937); G. W. Harley, *Notes on the Poro in Liberia*, Papers of the Peabody Museum of American Archaeology and Ethnology, XIX, 2 (Cambridge, Mass., 1941); K. L. Little, "The Poro Society as an Arbiter of Culture," *African Studies*, VII (1948), 1-15.

35. Cf. E. Andersson, *Contribution à l'ethnographie des Kuta* (Uppsala, 1953), I, 210 ff.; our "Mystère et régénération," p. 71.

36. Cf. our *Le Chamanisme et les techniques archaïques de l'extase* (Paris, 1951), pp. 47 ff., 55 ff., 65 ff.

37. Andersson, *Ethnographie des Kuta*, p. 213.

38. *Ibid.*, p. 214.

39. *Ibid.*, pp. 264 ff.

40. *Ibid.*, p. 266, note 1.

41. L. Bittremieux, *La Société secrète des Bakhimba au Mayombe* (Brussels, 1936). Cf. our "Mystère et Régénération," pp. 72 ff.

42. Bittremieux, *Société secrète*, p. 47.

43. *Ibid.*, p. 50.

44. *Ibid.*, p. 51.

45. *Ibid.*, p. 52.

46. See, for example, the initiation into the *nkita* society of the lower Congo, which includes, among other things, a long seclusion in the bush, during which the "dead man's" body is believed to decompose to the state of a skeleton; it is from his bones that the novice is mystically resuscitated, as was the society's divine patron, the Great Fetish. Cf. A. Bastian, *Die deutsche Expedition an der Loango Küste* (Jena, 1875), II, 17 ff.; J. H. Weeks, *Among the Primitive Bakongo* (London, 1914), pp. 158 ff.; Frobenius, "Masken und Geheimbünde," pp. 51 ff. On the theme of mystical death represented as reduction to a skeleton, see Chapter V, p. 92 ff. On the myths and initiation rites of the Bantu *Ryangombe* mystery, cf. Johanssen, *Mysterien eines Bantu-Volkes*, pp. 13 ff., 29 ff.. and *passim;* A. Friedrich, *Afrikanische Priestertümer* (Stuttgart, 1939), pp. 62 ff., 367 ff.

47. Cf. G. Catlin, *O-Kee-Pa* (London, 1867), pp. 13 ff., 28 ff.; and *Annual Report of the Smithsonian Institution for 1885* (Washington, 1886), Part 2, pp. 309 ff. A summary of the ceremony is given in Jensen, *Beschneidung*, pp. 122-123. Equally cruel are the initiation rites of the *hawinalal*, the war dance of the Kwakiutl; cf. Boas, "Secret Societies," pp. 496 ff.

48. Chamacoco and Vilela: A. Métraux, "A Myth of the Chamacoco Indians and Its Social Significance," *Journal of American Folklore*, LVI (1943), pp. 114, 117. Mandan: A W. Bowers, *Mandan Social*

and Ceremonial Organization (Chicago, 1950), pp. 115 ff. Kwakiutl: Boas, "Secret Societies," p. 446; Drucker, "Kwakiutl Dancing Societies, " pp. 208 ff. Pomo: E. Loeb, "Pomo Folkways," *University of California Publications in American Archaeology and Ethnology,* XIX (Berkeley, 1926), 372-374; and "The Eastern Kuksu Cult," *ibid.,* XXXIII (1933), pp. 172 ff., 181.

49. Ge and Tupi: J. Haekel, "Zur Problem des heiligen Pfahles bei den Indianers Brasiliens," *Añais do XXXI Congr. Internacional de Americanistas* (São Paulo, 1955), pp. 230 ff.; "Plains Indians," *ibid.,* pp. 235 ff.; and "Zum ethnologischen Aussagenwert von Kulturparallelen," *Wiener Völkerkundliche Mitteilungen,* III, 2 (1955), *passim.*

50. Yaruro: V. Petrullo, "The Yaruros of the Capanaparo River, Venezuela," Bureau of American Ethnology, *Bulletin 123* (Washington, 1939), pp. 249 ff. Araucanian: our *Le Chamanisme,* pp. 122 ff., 293 ff.; J. Cooper, "The Araucanians," *Handbook of South American Indians* (Washington, 1946), II, 742 ff. Maidu: Haekel, "Zur Problem des heiligen Pfahles," p. 238.

51. Haekel, "Zur Problem des heiligen Pfahles," pp. 239-240.

52. Cf. our *Le Chamanisme,* pp. 299 ff., especially p. 301, note 1 (Bibliography).

53. Cf. G. Tessmann, *Die Pangwe* (Berlin, 1913), II, 39.

54. Andersson, *Ethnographie des Kuta,* pp. 219-221.

55. U. Harva, *Die Religiösen Vorstellungen der Mordwinen* (Helsinki, 1952), pp. 386 ff.

56. Andersson, *Ethnographie des Kuta,* p. 218.

57. Harva, *Mordwinen,* p. 387.

58. On women's secret ceremonies, cf. R. Wolfram, "Weiberbünde," *Zeitschrift für Volkskunde,* XLII (1933), pp. 143 ff.; O. Loorits, "Das sogenannte Weiberfest bei den Russen und Setukesen," *Comm. Archivii traditionum popularium Estoniae,* XIV (1940), and *Die Grundzüge des estnischen Volksglauben* (Lund, 1949 ff.), II, 394 ff.; Peuckert, *Geheimkulte,* pp. 230 ff.; our "Mystère et régénération," pp. 82 ff.; E. Gasparini, *La civiltà matriarcale degli Slavi* (Venice, 1956), pp. 75 ff.

59. B. Malinowski, *The Sexual Life of Savages* (London, 1929), pp. 273-275, 422-423. The same custom obtains in the Caucasus; cf. R. Bleichsteiner, "Masken und Festnachtsbräuche bei den Völkern des Kaukasus," *Oesterr. Zeitschrift für Volkskunde,* n. s., VI (1952), 64 ff.

60. See above, Chapter III, p. 46.

CHAPTER V. HEROIC AND SHAMANIC INITIATIONS

1. *Ynglingasaga,* Chapter VI, trans. W. Morris and E. Magnusson, in *Heimskringla* (The Saga Library, III, London, 1893), I, 16-17.

2. L. Weiser, *Altgermanische Jünglingsweihen und Männerbünde*

(Baden, 1927), p. 44; O. Höfler, *Kultische Geheimbünde der Germanen* (Frankfurt on the Main, 1934), pp. 170 ff.; J. de Vries, *Altgermanische Religionsgeschichte*, 2nd ed. (Berlin, 1956), I, 454-455; cf. also Pl. XI, reproduction of the "altschwedischen Bronzeplatten von Torslunda auf Öland," showing a warrior clad in a wolfskin and carrying a wolf's head.

3. Tacitus, *Germania*, 31.

4. For the Taifali, cf. Ammianus Marcellinus, 31, 9, 5; for the Heruli, cf. Procopius, *De Bello Persico*, II, 25. See also Weiser, *Altgermanische Jünglingsweihen*, p. 42, and "Zur Geschichte der Altgermanischen Todesstrafe und Friedlosigkeit," *Archiv. für Religionswissenschaft*, XXX (1933), 216. On the *exercitus feralis* (army of shades) of the Harii (Tacitus, *Germania*, 43), cf. L. Weniger, "Feralis exercitus," *Archiv für Religionswissenschaft*, IX (1906), 201-247; X (1907), 61-81, 229-256; Weiser, *Altgermanische Jünglingsweihen*, pp. 39 ff.; Höfler, *Kultische Geheimbünde*, pp. 166 ff.

5. *Volsunga Saga*, Chapters 7-8; Weiser, *Altgermanische Jünglingsweihen*, pp. 40 ff.; Höfler, *Kultische Geheimbünde*, pp. 188 ff.

6. Cf. M. Danielli, "Initiation Ceremonial from Norse Literature," *Folk-Lore*, LVI (June, 1945), 229-230.

7. Georges Dumézil, *Mythes et Dieux des Germains* (Paris, 1939), pp. 94 ff.; Danielli, "Initiation Ceremonial," pp. 236 ff. Jan de Vries is inclined to see an initiatory pattern in the myth of the death of Balder; cf. "Der Mythos von Balders Tod," *Archiv för Nordisk Filologi*, LXX (1955), 41-60, especially 57 ff. The berserker is not a religious phenomenon peculiar to Indo-European societies. For China, see M. Granet, *Danses et légendes de la Chine ancienne* (Paris, 1928), pp. 261-262.

8. Weiser, *Altgermanische Jünglingsweihen, passim;* Höfler *Kultische Geheimbünde;* Dumézil, *Mythes et Dieux des Germains*. Cf. also Höfler, "Der Germanische Totenkult und die Sagen vom Wilden Heer," *Oberdeutschen Zeitschrift für Volkskunde*, X (1936), 33 ff.; A. Endter, *Die Sage vom Wilden Jäger und von der Wilden Jagd* (Dissertation, Frankfurt, 1933). Some of Höfler's conclusions have been criticized; cf. H. M. Flasdieck, "Harlekin," *Anglia*, LXI (1937), 293 ff.

9. S. Wikander, *Der arische Männerbund* (Lund, 1938), pp. 82 ff.; G. Widengren, *Hochgottglaube im alten Iran* (Uppsala, 1938), pp. 311 ff. Cf. also Widengren, "Stand und Aufgaben der iranischen Religionsgeschichte," *Numen*, I (1954), 65 ff.

10. Terrorization of women: H. Webster, *Primitive Secret Societies: A Study in Early Politics and Religion* (New York, 1908), pp. 101 ff., 118 ff. Right to steal: H. Schurtz, *Altersklassen und Männerbünde* (Berlin, 1902), pp. 423 ff. (Africa); Höfler, *Kultische Geheimbünde*, pp. 25 ff., 259 (Germans); Widengren, *Hochgottglaube*, p. 330 (Iran);

R. Bleichsteiner, "Masken und Fastnachtsbräuche bei den Völkern des Kaukasus," *Oesterreichische Zeitschrift für Volkskunde,* n.s., VI (1952), 18 ff., 70 (Caucasus).

11. For the Germanic world, cf. Höfler, *Kultische Geheimbünde,* pp. 12, 129, 287 ff., etc. Noises and uproar in the rituals of the Japanese secret fraternities: A. Slawik, "Kultische Geheimbünde der Japaner und Germanen," *Wiener Beiträge zur Kulturgeschichte und Linguistik,* IV (1936), 724, 732.

12. G. Dumézil, *Horace et les Curiaces* (Paris, 1942), pp. 16 ff.

13. *Ibid.,* pp. 21 ff.

14. J. Vendryès, "Les développements de la racine *nei-* en celtique," *Revue Celtique,* XLVI (1929), 265 ff.; Dumézil, *Horace et les Curiaces,* p. 20.

15. M. L. Sjoestedt, *Dieux et héros des Celtes* (Paris, 1941), pp. 80 ff.; cf. Dumézil, *Horace et les Curiaces.*

16. Sjoestedt, *Dieux et héros,* p. 81.

17. *Tain Bo Cualnge,* trans. Joseph Dunn (London, 1914), pp. 60-78. Cf. Dumézil, *Horace et les Curiaces,* pp. 35-38.

18. Dumézil, *Mythes et Dieux des Germains,* pp. 103 ff.

19. Dumézil, *Horace et les Curiaces,* pp. 40 ff.

20. Cf. our "Puissance et sacralité dans l'histoire des religions," *Eranos-Jahrbuch,* XXI (1953), p. 36.

21. Our *Le Chamanisme et les techniques archaïques de l'extase* (Paris, 1951), pp. 412 ff. The test by fire also forms part of the berserker initiation; cf. Weiser, *Altgermanische Jünglingsweihen,* pp. 75 ff. The berserker can pass unharmed over fire (*ibid.,* pp. 76-77), like shamans and ecstatics. The wild hunt (*Wilde Jagd*) is sometimes called the fiery hunt (*feurige Jagd*). On the relations between fire and the Ancestor cult in Japan and among the Germans, see Slawik, "Kultische Geheimbünde der Japaner und Germanen," p. 746 ff.

22. Cf. the references in our "Puissance et sacralité," p. 35, and *Le Chamanisme,* pp. 370 ff.

23. J. Abbott, *The Keys of Power: A Study of Indian Ritual and Beliefs* (London, 1932), pp. 5 ff.

24. Our "Puissance et sacralité," p. 37, citing K. Rönnow, "Ved. *Kratu,* eine wortgeschichtliche Untersuchung," *Le Monde Oriental,* XXVI (1932), 1-90; and G. Dumézil, *Naissance d'archanges* (Paris, 1945), pp. 145 ff.

25. Our "Puissance et sacralité," p. 38, citing D. J. Hoens, *Shanti: A Contribution to Ancient Indian Religious Terminology* (The Hague, 1951), pp. 177 ff.

26. Cf. our *Forgerons et alchimistes* (Paris, 1956), pp. 100 ff. and *passim.*

27. For the different interpretations of the terms shaman and shamanism, cf. our *Le Chamanisme,* pp. 17 ff., 430 ff. and *passim.*

28. *Ibid.*, pp. 26 ff.; see also A. P. Elkin, *Aboriginal Men of High Degree* (Sydney, 1946), pp. 25 ff.

29. See the examples in our *Le Chamanisme*, p. 28.

30. Pripuzov and Mikhailowski, cited, *ibid*, p. 29.

31. S. Shirokogorow, *Psychomental Complex of the Tungus* (Shanghai and London, 1935), pp. 346 ff., 351 ff.; our *Le Chamanisme*, p. 30.

32. Mikhailowski, cited in our *Le Chamanisme*, pp. 31 ff.

33. See some examples in our *Le Chamanisme*, pp. 31, 68 ff.

34. Krivoshapkin, 1861; V. G. Bogoraz, 1910; Vitashevskij, 1911; M. A. Czaplicka, 1914. Cf., more recently, A. Ohlmarks, *Studien zum Problem des Schamanismus* (Lund and Copenhagen, 1939), pp. 11, 100 ff., 122 ff., and *passim*. See the critique of Ohlmarks's method in our article "Le problème du chamanisme, *Revue de l'Histoire des Religions*, 131 (1946), 5-52, especially 9 ff.; cf. *Le Chamanisme*, pp. 36 ff. See also A. P. Elkin, *Aboriginal Men of High Degree* (Sydney, 1946), pp. 22-25, on the "normality" of Australian medicine men.

35. We have elsewhere discussed the meaning of the ritual return to Chaos; cf. our *Traité d'histoire des religions* (Paris, 1949), pp. 306 ff., 340 ff., and *The Myth of the Eternal Return* (New York, 1954), pp. 17 ff., 51 ff.

36. G. W. Ksenofontov, *Legendy i rasskazy o schamanach u jakutov, burjat i tungusov*, 2nd ed. (Moscow, 1930), pp. 44 ff., used in our *Le Chamanisme*, pp. 47-48. See the German translation in A. Friedrich and G. Buddrus, *Schamanengeschichten aus Sibirien* (Munich, 1955), p. 137.

37. Ksenofontov, cited in our *Le Chamanisme*, p. 48; Friedrich and Buddrus, *Schmanengeschichten*, pp. 139 ff.

38. Ksenofontov, cited in our *Le Chamanisme*, pp. 48 ff.; Friedrich and Buddrus, *Schamanengeschichten*, pp. 156 ff.

39. T. Lehtisalo, *Entwurf einer Mythologie der Jurak-Samojeden*, Mémoires de la Société Finno-Ougrienne, LIII (Helsinki, 1927), 146; our *Le Chamanisme*, p. 49.

40. A. A. Popov, *Tavgijcy. Materialy po etnografii avamskich i vedeevskich tavgicev*, Trudy Instituta Antropologii i Etnografii, 1, 5 (Moscow and Leningrad, 1936), pp. 84 ff.; our *Le Chamanisme*, pp. 50 ff.

41. Ksenofontov, cited in our *Le Chamanisme*, p. 54; Friedrich and Buddrus, *Schamanengeschichten*, pp. 212-213.

42. Ksenofontov, cited in our *Le Chamanisme*, p. 54; Friedrich and Buddrus, *Schamanengeschichten*, pp. 209-210.

43. Dyrenkowa, cited in our *Le Chamanisme*, p. 54.

44. A. V. Anochin, cited in our *Le Chamanisme*, p. 54.

45. A. Métraux, "Le shamanisme araucan," *Revista del instituto de Antropología de la Universidad nacional de Tucumán*, II (1942), 313-

314; our *Le Chamanisme,* pp. 63-64.

46. E. M. Loeb, "Tribal Initiation and Secret Societies," *University of California Publications in American Archaeology and Ethnology,* XXV, 3 (Berkeley, 1929), p. 269.

47. S. F. Nadel, cited in our *Le Chamanisme,* p. 65.

48. E. M. Loeb, "Shaman and Seer," *American Anthropologist,* XXXI (1929), 66 ff.

49. H. Ling-Roth, *Natives of Sarawak and British North Borneo* (London, 1896), I, 280-281; our *Le Chamanisme,* p. 66.

50. We shall soon devote a separate study to this problem.

51. W. Thalbitzer, "Les magiciens esquimaux, leurs conceptions du monde, de l'âme et de la vie," *Journal de la Société des Américanistes,* n. s., XXII (1930), 78.

52. K. Rasmussen, "Intellectual Culture of the Iglulik Eskimos," *Report on the Fifth Thule Expedition 1921-1924,* VII, No. I (Copenhagen, 1929), 114.

53. Cf. our *Le Chamanisme,* pp. 384 ff.; cf. also Chapter VI, p. 105.

54. Cf. our *Le Chamanisme,* pp. 151 ff.

55. Cf. A. Friedrich, "Knochen und Skelett in der Vorstellungswert Nordasiens," *Wiener Beiträge zur Kulturgeschichte und Linguistik,* V (1943), 189-247; Friedrich and Buddruss, *Schamanengeschichten,* pp. 30 ff.; H. Nachtigall, "Die erhöhte Bestattung in Nord- und Hochasien," *Anthropos,* XLVIII (1953), 44-70.

56. Cf. H. Nachtigall, "Die Kulturhistorische Wurzel der Schamanenskelettierung," *Zeitschrift für Ethnologie,* LXXVII (1952), 188-197, especially 191 ff.

57. Cf. our *Le Chamanisme,* pp. 116-120, after N. N. Agapitov, M. N. Changalov, and J. Partanen.

58. Uno Harva, *Der Baum des Lebens* (Helsinki, 1922), pp. 140 ff., and *Die religiöse Vorstellungen der altaischen Völker,* F. F. Communications, No. 125 (Helsinki, 1938), pp. 492 ff. Cf. also our *Le Chamanisme,* pp. 121 ff.

59. Cf. our *Le Chamanisme,* pp. 237 ff., *Images et symboles* (Paris, 1952), pp. 47 ff., and "Centre du monde, temple, maison," *Symposion de l'Istituto Italiano per il Medio ed Estremo Oriente* (Rome, 1957).

60. Cf. our *Le Chamanisme,* pp. 175 ff.

61. Cf. E. Emsheimer, "Schamanentrommel und Trommelbaum," *Ethnos,* IV (1946), 166-181; our *Le Chamanisme,* pp. 159 ff.

62. Cf. our *Le Chamanisme,* pp. 123 ff.

63. Cf. *ibid.,* p. 128.

64. On all this, see *ibid.* Cf. also D. Schröder, "Zur Struktur des Schamanismus," *Anthropos,* L (1955), 848-881.

65. Cf. also H. Petri, "Der australische Medizinmann," *Annali Lateranensi,* XVI (1952), 159-317; XVII (1953), 157-225; our *Le Chamanisme,* pp. 55 ff.

66. Elkin, *Aboriginal Men*, p. 43.

67. *Ibid.*, p. 31. Cf. also A. W. Howitt, *The Native Tribes of South-East Australia* (London, 1904), pp. 404 ff.; K. L. Parker, *The Euahlayi Tribe* (London, 1905), pp. 25 ff.; Elkin, *Aboriginal Men*, pp. 119 ff., etc.

68. Elkin, *Aboriginal Men*, p. 31; cf. also p. 116.

69. A. P. Elkin, *The Australian Aborigines* (Sydney, 1938), p. 223; cf. also his *Aboriginal Men*, p. 116.

70. B. Spencer and F. J. Gillen, *The Native Tribes of Central Australia* (London, 1899), pp. 522 ff., and *The Arunta* (London (1927), II, 391 ff. In these last two examples, note the importance of the cave as privileged space for initiations.

71. B. Spencer and F. J. Gillen, *The Northern Tribes of Central Australia* (London, 1904), pp. 480-481.

72. R. and C. Berndt, "A Preliminary Report of Field-Work in the Ooldea Region, Western South Australia," *Oceania*, XIV (1943), 56-61; Elkin, *Aboriginal Men*, pp. 112-113. Elkin reports a similar initiation among the aborigines of the Forrest River district, northern Kimberley. The medicine men's power comes from the Rainbow Serpent, but it is a "fully qualified practitioner" who performs the initiation; that is, carries the postulant to the sky, the Rainbow Serpent's domain. The master takes the form of a skeleton and, transforming the postulant into an infant, puts him into a pouch, which he fastens to his waist. "When near the sky, the latter throws the postulant out of the pouch on to the sky, thus making him 'dead'. Having reached the sky, the doctor inserts into the young man some little rainbow-snakes and some quartz crystals." After bringing him back to earth, the doctor introduces other magical substances into the postulant through the navel and finally awakens him by touching him with a magical stone. "The young man returns to his normal size, if he had been changed, and next day he tries himself to go up to the sky." His instruction proper begins after this ecstatic experience. Elkin, *Aboriginal Men*, pp. 139-140. Elkin rightly remarks that the reduction to infant size and the resemblance between the doctor's pouch and the kangaroo pouch indicate that this is a ritual of rebirth.

73. Cf. Elkin, *Aboriginal Men*, pp. 43 ff. Medicine men's journeys to the sky: Howitt, *Native Tribes*, pp. 358 ff., 389, 405, 436, 491, etc.; Elkin, *Aboriginal Men*, pp. 95 ff. (from R. M. Berndt's field notes collected among the Menindee of New South Wales), 107, 121 ff., etc. On the ritual value of quartz crystals in the making of medicine men, cf. Elkin, *Aboriginal Men*, pp. 93, 98, 103, 107 ff., etc. Rock crystals are introduced into the bodies of future South American shamans; cf. A. Métraux, "Le Chamanisme chez les Indiens de l'Amérique du Sud tropicale," *Acta Americana*, II (1944), 215 ff. Cf. also our *Le Chamanisme*, pp. 62, 135 ff., etc.

74. Cf. Howitt, *Native Tribes,* pp. 405 ff., 383, 376 (burial ground); Elkin, *Aboriginal Men,* pp. 90 (journey to the bottom of a lake), 93 (dive to the bottom of a river), 105-106 (burial ground), etc.

75. Elkin, *Aboriginal Men,* pp. 91, 129, etc. Like the Asiatic and American shamans, the Australian medicine men walk on fire un-harmed (*ibid.,* pp. 63 ff). On this specifically shamanic power, cf. our *Le Chamanisme,* pp. 233, 385 ff., 412 ff., etc.

76. Elkin, *Aboriginal Men,* p. 36.

77. *Ibid.,* pp. 40-41. On the relations between dismemberment of the body and mummification, see A. Hermann, "Zergliedern und Zu-sammenfügen: Religionsgeschichtliches zur Mumifizierung." *Numen,* III (1956), 81-96.

78. Elkin, *Aboriginal Men,* pp. 76-77.

79. Cf. our *Le Chamanisme,* especially pp. 430 ff.

80. Cf. our "Symbolisme du 'Vol Magique,'" *Numen,* III (1956), 1-13. On the "nostalgia for paradise" traceable in the ideology of shamanism, cf. our "La Nostalgie du paradis dans les traditions prim-itives," *Diogène,* III (July, 1953), 31-45.

81. For the memory of prenatal existences among North American shamans, see P. Radin, *The Road of Life and Death* (New York, 1945), p. 8; A. Hultkrantz, *Conceptions of the Soul among North American Indians* (Stockholm, 1953), pp. 418 ff.

CHAPTER VI. PATTERNS OF INITIATION IN HIGHER RELIGIONS

1. Cf. G. W. Briggs, *Gorakhnath and the Kanphata Yogis* (Cal-cutta and Oxford, 1938), p. 72; S. Dasgupta, *Obscure Religious Cults* (Calcutta, 1945), p. 244. For the Buddhist and Tantric mysteries, cf. H. von Glasenapp, *Buddhistische Mysterien* (Stuttgart, 1940); W. Koppers, "Zum Ursprung des Mysterienwesen im Lichte von Völker-kunde und Indologie," *Eranos-Jahrbuch,* XI (1944), 215-275; W. Ruben, "Indische Mysterien," *Anthropos,* XLV (1950), 357-362.

2. Cf. Dasgupta, *Obscure Religious Cults,* pp. 259 ff.; our *Le Yoga. Immortalité et liberté* (Paris, 1954), pp. 312 ff.

3. Cf. our *Le Chamanisme et les techniques archaïques de l'extase* (Paris, 1951), pp. 195 ff. The famous rope trick of the yogis also be-longs to a shamanic mythico-ritual complex; but since it does not in-volve an initiatory ritual, it will not concern us here. On the rope trick, see our *Le Chamanisme,* pp. 379 ff.; and *Le Yoga,* pp. 319 ff. Some features of the initiation into the Ajivika order—a movement led by Makkhali Gosala, the most dangerous rival of the Buddha—display an extremely archaic character; for example, the candidate was buried to the neck and his hairs were pulled out one by one; cf. A. L. Basham, *History and Doctrines of Ajivikas* (London, 1951), p. 106; our *Le Yoga,* p. 195.

4. R. Bleichsteiner, *L'Eglise jaune,* French trans. (Paris, 1937); our *Le Yoga,* p. 321.

5. Another Tantric rite whose initiatory structure has been clearly preserved is ceremonial entrance into a mandala. Homologous with the Australian *bora* and, in general, with any sacred space, the mandala is at once an image of the world (*imago mundi*) and a pantheon. By entering the mandala, the novice in some sort approaches the center of the world; at the heart of the mandala he can accomplish the rupture of planes and gain access to a transcendental mode of being; cf. G. Tucci, *Teoria e pratica del mandala* (Rome, 1949); our *Le Yoga,* pp. 223-231, 392-393.

6. *Shiva-samhita,* I, 69-77; our *Le Yoga,* pp. 272 ff.

7. *Majjhima-Nikaya,* II, 17; cf. A. K. Coomaraswamy, "Some Pali Words," *Harvard Journal of Asiatic Studies,* IV (1939), 144 ff.

8. Cf. Dasgupta, *Obscure Religious Cults,* pp. 293 ff.; our *Le Yoga,* pp. 282, 315.

9. On "Theseus' dive," see H. Jeanmaire, *Couroï et Courètes. Essai sur l'éducation spartiate et sur les rites d'adolescence dans l'antiquité hellénique* (Lille, 1939), pp. 330 ff.

10. *Ibid.,* pp. 323 ff., 338 ff.

11. Cf. scholiast on Plato, *Laws,* 633 B, quoted in Jeanmaire, *Couroï,* p. 552. On the *krypteia* and lycanthropy, see *ibid.,* pp. 540 ff. See also Chapter V, pp. 81 ff.

12. Cf. J. Harrison, *Themis* (Cambridge, 1912).

13. S. Wikander, *Der arische Männerbund* (Lund, 1938); G. Dumézil, *Horace et les Curiaces* (Paris, 1942).

14. The bibliography is immense. The essential references will be found at the end of R. Pettazzoni's "Les Mystères Grecs et les religions à mystère de l'antiquité. Recherches récentes et problèmes nouveaux," *Cahiers d'Histoire Mondiale,* II, 2 and 3 (Paris, 1955), 303-312, 661-667, Bibliography.

15. For the literary sources, see L. R. Farnell, *Cults of the Greek States* (Oxford, 1907), III, 29-213. For archaeological exploration, see F. Noack, *Eleusis: die baugeschichtliche Entwicklung des Heiligtums* (Berlin and Leipzig, 1927); K. Kuruniotis, "Das eleusinische Heiligtum von den Anfängen bis zur vorperikleische Zeit," *Archiv für Religionswissenschaft,* XXXII (1935), 52-78; G. E. Mylonas, *The Hymn to Demeter and Her Sanctuary at Eleusis,* Washington University Studies in Languages and Literature, XIII (St. Louis, 1942). Cf. also M. P. Nilsson, "Die eleusinische Gottheiten," *Archiv für Religionswissenschaft,* XXXII (1935), 79-141; S. Eitrem, "Eleusinia: les mystères et l'agriculture," *Symbolae Osloenses,* XX (1940), 133-151; W. F. Otto, "Der Sinn der eleusinischen Mysterien," *Eranos-Jahrbuch,* IX (1939), 83-112 (translated as "The Meaning of the Eleusinian Mysteries," in *The Mysteries, Papers from the Eranos Yearbooks,* II [New York, 1955], 14-31).

16. Cf., among others, K. H. E. de Jong, *Das antike Mysterienwesen in religionsgeschichtlicher, ethnologischer und psychologischer Beleuchtung* (Leiden, 1909), pp. 20 ff.; A. Körte, "Zu den eleusinischen Mysterien," *Archiv für Religionswissenschaft*, XVIII (1915), pp. 116–127. But see the pertinent remarks of W. F. Otto, directed especially against the sexual interpretations of A. Dieterich and A. Körte, "Meaning of the Eleusinian Mysteries," pp. 22 ff.

17. Stobaeus, *Florilegium*, 120, 28, reproducing a fragment.of Themistius or Plutarch.

18. Hippolytus, *Philososphoumena*, V, 8; cf. Farnell, *Cults*, III, 177; A. Dieterich, *Eine Mithrasliturgie* 3rd ed. (Leipzig, 1922), p. 138.

19. Otto, "Meaning of the Eleusinian Mysteries," p. 25, developing a conjecture of L. Deubner, *Attische Feste* (Berlin, 1932), p. 86.

20. Cf. R. Pettazzoni, *I Misteri* (Bologna, 1924), pp. 21 ff.; W. K. C. Guthrie, *Orpheus and the Greek Religion* (London, 1935; 2nd ed., 1952), pp. 121 ff. On the bull-roarer in primitive religions, see above, Chapters I–II, and Pettazzoni, "Les Mystères dans l'antiquité," pp. 308 ff.

21. Cf. A. E. Jensen, *Die religiöse Weltbild einer frühen Kultur* (Stuttgart, 1948), pp. 66 ff.

22. *Metamorphoses*, XI, 21, 24, reading, with S. Angus (*The Mystery-Religions and Christianity* [London, 1925], p. 96, note 4), *sacrum*. Cf. also de Jong, *Antike Mysterienwesen*, pp. 207 ff.

23. H. Hepding, *Attis, seine Mythen und sein Kult* (Giessen, 1903), p. 196; Angus, *Mystery-Religions*, p. 97.

24. Firmicus Maternus, *De Errore profanarum religionum*, 18; cf. de Jong, *Antike Mysterienwesen*, pp. 203 ff.

25. Sallustius, *De Diis et Mundo*, 4.

26. Dieterich, *Mithrasliturgie*, p. 10, fragment translated by S. Angus, *Mystery-Religions*, p. 100.

27. Cf. R. Reitzenstein, *Die hellenistische Mysterienreligionen*, 2nd ed. (Leipzig, 1920), pp. 29 ff.; Angus, *Mystery-Religions*, pp. 106 ff. These concepts, it should be noted, belong to the Hellenistic period and differ radically from the religious horizon of Homer and Hesiod. For Egypt of the Greco-Roman period, cf. H. I. Bell, *Cults and Creeds in Graeco-Roman Egypt* (Liverpool, 1953), pp. 87 ff., 102 ff.

28. *De Republica*, VI, 17.

29. Cf. Angus, *Mystery-Religions*, p. 110, note 5.

30. *Protrepticus*, VIII, 4.

31. *Institutiones Divinae*, VI, 21; Angus, *Mystery-Religions*, p. 106.

32. *Hymn to Demeter*, vv. 480-482; Pindar, *Threnoi*, Frag. X; Sophocles, Frag. 719 (Dindorf), 348 (Didot). Cf. Angus, *Mystery-Religions*, pp. 238 ff. A difference between the post-mortem destiny of initiates into the secret societies and noninitiates is already to be found among some primitive peoples (e.g., Melanesians, Africans).

33. Cf. A. D. Nock, *Conversion* (Oxford, 1933), especially pp. 138-155 ("The Conversion of Lucius").

34. Research viewpoints and bibliography will be found in K. Prümm, *Religionsgeschichtliches Handbuch für den Raum der altchristlichen Umwelt* (Freiburg, 1943), pp. 308–356; A. D. Nock, "Hellenistic Mysteries and Christian Sacraments," *Mnemosyne*, Series 4, V (1952), 117-213; H. Rahner, "The Christian Mystery and the Pagan Mysteries," in *The Mysteries, Papers from the Eranos Yearbooks*, II (New York, 1955), 337-401. Cf. also O. Casel, *Das christliche Kultusmysterium*, 2nd ed. (Regensburg, 1935), and *Das christliche Festmysterium* (Paderborn, 1941).

35. For the following, we use the translations and commentaries of T. H. Gaster, *The Scriptures of the Dead Sea Sect* (New York, 1956), and especially the studies of Krister Stendhal, Oscar Cullman, and Karl Georg Kuhn in K. Stendhal (ed.), *The Scrolls and the New Testament* (New York, 1957).

36. Stendhal, *The Scrolls*, p. 10; Kuhn, *ibid.*, p. 78.

37. Nock, "Hellenistic Mysteries," p. 199.

38. *Ibid.*, p 100.

39. Rahner, "The Christian Mystery," p. 362.

40. See the references to patristic texts in our *Images et symboles* (Paris, 1952), pp. 213 ff.; and Rahner, "The Christian Mystery," pp. 380 ff.

41. Cf. the references in Rahner, "The Christian Mystery," p. 392, note 20.

42. James of Sarug, *Consecration of the Baptismal Water*, cited *ibid.*, p. 395.

43. *Protrepticus*, XII, 119, 3; 120, 1 (trans. Butterworth), cited *ibid.*, p. 369.

44. *Ibid.*, p. 365, citing G. Anrich, *Antike Mysterienreligionen und Urchristentum* (Munster, 1932), pp. 157, 158; and *Ecclesiastica hierarchia* I, 1 (J.-P. Migne, *Patrologiae Cursus Completus: Series Graeca* [Paris, 1857-86], III, 372 A).

45. The documentary material will be found in O. Höfler, *Kultische Geheimbünde der Germanen*, (Frankfurt on the Main, 1934), I; R. Wolfram, *Schwerttanz und Männerbund* (Kassel, 1935); H. Métraux, *Schweizer Jugendleben in fünf Jahrhunderten. Geschichte und Eigenart der Jugend und ihre Bünde im Gebiet der protestantischen deutschen Schweiz* (Aarau, 1942); U. Helfenstein, *Beiträge zur Problematik der Lebensalter in der mittleren Geschichte* (Zurich, 1952).

46. Cf. our *Comentarii la legenda Mesterului Manole* (Bucharest, 1943) and *Forgerons et alchimistes* (Paris, 1956).

47. Text edited and translated by M. Bertholet, *Collection des anciens alchimistes grecs* (Paris, 1887), pp. 107-112, 115-118; see also the new English translation by F. S. Taylor, *Ambix,* I (1937), pp.

88-92. Cf. C. G. Jung, "Die Visionen des Zosimus," in *Von den Wurzeln des Bewusstseins* (Zurich, 1954), pp. 153 ff.; our *Forgerons et alchimistes,* p. 153.

48. J. G. Gichtel, *Theosophia Practica,* III, 13, 5, cited in our *Forgerons et alchimistes,* p. 164.

49. Out of the immense literature devoted to this problem, I mention especially G. L. Kittredge, *A Study of Sir Gawain and the Green Knight* (Cambridge, Mass., 1916); A. Brown, *The Origin of the Grail Legend* (Cambridge, Mass., 1943); and R. S. Loomis, *Celtic Myth and Arthurian Legend* (New York, 1927).

50. Cf. J. Marx's analysis, *La Légende arthurienne et le Graal* (Paris, 1952), pp. 281 ff.

51. Cf. A. Fierz-Monnier, *Initiation und Wandlung. Zur Geschichte des altfranzösischen Romans im 12 Jahrhundert,* Studiorum Romanorum, V (Bern, 1951).

52. P. Saintyves, *Les Contes de Perrault et les récits parallèles* (Paris, 1923); J. de Vries, *Betrachtungen zum Märchen, besonders in seine Verhältnis zu Heldensage und Mythos,* FF Communications, No. 150 (Helsinki, 1954). Cf. also H. von Beit, *Symbolik des Märchens. Versuch einer Deutung* (Bern, 1952), I, for an interpretation of initiatory themes in terms of the psychology of C. G. Jung.

53. Cf. L. Valli, *Il linguaggio segreto di Dante e dei Fedeli d'Amore* (Rome, 1928); R. Ricolfi, *Studi sui "Fedeli d'Amore,"* (Milan, 1933), I.

54. "D'amur ne doivent reveler
    Les consiaus, mas très bien celer . . ."

C'est des fiez d'amours, 11: 499-500, cited by Ricolfi, *Studi,* pp. 68-69.

55. "*A* signifies 'without' and *mor* signifies 'death'; put them together and we have 'without death.'" Original cited *ibid.,* p. 63.

56. See our article, "Les Mythes du monde moderne," *La Nouvelle NRF* (September, 1953).

57. From a certain point of view, psychoanalysis can be regarded as a secularized form of initiation, that is, an initiation accessible to a desacralized world. But the pattern is still recognizable: the descent into the depths of the psyche, peopled with monsters, is equivalent to a descent to the Underworld; the real danger implied by such a descent could be connected, for example, with the typical ordeals of traditional societies. The result of a successful analysis is the integration of the personality, a psychic process not without resemblance to the spiritual tranformation accomplished by genuine initiations.

58. Cf. H. Webster, *Primitive Secret Societies: A Study in Early Politics and Religion* (New York, 1908), pp. 191 ff.

INDEX

Achilles, 109
Adonis, 117
Africa, 22, 23-25, 26, 30-33, 35, 37, 42, 73, 74-76, 77, 92, 130
Agastya, 57
Alchemy, initiatory patterns in, 123-24
and new body, 108
and return to womb, 57-58, 124
Alchera times, 6-7, 12
Altaic people, 91, 94
Altar, 120
Ammasilik Eskimos, 92
Ancestors, x, xii, xiv, 5, 19, 23, 29, 34, 37 ff., 67, 74, 84, 129, 132
Angakuts, 92
Animals, and initiation ceremonies, 23-24, 35, 38, 44
See also Beasts of prey
Antero, 64
Anthropology, ix
Anthroposophy, 133
Anula tribe, 22
Aphrodite, 109
Apuleius, 112
Araucanian people, 77, 91
Argonauts, 65
Ariadne, 109
Arioi Society, 26
Aristotle, 110
Arm-blood, 49-50
Arnhem Land, 43, 47
Arthurian cycle, 124-26
Arunta tribe, 7, 12, 97
circumcision and subincision, 21-22, 25
Ascension, symbols of, 14, 17-18, 70, 75, 77-78, 80, 89, 93-94, 97, 99 ff., 130
Asceticism, 67-68, 85-86, 106-7
Ashley-Montagu, M. F., 27
Asia, 67, 77-78, 110
influences in Australia, 99-102
shamanism, *see* Shamanism

Australia, Asiatic influences in, 99-102
initiation mysteries, 4-20, 67, 74, 77, 92, 129, 130
of girls, 41 ff.
of medicine men, 96-100, 105, 111
initiatory ordeals, 21-28, 30, 35, 37-40
Kunapipi cult, 26, 47-51, 58
Avam-Samoyeds, 90

Babali tribe, 37
Bâd tribe, 6
Baiamai, 5-6
Baiame, 13-14
Baisieux, Jacques de, 126-27
Bakhimba society, 75
Bali, 56, 100
Banda tribe, 75
Banquets, ritual, 116-17
Bantu peoples, 54, 56
Bapedi tribe, 25
Baptism, ix, 116, 117, 120
Barberino, Francesco da, 126
Barrier, revolving, 65
Bastian, A., 31
Baths, ritual, 67, 72, 85, 116
Bear, 72, 81, 83, 92
Beasts of prey, 23-24, 72, 81-84, 130
See also Animals
Bella Bella tribe, 69, 70
Berndt, R. and C., 97-98
Berndt, R. M., 26, 43, 49-50
Berserkers, 1, 72, 81-84
Biamban (Great Master), 11, 12
Binbinga tribe, 14
Birds, beaks of, 65, 66, 70
Birth, *see* Childbirth; Rebirth
Bisexuality, 25-26
Bismarck Archipelago, 27
Bittremieux, Léo, 75
Blood, 5, 18, 33, 34, 38
arm-blood, 49-50

Blood—*Continued*
  and female initiations, 44-45
  and shamanism, 90 ff., 93, 96
  and subincision, 25-28
Body, new, 107-8
Böhdvar, 83
Bones, 90, 92, 97, 99
Bora ceremony, 4-7, 17
Boubia tribe, 26
Brahmanic initiations, 52, 53-57,
    104, 114
Breathing, embryonic, 57, 58
Bremen, Adam von, 84
Bridge, crossing over, 52
Brimo and Brimos, 111
Brown, Arthur, 125
Buddha, 57, 86
Buddhism, 53-54, 58, 92, 107, 114
  Mahayana, 106
Bugari times, 6
Bull-roarers, 4, 8, 9, 10-11, 12-14,
    16, 47, 49, 50, 83, 111, 129
  and circumcision, 21-24
Buriat people, 88, 91, 93-94
Bushongo tribe, 32-33

Cabin initiatory, symbolism of, 35-
    37, 42-44, 63
  as womb, xiv, 55, 56, 59
Call, *see* Vocation
Cannibal Society, 69-72
Cannibalism, 69, 71, 73
Cathba, 84
Cattle stealing, 83
Caul, 54
Caves, symbolism of, 58, 69, 97
Celestial Beings, 37, 74, 77
Ceram, 31, 35
Chamacoco tribe, 77
Chaos, xiii, xiv, 89
Chastity, 53
Chatti people, 81
Chepara tribe, 17
Chick, symbolism of, 54
Childbirth, 45, 51, 52, 80
China, 58, 59, 100
Christianity, ix, 103-4, 113, 115-21,
    132-33
Cicero, 112
Circumcision, 4, 16, 18, 31, 35, 37,
    38, 47, 129, 130
  and bull-roarer, 21-25
Clam, giant (*Tridacna deresa*), 62
Clement of Alexandria, 110, 113,
    120

Clown Society, Fort Rupert, 69, 70
Cold, resistance to, 85
Comorin, 57
Conchobar, 84
Confraternities, 2, 38, 45, 74, 76
Conversion, 135
Coomaraswamy, A. K., 65
Copper pillar, 69-70
Cord, magic, 17, 100
Coroado tribe, 42
Cosmic Tree, 78, 119
Cosmocrator, 121
Cow, 56-57
Crab Woman, 62
Crocodiles, 23, 35, 36
Cross, symbolism of, 119-20
Crystals, 17, 97, 99
Cuchulainn, initiation of, 84-85
Curetes, 109

Dancing Societies, Kwakiutl, 67, 68-
    72, 77, 78, 85
Dante Alighieri, 127
Daramulun (Dharamulun), 8, 11-14
Darkness, xiv, 9, 16, 36, 42, 56
Dayaks, 92
Deacon, A. B., 62
Dead Sea manuscripts, 115, 117
Death, 80, 83
  and circumcision, 23-24
  in darkness, 9
  initiatory, symbolism of, 13-14,
    18, 29, 30-35, 36-37, 38-39,
    51, 52, 57, 59, 89-93, 101-2,
    106-8, 110-12, 130, 131-32,
    136
  and resurrection, xii ff., 12-13, 29,
    34, 38, 73-76, 91, 108, 122,
    130, 135
  and speech, 15-16
  temporary, 95
  and Underworld, 61-64
Demeter, 110, 111
Denmark, 45
Dephinas, 58
Destiny, and spinning, 45-46
Dieiri tribe, 26, 38
Dietary taboos and prohibitions, 5,
    12, 14, 15, 27, 33, 38-39,
    42-43, 67
Diksha ritual, 54-55, 58-59, 104
Dionysius the Pseudo-Areopagite,
    120
Dionysus, rites of, 109-12

Dismemberment, 74, 89, 90-92, 96, 98, 101, 105-6, 108, 130
Divine Beings, 6, 9, 10, 13-14, 19, 22 ff., 47, 129, 132
Djamar, 6
Djunggawon ritual, 49
Dluwulaxa tribe, 69
Dogs, 81, 84
Door, active, 65
Dream Time, 6, 19
Dreaming Period, 48, 49
Dreams, 87, 89, 106, 128, 135
Drinking, prohibitions against, 15
Dumézil, Georges, 83, 85
Dvi-ja (twice-born), 53-54, 104
Dyaks, 44

Eagle, beak of, 65, 66
Earth Spirit, 29
Ecstasy, 3, 39, 64, 83, 87, 93, 100-101, 102
  techniques of, 94-96
Egg, symbolism of, 54, 79
Elema tribe, 33
Eleusinian mysteries, 103, 109-15
Eliot, T. S., 134
Elkin, A. P., 96-97, 99-100
Embryonic breathing, 57, 58
Embryonic state, *see* Womb, return to
Emu, 5, 97
Epilepsy, 88
Epopteia, 111
Eravo (Men's House), 33
Eskimos, 88, 92
Essenes, 115-17
Ethnology, 1-2, 16, 21, 25, 41, 43
Eucharist, 116-17

Fairy tales, 126
Fakirs, 73, 100
Fasting, 67
Fedeli d'Amore, 126-27
Fertility, 14, 42, 46, 48, 79-80
Fiji, 33
Fingers, eating with, 37
Finland, 63
Fire, mastery over, 85-86, 95
  roasting at, 7-8, 99
  throwing of, 16-17, 50
  walking on, 100
Firmicus Maternus, 112
Fish, 36, 63
Fisher King, 124
Flight, magic, 100, 101

Food, *see* Dietary taboos and prohibitions
Forest, symbolism of, 31, 36-37, 42, 69
Forest Spirit, 31
Fort Rupert, Clown Society of, 69, 70
Fraternities, 2
Frau Holle, 46
Frazer, Sir J. G., 44
Freemasonry, 133
Frobenius, L., 73
Fury (*furor*), 72, 81, 84-85, 87, 88, 130

Gabun, 78
Ganda, ceremony, 32-33
Gates, symbolism of, 65
Ge festival, 77
Gestation, 53-57
Ghosts, 15, 31, 32, 37, 83
Gichtel, J. G., 124
Gilgamesh, 64
Gillen, F. J., 12, 14, 97
Girls' initiation, 41-44, 67
  degrees in, 44-47
Gnabaia, 22
Gnosticism, 112, 113, 115, 119, 121
Goddesses, 105, 110
  of Death, 63-64
  of Destiny, 45
Gods, xii-xv, 19, 21, 22, 40, 46, 68, 72, 74, 77, 88, 96, 107, 121, 129, 132
Gold, symbolism of, 56, 124
Gorakhnath, 105
Grail quest, 124-25
Great Master (*biamban*), 11, 12
Great Mother, 47-51, 52, 56-57, 58, 61 ff., 112
Great Spirit, 21-22
Greco-Oriental mysteries, *see* Mysteries
Guilds, 122
Guringal ceremony, 8
Gusinde, M., 28, 29

Haddon, A. C., 26
Haeckel, Josef, 77
Hag of Hiisi, 63
Hair, pulling out of, 4, 18
Halakwulup tribe, 28-29
Hamatsa Dance, 69-72
Harva, Uno, 93
Hathayoga, 108

Healer, 71, 72
Heating, body, 72, 84-85
  symbolism of, 85-87
Heaven, 66, 69, 75, 77-78, 80, 89 ff.,
    93-96, 97, 99, 119-20, 130
  kingdom of, 118-19
Helios, 110
Hell, 62, 64, 90, 91, 94 ff., 106, 110,
    125, 130
  See also Underworld
Hentze, C., 62
Hermeticism, 112, 113, 123
Herodotùs, 56
Heroes, x, xi, xv, 19, 21, 52, 74, 97,
    99, 121, 125, 134-35
  initiations of, 61-63, 66, 130
    berserkers, 1, 72, 81-84, 87
    Cuchulainn, 84-85
    heat symbolism, 85-87
Heruli people, 81
Hiisi, Hag of, 63
Hinduism, 92, 100, 106
Hine-mi-te-po, 61
Hiranyagarbha rite, 56-57, 58, 104
Höffler, Otto, 83
Horse, symbolism of, 79
Höttri, 83
House, ceremonial, symbolism of, 69
Howitt, A. W., 7, 14
Hunting magic, 80
Hut, see Cabin
Huysmans, J. K., 132-33
Hymn to Demeter, 113

Iamblichus, 114
Iglulik Eskimos, 92
Ilmarinen, 63
Imagination, 125-26, 135
Immortality, 56, 59, 62, 64, 125,
    134
Incest, 58
India, 42, 65, 86, 100, 103
  initiations, 53-57, 104-8, 114
Individuation, 135
Indra, 55, 86
Initiation, ix-xv
  and Christianity, 115-21
  Europe, see Europe
  Greece, 108-15
  heroic, see Heroes
  India, see India
  individual, 66-72
  and literary themes, 124-28
  primitive religions, see Primitive
    religions

Initiation—Continued
  shamanic, see Shamanism
  Symplegades, 64-66
  types of, 2-3
Iran, 94, 100, 109
Ireland, 84-85, 125
Iruntarinia, 97
Isis, 112
Itchumundi tribe, 27
Ituri pygmies, 22, 37

Jabim tribe, 36
Jaguars, 23
Jaiminiya Upanishad Brahmana, 65
Japan, 34, 46, 83
Jason, 65
Jaws, 65
Jeanmaire, H., 109
Jelmalandji, 49
Jeraeil mysteries, 10-11
Jesus Christ, 116-18, 120
Jewish people, 115-17
John, St., 116
Joyce, James, 134
Joyce, T. A., 32
Julunggul, 48-49
Jung, C. G., 135

Kai tribe, 36
Kaiemunu, 36
Kaitish tribe, 14
Kalevala, 63
Kamilaroi tribe, 5
Karadjeri tribe, 16, 17, 22, 25, 26-27,
    38
Kavirondo Bantu, 54
Kittredge, George Lyman, 125
Knights Templars, 124
Koppers, W., 28, 29
Kore, 110, 111
Kovave, 33
Kra, 29
Kran, 29
Kukata tribe, 22
Kuksu society, 91
Kuman tribe, 27
Kunapipi cult, 26, 47-51, 58
Kundalini, 86
Kurnai tribe, 7, 17
  initiation mystery, 10-11, 22, 28,
    130
Kuta confraternity, 74
Kuta Lisimba society, 79
Kwakiutl Dancing Societies, 68-72,
    77, 78, 85

Labyrinth, 62, 108-9
Lactantius, 113
Ladder, 94
Language, new, 31, 75
  special, 37, 87, 126
Lapland, 64
Laribuga ceremony, 17
Last Supper, 116-17
Laws of Manu, 53
Layard, J., 62
Le-hev-hev, 62
Lehtisalo, T., 90
Lenape tribe, 77
Leopards, 23, 32, 72, 78-79
Leviathan, 64
Lions, 23
Literary themes, and initiation, 124-128, 134-35
Lommel, Herman, 54
Loomis, Roger Sherman, 125
Lu'ningu, 49
Lycurgus, 109

Maamba, 17
Madness, 72, 79
  See also Fury; Heating
Magic, 64, 72, 100, 107, 130
  and female initiations, 47, 80
  heat, *see* Heating
  substances, 12, 97, 98-99
Magwanda tribe, 25
Maidu tribe, 77
Maier, Michael, 58
Mairya societies, 83
Maitrayani Samhita, 55
Makua tribe, 31
Malekula, 62, 92
Manangs, 92
Mandan Indians, 76, 77
Mandja tribe, 75
Männerbunde, 2, 81, 125
Maoris, 61
Marsaba, 35
Marshall Islands, 42
Masai tribe, 26
Masks, 36, 39, 71, 83
  Societies of, 73, 74
Masons, 122
Mathews, R. H., 5, 8
Matsyendranath, 105
Matter of Britain, 124-25
Maui, 52, 61
Mayanamati, Queen, 105
Mayombe, 75

Medicine men, 2-3, 12, 38, 39, 73, 78, 85, 87, 92, 101-2
  Australian, initiations of, 96-100, 105
Melanesia, 25, 26, 28, 30, 33, 50, 76, 99, 130
Menstruation, 27, 41 ff., 47, 67, 80
Meriah, 92
Mesopotamia, 57, 94, 100
Messiah, 116-18
Metanira, Queen, 110
Military organizations, 79, 83-84, 85, 87, 109, 122
Millstones, 52
Mithraism, 93-94, 112
Mitla tribe, 69
Mohammedanism, 86
Moksha, 106
Monkeys, 32
Monsters, xiv, 23, 83
  swallowing by, *see* Swallowing
Moon, connection of, with women, 42, 45-46
Moon Woman, 29
Mordvins, 79
Mother, separation from, 7-10, 30, 130
Mother Earth, 51, 52, 58, 61-62, 63, 66, 93, 104
Mountains, 65
  crevasses, 58
Mukti, 106
Mummification, 99-100
Mungan-Ngaua, 10
Murder, initiatory, 23-24
Murring tribe, 8, 11
Musgrave Ranges aborigines, 16
Mycerinus, 56
Mysteries, and Christianity, 118-21
  Greco-Oriental, ix, 1, 2, 22, 103-4, 109-15, 123, 130
Mysticism, 1, 38, 52, 55, 65, 72, 73, 78, 107

Names, new, 28, 31, 68, 74, 75
Nanda ceremony, 33-34
Nandi tribe, 26
Narriniyeri tribe, 15
Necht, sons of, 84-85
Neo-Buddhism, 133
Neoplatonism, 114, 115, 120-21
Neo-Vedantism, 133
Nereids, 108
Nettles, symbolism of, 74
New birth, *see* Rebirth

New Guinea, 21, 26, 27, 30, 33, 35-36, 37, 39
New Hebrides, 42
New Year rites, xiii
New Zealand, 42
Ngakola society, 75
Nganaoa, 63
Ngarigo tribe, 15
Ngoye (Ndassa) tribe, 74
Night watch, 125
Nilles, John, 27
Nirvana, 106
Niyami, 33
Nootka Indians, 70
North America, 15, 22, 30, 31, 39, 42
    initiations, 66-72, 77-78, 87, 94
    secret societies, 68-73, 76
Nose, perforation of, 27
Nuba tribe, 26
Nudity, ritual, 26, 32
Nyembe association, 78-79

Occultism, 133-34
Ocher, 8, 12, 17, 26, 43, 49, 50, 98
Olim, 30
Olympiodorus, 114
Opossum game, 17
Opus alchymicum, 123-24
Ordeals, *see* Primitive religions, initiatory ordeals
Orphism, 109-12, 115
Osiris, 92, 111, 112
Other World, 64-66, 69, 90, 113, 126
Otto, Walter, 111

Palestine, 116
Pangwe tribe, 31-32, 78
Papua, 30, 36, 100
Paracelsus, 57-58
Paradoxical passage, 52, 65, 130
Patasiva tribe, 31
Patwin tribe, 91
Paul, St., 114, 116, 118
Pearl shell, 99
Percival, 124, 125
Personality, disintegration of, 68, 72, 89
Pflanzervölker, 43
Phrygia, 112
Piddington, R., 17
Pillar, copper, 69-70
Pindar, 113
Pitjandara tribe, 22
Pitta-Pitta tribe, 26

Plains Indians, 77
Plato, 111
Platonism, 114
Pole, symbolism of, 5, 17, 49, 50, 67, 69-70, 77-78, 89, 94
Pomo tribe, 77
Popov, A. A., 90
Possession, 68, 70-72
Pot, symbolism of, 54, 56-57
Potanin, 93
Prajapati, 56, 86
Primitive religions:
    initiation mysteries, 1-4
        Australian medicine men, 96-100
        and collective regeneration, 18-20
        death, symbolism of, 13-14
        descent to Underworld, 61-63
        girls, *see* Girls' initiation
        Kurnai tribe, 10-11, 22, 28, 130
        North America, 66-72, 77-78, 87, 94
        return to womb, *see* Womb
        sacred ground, 4-7, 34, 49-50
        and secret societies, 77-80
        separation from mother, 7-10
        Yuin tribe, 11-13, 22
    initiatory ordeals, xii ff.
        bull-roarer and circumcision, 21-25
        death, initiatory, 30-35
        Kunapipi cult, 26, 47-51, 58
        meaning of, 14-18
        revelation, degrees of, 37-40
        subincision, symbolism of, 25-28
Proclus, 114
Psychology, 25, 36, 80, 126, 128, 134
Puberty rites, *see* Primitive religions, initiation mysteries and initiatory ordeals
Pythagoreanism, 114

Quartz crystals, 17, 99
Quest, 3, 87, 96

Rahner, Hugo, 120
Rapine, right of, 83
Ravishing, 69
Rebirth, xii, xiii, 18, 28-29, 31-32, 36-37, 51, 63, 101, 130
    Indian initiations, 53-57, 107-8
Reeds, dancing, 65
Regeneration, collective, 18-20

Resurrection, 12-13, 29, 34, 38, 73-76, 91, 108, 122, 130, 135
of Jesus, 117-18
Revelation, 3, 29, 134
degrees of, 37-40
Rig-Veda, 53, 54, 56
Rocks, clashing, 52, 65
Rome, 108, 109, 119, 121
Rooke Island, 35
Roth, W. E., 25-26
Russia, 46

Sacrality, 58-59, 70, 80, 86, 104
Sacred ground, 4-7, 34, 49-50
Sacred history, x-xi, xiv, 20, 47
Sacred Time, 68
Saintyves, Paul, 126
Sallustius, 112
Salt water, 71, 85
Samoa, 37
Samoyeds, 90, 94
Sanskrit, 86
Scarification, 4, 18, 67
Schleswig, 45
Schmidt, Wilhelm, 21, 26, 28, 44
Schurtz, Heinrich, 1
Secret societies, 2, 3, 31, 33, 38, 39, 41, 67-68, 122, 129, 133
Kwakiutl Dancing Societies, 68-72, 77, 78, 85
men, 72-77, 81, 83, 125
and puberty rites, 77-80
women, 45, 78-80
Segregation, 4, 15, 26, 29, 32, 35, 67-68, 130
of girls, 41-44
Selish tribe, 77
Selknam tribe, 29-30
Semen, 54, 55, 58
Sexuality, 3, 14, 18, 24-25, 27, 38-39, 42, 62
and female initiations, 46-47
Shamanism, 2-3, 17-18, 38, 52, 64, 72, 80, 105 ff., 109, 129
dissemination of, 100-102
initiations, 66-68, 73, 74, 76-77, 78, 123, 130
ordeals, 90-93
public rites, 93-94
techniques of ecstasy, 94-96
vocation, 87-89
and magical heat, 72, 85-87
Shushwap tribe, 42
Siberia, 85, 87-91, 94, 96, 105, 111
Sickness, initiatory, 72, 76, 88-91, 106

Siddhas, 105
Siggeir, King, 81-82
Sight, prohibitions against, 16
Sigmund, 82
Signy, 82
Sinfjotli, 82
Sjoestedt, Marie-Louise, 84
Skeleton, 92-93, 96, 102, 105
Skin, wrapping in, 54, 55-56
Sky, ascent to, *see* Ascension
Sky God, 7, 17, 22
Sleep, prevention of, 14-15
Smiths, 64, 86, 122
Snakes, 35, 48-50, 82, 97-98, 99
Socrates, 114
Soma sacrifice, 54, 55, 104
Sophocles, 113
Sotho tribe, 26
Soul, and mysteries, 114-15
of shaman, 88, 95, 100
of woman, 46
South America, 22, 23, 62-63, 70, 77, 94
Soyot people, 88
Speech, prohibitions against, 15-16
Spencer, B., 12, 14, 97
Spinning, 45-46
Spiral, bark, 14
Spirit, tutelary, 66-68
Spirits, ancestral, 87 ff., 90-92, 95-96
Stealing, 31, 83, 109
Stendhal, Krister, 116
Sticks, eating with, 37
Stone, sacred, of Ngakola, 75
Strehlow, C., 22
Subincision, 4, 18, 21, 38
symbolism of, 25-28
Sun, 56, 59
prohibition against seeing, 42
Sun Man, 29
Superhuman Beings, 19, 21 ff., 95
Supernatural Beings, x ff., xiv, xv, 24, 30, 39-40, 48, 83, 96 ff., 101, 129, 131, 132
Supreme Beings, 5-6, 11, 17-18, 19, 22, 23, 38, 74, 80
Tierra del Fuego, 28-30
Wiradjuri tribe, 13-14
Yuin tribe, 11-13
Swahili tribe, 42
Swallowing, initiatory motif of, 13-14, 35-37, 48-49, 51, 52, 62-64, 73, 75, 77, 78, 98
Symbolism, 2
Symplegades, 64-66, 130

Synesius, 114
Syria, 116, 120

Taboos, *see* Dietary taboos and prohibitions
Tacitus, 81
Tahiti, 26
Taifali people, 81
Tantrism, 1, 86, 105-8
Taoism, 57
Tathagata, 57
Tattooing, 18, 31, 43
Tchoed rite, 105, 107
Teacher of Righteousness, 117
Teeth, blackening of, 43
    extraction of, 4, 12, 13-14, 18, 38
Telekut people, 91
Tessmann, Günther, 31-32
Theseus, 108-9
Theosophical Society, 133
Thurmulun, 14
Tibet, 100, 105
Tierra del Fuego, 15
    puberty rites, 28-30, 41, 129
Time, beginning of, x ff., xiv
    reintegration of, 6-7, 40, 129
    and spinning, 45-46
Tindale, Norman B., 16, 38
Tomb, and baptismal font, 120
Torday, E., 32
Torres Strait, 26, 99
Tossing of novices, 16-17
Totemism, 43
Trance, 64, 69, 87, 95
Transcendental state, 52, 65-66, 72, 101, 104, 106
Transition rites, x, 2, 122, 136
Transmutation, 77, 123-24
Traveling, fast, 100
Trees, symbolism of, 5, 6, 17-18, 67, 77-78, 89, 90, 93-94, 100, 119, 130
Trobriand Islands, 79-80
Tundum, 10
Tungus people, 88, 91
Tupi tribe, 77
Turrbal tribe, 14
Tutelary spirit, 66-68
Twanyirrika, 21
Twice-born, 53-54, 55, 58-59, 104

Ukraine, 46
Umba ceremony, 17
Unconscious, 128, 134

Underworld, descent to, 61-63, 78, 97, 102, 110-12, 130
    See also Hell
Unmatjera tribe, 14, 97
Unthippa women, 7
Upanayana ceremony, 53 ff., 58, 104
Urns, 57

Vagina dentata, 51, 52, 63, 66
Vaïnämoïnen, 63-64
Vangla-Papua tribe, 27
Vasishta, 57
Veddah tribe, 42
Vendryès, J., 84
Vilela tribe, 77
Visions, 87, 106
Vocation, mystical, 2-3, 87-89, 96, 129
Volsunga Saga, 81-83
Vries, Jan de, 126
Vulva, and subincision, 26

Warburton Ranges, 97
Warriors, initiations of, 66, 67, 69, 81-85, 86-87
Watauineiwa, 29
Wauwalak Sisters, 48-50
Weaving, 45-46
Webster, Hutton, 1
Weiser, Lily, 83
Weule, Karl, 31
Whale, 36, 63-64
Wheat, ear of, 111
Widengren, G., 83
Wikander, Stig, 83
Wikeno Dancing Societies, 69, 70
Wildcat, 97
Winter season, 68, 83-84, 123
Winthuis, J., 25
Wintun tribe, 42
Wiradjuri tribe, 5, 8, 17
    death symbolism of, 13-14
Wirz, Paul, 26
Witches, trials of, 124
Wizards, 5, 64, 887
Wolf, 72, 81-83, 109
Womb, 64, 120
    cabin as symbol of, 36-37, 42
    return to, xiv, 49-53, 61, 93, 98, 124
    in Indian initiations, 53-57, 104
    multiple meanings of, 57-60
Women, exclusion of, from initiations, 4, 5, 7, 8, 16, 33
    and *Fedeli d'Amore*, 126-27

Women—*Continued*
  and heroic initiations, 84-85
  initiations, *see* Girls' initiations
  and men's secret societies, 69, 71,
    73, 83
  secret societies, 45, 78-80
  symbolic transformation into, 25-
    26
Wonghibon subtribe, 14
World, center of, 70, 94, 95, 100,
    119-20
  creation of, x-xi, xv, 36, 45-46,
    59
  image of, 6, 69-70
  sacred, 9-10
World Tree, 17, 89, 94

Xalpen, 30

Yakut people, 88, 90
Yamana tribe, 15
  initiation ceremony, 28-29
Yao tribe, 44-45
Yaruro tribe, 77
Yetaita, 29
Yoga, 100, 106-8
Yuin tribe, 5, 7-8
  Supreme Being and initiation cere-
    mony, 11-13, 22
Yuri-ulu tribe, 15

Zagreus, 22
Zosimus, 123

In the Same Vein...

Spirits of the Night:
The Vaudun Gods of Haiti • Selden Rodman and Carole Cleaver

A living polytheistic culture and religion? Yes, Haiti's! Filled with the authors' over fifty years knowledge and experience of Haiti, it combines a sense of art, culture, and history to reveal the pleasure in a polytheistic "voodoo." Includes a bibliography, black and white photos, and illustrations of Haitian art.

144 pp. ISBN 0-88214-354-9

Santeria:
A Practical Guide to Afro-Caribbean Magic • Luis Manuel Nuñez

Santeria is a religion like Voodoo, but Hispanic rather than French. With millions of participants in the Americas, its rituals are a major assault on the Western Christian mind, long accustomed to a distant God and to orderly liturgies. This Spring best-seller presents the gods, oracles, spells, and ceremonies of a growing underground religion that we guarantee will make you shake in your bed.

163 pp. ISBN 0-88214-349-2

Women's Dionysian Initiation • Linda Fierz-David

A fresco in ancient Pompeii—before Vesuvius buried it all for centuries—depicts an initiation ceremony for women. Jungian analyst Linda Fierz-David explores what it was all about. With color plates to show you the ceremony itself. "...Provides one of the clearest, most readable accounts of the archetypal structure of a woman's experience of the world this reviewer has ever read."—Small Press

149 pp. ISBN 0-88214-510-X

The Inner King and Queen • Robert Bly & Michael Meade

Bly's and Meade's success has partly to do with their brilliant and sensitive re-working of "Jungian" ideas into language that talks and walks. These tapes, filled with stories, are a further popularizing of Jung's ideas delivered in Bly's and Meade's tag team, witty style.

Available only to individuals
2 audio tapes: 2 hrs. ISBN 1-879323-05-2

Spring Publications, Inc.
299 East Quassett Road, Woodstock, CT 06281